Go Machine Learning Pı ,

Eight projects demonstrating end-to-end machine learning
and predictive analytics applications in Go

Xuanyi Chew

BIRMINGHAM - MUMBAI

Go Machine Learning Projects

Commissioning Editor: Pravin Dhandre
Acquisition Editor: Nelson Morris
Content Development Editor: Snehal Kolte
Technical Editor: Dharmendra Yadav
Copy Editor: Safis Editing
Project Coordinator: Manthan Patel
Proofreader: Safis Editing
Indexer: Tejal Daruwale Soni
Graphics: Jisha Chirayil
Production Coordinator: Deepika Naik

First published: November 2018

Production reference: 1301118

Published by Packt Publishing Ltd.
Livery Place
35 Livery Street
Birmingham
B3 2PB, UK.

ISBN 978-1-78899-340-1

www.packtpub.com

`mapt.io`

Mapt is an online digital library that gives you full access to over 5,000 books and videos, as well as industry leading tools to help you plan your personal development and advance your career. For more information, please visit our website.

Why subscribe?

- Spend less time learning and more time coding with practical eBooks and Videos from over 4,000 industry professionals

- Improve your learning with Skill Plans built especially for you

- Get a free eBook or video every month

- Mapt is fully searchable

- Copy and paste, print, and bookmark content

Packt.com

Did you know that Packt offers eBook versions of every book published, with PDF and ePub files available? You can upgrade to the eBook version at `www.packt.com` and as a print book customer, you are entitled to a discount on the eBook copy. Get in touch with us at `customercare@packtpub.com` for more details.

At `www.packt.com`, you can also read a collection of free technical articles, sign up for a range of free newsletters, and receive exclusive discounts and offers on Packt books and eBooks.

Contributors

About the author

Xuanyi Chew is the Chief Data Scientist of a Sydney-based logistics startup. He is the primary author of Gorgonia, an open source deep learning package for Go. He's been practicing machine learning for the past 12 years, applying them typically to help startups. His goal in life is to make an artificial general intelligence a reality. He enjoys learning new things.

I would like to thank my incredible wife, SML for her patience . To my friends, Darrell C., Gareth S., Makoto I. and Samaneh F. for providing me feedback and a bouncing board for ideas. A great thank you to Barry J. for teaching me to write, and Daniel W. for introducing me to the editors. Snehal K. and the various editors at Packt also deserve a much vaunted thank you for all they went through to bring this book to reality.

About the reviewer

Dr. Janani Selvaraj works as a senior research and analytics consultant for a start-up in Trichy, Tamil Nadu. She is a mathematics graduate with an interdisciplinary Ph.D in environmental management. Her research interests include mathematical and statistical modeling, spatial modeling, and environmental epidemiology. She currently trains students in data science and works as a consultant on several data-driven projects in a variety of domains. She is an R programming expert and founder of the R-Ladies Trichy group, a group that promotes gender diversity.

Packt is searching for authors like you

If you're interested in becoming an author for Packt, please visit `authors.packtpub.com` and apply today. We have worked with thousands of developers and tech professionals, just like you, to help them share their insight with the global tech community. You can make a general application, apply for a specific hot topic that we are recruiting an author for, or submit your own idea.

Table of Contents

Preface

Go is the perfect language for machine learning. Its simple syntax helps to clearly describe complex algorithms, but does not obscure developers from understand how to run efficient optimized code. This book will teach you how to implement machine learning in Go to make programs that are easy to deploy and code that is not only easy to understand and debug, but that can also have its performance measured.

The book begins by guiding you in setting up your machine learning environment with Go libraries and capabilities. You will then plunge into regression analysis of a real-life house pricing dataset and build a classification model in Go to classify emails as spam or ham. Using Gonum, Gorgonia, and STL, you will explore time series analysis, along with decomposition and how to clean up your personal Twitter timeline by clustering tweets. In addition to this, you will learn how to recognize handwriting using neural networks and convolutional neural networks, both of which are deep learning techniques. Once you've covered all the techniques, you'll learn how to choose the most appropriate machine learning algorithms to use for your projects with the help of a facial detection project.

By the end of this book, you will have developed a solid machine learning mindset, a strong hold on the powerful Go libraries, and a sound understanding of the practical implementations of machine learning algorithms in real-world projects.

Who this book is for

If you're a machine learning engineer, data science professional, or Go programmer who wants to implement machine learning in your real-world projects and make smarter applications more easily, this book is for you.

What this book covers

Chapter 1, *How To Solve All Machine Learning Problems*, introduces two classes of machine learning: regression and classification. By the end of this chapter, you should feel comfortable with the data structures used to build machine learning programs. Most machine learning algorithms are built based on the data structures introduced here. We are then going to introduce Go machine learning and get you up and running for further projects.

Chapter 2, *Linear Regression – House Price Prediction,* goes into a regression analysis on a real-life dataset on house pricing. We will start off by building the necessary data structures to perform such analyses, along with initial exploration of the dataset.

Chapter 3, *Classification – Spam Email Detection,* covers the construction of a classification model in Go. The dataset is the classic spam and ham email dataset in which our goal is to build a model that classifies the emails as spam or ham. Then, we will learn how to write the algorithms themselves, while leveraging external libraries (such as Gonum) for data structure support.

Chapter 4, *Decomposing CO2 Trends Using Time Series Analysis,* introduces us to the subtleties of time series analysis. Data in time series can often be decomposed for descriptive purposes. This chapter shows us how to perform such decompositions, and how to display them using Gonum's plotting tools as well as gnuplot.

Chapter 5, *Clean Up Your Personal Twitter Timeline by Clustering Tweets,* covers the clustering of tweets on Twitter. We will be using two different clustering techniques, K-Means and DBSCAN. For this chapter, we're going to rely on a number of skills we built up in Chapter 2, *Linear Regression – House Price Prediction.* We will also be using the same libraries used in the aforementioned chaper. On top of that, we will also be using the clusters library by Marcin Praski

Chapter 6, *Neural Networks – MNIST Handwriting Recognition,* opens up the rich world of image recognition to us. Images are difficult, because useful features are nonlinear products of the input features. The aim of this project is to introduce the various methods of handling high-dimensional data; specifically, the use of PCA algorithms in the Gonum library to whiten data.

Chapter 7, *Convolutional Neural Networks – MNIST Handwriting Recognition,* explains how to use recent advancements in deep learning to perform handwriting recognition, by building a convolutional neural network using Gorgonia tp achieve 99.87% accuracy.

Chapter 8, *Basic Facial Detection,* explores a basic implementation of facial detection. By the end of this chapter, we will have implemented a usable facial detection system using GoCV and PIGO. This chapter teaches an important lesson in learning to choose the correct algorithm for the job.

Chapter 9, *Hot Dog or Not Hot Dog - Using External Services* culminates the book by showing how one may integrate external services in machine learning projects, and what to look out for when doing so.

Chapter 10, *What Is Next,* lists the further avenues for machine learning in Go.

To get the most out of this book

Some coding experience in Golang and knowledge of basic machine learning concepts will aid you in understanding the concepts covered in this book.

Download the example code files

You can download the example code files for this book from your account at `www.packt.com`. If you purchased this book elsewhere, you can visit `www.packt.com/support` and register to have the files emailed directly to you.

You can download the code files by following these steps:

1. Log in or register at `www.packt.com`.
2. Select the **SUPPORT** tab.
3. Click on **Code Downloads & Errata**.
4. Enter the name of the book in the **Search** box and follow the onscreen instructions.

Once the file is downloaded, please make sure that you unzip or extract the folder using the latest version of:

- WinRAR/7-Zip for Windows
- Zipeg/iZip/UnRarX for Mac
- 7-Zip/PeaZip for Linux

The code bundle for the book is also hosted on GitHub at `https://github.com/PacktPublishing/Go-Machine-Learning-Projects`. In case there's an update to the code, it will be updated on the existing GitHub repository.

We also have other code bundles from our rich catalog of books and videos available at `https://github.com/PacktPublishing/`. Check them out!

Conventions used

There are a number of text conventions used throughout this book.

`CodeInText`: Indicates code words in text, database table names, folder names, filenames, file extensions, pathnames, dummy URLs, user input, and Twitter handles. Here is an example: "We sketched out a dummy `Classifier` type that does nothing."

A block of code is set as follows:

```
Word: she - true
Word: shan't - false
Word: be - false
Word: learning - true
Word: excessively. - true
```

Any command-line input or output is written as follows:

```
go get -u github.com/go-nlp/tfidf
```

Bold: Indicates a new term, an important word, or words that you see on screen. For example, words in menus or dialog boxes appear in the text like this. Here is an example: "Select **System info** from the **Administration** panel."

Warnings or important notes appear like this.

Tips and tricks appear like this.

Get in touch

Feedback from our readers is always welcome.

General feedback: If you have questions about any aspect of this book, mention the book title in the subject of your message and email us at customercare@packtpub.com.

Errata: Although we have taken every care to ensure the accuracy of our content, mistakes do happen. If you have found a mistake in this book, we would be grateful if you would report this to us. Please visit www.packt.com/submit-errata, selecting your book, clicking on the Errata Submission Form link, and entering the details.

Piracy: If you come across any illegal copies of our works in any form on the internet, we would be grateful if you would provide us with the location address or website name. Please contact us at copyright@packt.com with a link to the material.

If you are interested in becoming an author: If there is a topic that you have expertise in, and you are interested in either writing or contributing to a book, please visit authors.packtpub.com.

Reviews

Please leave a review. Once you have read and used this book, why not leave a review on the site that you purchased it from? Potential readers can then see and use your unbiased opinion to make purchase decisions, we at Packt can understand what you think about our products, and our authors can see your feedback on their book. Thank you!

For more information about Packt, please visit packt.com.

How to Solve All Machine Learning Problems

1

Welcome to the book *Go Machine Learning Projects*.

This is a rather odd book. It's not a book about how **machine learning** (**ML**) works. In fact, originally it was decided that we will assume that the readers are familiar with the **machine learning** (**ML**) algorithms I am to introduce in these chapters. Doing so would yield a rather empty book, I feared. If the reader knows the ML algorithm, what happens next is to simply apply the ML algorithm in the correct context of the problem! The ten or so chapters in this book would be completed in under 30 pages—anyone who's written a grant report for government agencies would have experience writing such things.

So what is this book going to be about?

It's going to be about applying ML algorithms within a specific, given context of the problem. These problems are concrete, and are specified by me on a whim. But in order to explore the avenues of the application of ML algorithms to problems, the reader must first be familiar with algorithms and the problems! So, this book has to strike a very delicate balance between understanding the problem, and understanding the specific algorithm used to solve the problem.

But before we go too far, what is a problem? And what do I mean when I say *algorithm*? And what's with this *machine learning* business?

What is a problem?

In colloquial use, a problem is something to be overcome. When people say they have money problems, the problem may be overcome simply by having more money. When someone has a mathematical problem, the problem may be overcome by mathematics. The thing or process used to overcome a problem is called a **solution**.

At this point, it may seem a little strange for me to define what is a common word. Ah, but precision and clarity of mind are required in order to solve problems with ML. You have to be precise about what exactly you are trying to solve.

Problems can be broken down into subproblems. But at some point, it no longer makes sense to break down those problems any further. I put it to the reader that there are different types of problems out there. So numerous are the types of problems that it is not worthwhile enumerating them all. Nonetheless, the urgency of a problem should be considered.

If you're building a photo organization tool (perhaps you are planning to rival Google Photos or Facebook), then recognizing faces in a photo is less urgent than knowing where to store, and how to retrieve a photo. If you do not know how to solve the latter, all the knowledge in the world to solve the former would be wasted.

I argue that urgency, despite its subjectivity, is a good metric to use when considering subproblems of the larger problem. To use a set of more concrete examples, consider three scenarios that all require some sort of ML solutions, but the solutions required are of different urgency. These examples are clearly made up examples, and have little or no bearing on real life. Their entire purpose is to make a point.

First, consider a real estate intelligence business. The entire survival of the business depends on being able to correctly predict the prices of houses to be sold, although perhaps they also make their money on some form of second market. To them, the ML problem faced is **urgent**. They would have to fully understand the ins and outs of the solution, otherwise they risk going out of business. In the view of the popular urgency/importance split, the ML problem can also be considered **important** and **urgent**.

Second, consider an online supermarket. They would like to know which groupings of products sell best together so they can bundle them to appear more competitive. This is not the core business activity, hence the ML problem faced is less urgent than the previous example. Some knowledge about how the solution works would be necessary. Imagine their algorithm says that they should bundle diarrhea medication with their home brand food products. They'd need to be able to understand how the solution came to that.

Lastly, consider the aforementioned photo application. Facial recognition is a nice *bonus* feature, but not the main feature. Therefore, the ML problem is least urgent amongst the three.

Different urgencies lead to different requirements when it comes to solving the problems.

What is an algorithm?

The previous section has been pretty diligent in the use of the term *algorithm*. Throughout this book, the term is liberally sprinkled, but is always used judiciously. But what is an algorithm?

To answer that, well, we must first ask, what is a program? A program is a series of steps to be performed by the computer. An algorithm is a set of rules that will solve the problem. A ML algorithm is hence a set of rules to solve a problem. They are implemented as a program on a computer.

One of the most eye-opening moments in truly and deeply understanding what exactly an algorithm is for me was an experience I had about 15 years ago. I was staying over at a friend's place. My friend had a seven year old child, and the friend was exasperated at trying to get her child to learn programming as her child had been too stubborn to learn the discipline of syntax. The root cause, I surmised, was that the child had not understood the idea of an algorithm. So the following morning, we tasked the child to make his own breakfast. Except he wasn't to make his own breakfast. He was to write down a series of steps that his mother was to follow to the letter.

The breakfast was simple—a bowl of cornflakes in milk. Nonetheless, it took the child some eleven attempts to get a bowl of cereal. It ended in tears and plenty of milk and cereal on the countertop, but it was a lesson well learned for the child.

This may seem like wanton child abuse. but it served me well too. In particular, the child said to his mother and me, in paraphrase, *But you already know how to make cereal; why do you need instructions to do so?* His mum responded, *think of this as teaching me how to to make computer games.* Here we have a meta notion of an algorithm. The child giving instructions on how to make cereal is teaching the child how to program; is itself an algorithm!

A ML algorithm can refer to the algorithm that is learned, or the algorithm that teaches the machine to use the correct algorithm. For the most part of this book, we shall refer to the latter, but it's quite useful to think of the former as well, if only as a mental exercise of sorts. For the most parts since Turing, we can substitute algorithm with machine.

Take some time to go through these sentences after reading the following section. It will help in clarifying what I mean upon a second read.

What is machine learning?

So what then is ML? As the word may hint, it's the ML to do something. Machines cannot learn the same way as humans can, but they can definitely emulate some parts of human learning. But what are they supposed to learn? Different algorithms learn different things, but the shared themes are that the machines learn a program. Or to put in less specific terms, the machine learns to *do* the correct thing.

What then is the correct thing? Not wanting to open a philosophical can of worms, the correct thing is what we, as human programmers of the computer, define as the correct thing.

There are multiple classification schemes of ML systems, but amongst the most common classification schemes, is one that splits ML into two types: supervised learning and unsupervised learning. Throughout this book we will see examples of both, but it's my opinion that such forms of classification are squarely in the *good to know but not operationally important* area of the brain. I say so because outside of a few well-known algorithms, unsupervised learning is still very much under active research. Supervised learning algorithms are too, but have been used in industry for longer than the unsupervised algorithms. That is not to say that unsupervised learning is not of value—a few have escaped the ivory towers of academia and have proven to be quite useful. We shall explore **K-means** and **k-Nearest Neighbors (KNN)** in one of the chapters.

Let's suppose for now we have a machine learning algorithm. The algorithm is a black box - we don't know what goes on inside. We feed it some data. And through its internal mechanisms, it produces an output. The output may not be correct. So it checks for whether the output is correct or not. If the output is not correct, it changes its internal mechanism, and tries again and again until the output is correct. This is how machine learning algorithms work in general. This is called **training**.

There are notions of what "correct" means of course. In supervised learning situations, we, the humans provide the machine with examples of correct data. In unsupervised learning situations, the notion of correctness relies on other metrics like distances between values. Each algorithm has its own specifics, but in general machine learning algorithms are as described.

Do you need machine learning?

Perhaps the most surprising question to ask, is whether you need machine learning to solve your problem. There is after all, a good reason why this section is the fourth in the chapter—we must understand what exactly is a problem is; and understand what an algorithm is before we can raise the question: do you need machine learning?

The first question to ask is of course: do you have a problem you need to solve? I assume the answer is yes, because we live in the world and are part of the world. Even ascetics have problems they need solved. But perhaps the question should be more specific: do you have a problem that can be solved with machine learning?

I've consulted a fair bit, and in my early days of consulting, I'd eagerly say yes to most enquiries. Ah, the things one does when one is young and inexperienced. The problems would often show up after I said yes. It turns out many of these consulting enquiries would be better served by having a more thorough understanding of the business domain and a more thorough understanding of computer science in general.

A common variant of a problem that is brought to me often requires information retrieval solutions, not machine learning solutions. Consider the following request I received several years ago:

> *Hi Xuanyi,*
> *I am XXXX. We met at YYYY meetup a few months ago. My company is currently*
> *building a machine learning system that extracts relationships between entities.*
> *Wondering if you may be interested to catch up for coffee?*

Naturally, this piqued my interest—relationship extraction is a particularly challenging task in machine learning. I was young, and ever so eager to get my hands on tough problems. So I sat down with the company, and we worked out what was needed based on surface information. I suggested several models, all of which were greeted with enthusiasm. We finally settled on an SVM-based model. Then I got to work.

The first step in any machine learning project is to collect data. So I did. Much to my surprise, the data was already neatly classified, and entities already identified. Further, the entities have a static, unchanging relationship. One type of entity would have a permanent relationship with another type of entity. What was the machine learning problem?

I brought this up after one and a half month's worth of data gathering. What was going on? We have clean data, we have clean relationships. All new data had clean relationships. Where is the need for machine learning?

It later emerged that the data came from manual data input, which was at the time required by law. The entity relationships were defined fairly strictly. The only data requirement they really needed was a cleaned up database entity-relationship diagram. Because their database structure was so convoluted, they could not really see that all they needed to do was to define a foreign-key relationship to enforce the relationship. When I had requested the data, the data had came from individual SQL queries. There was no need for machine learning!

To their DBA's credit, that was what their DBA had been saying all along.

This taught me a lesson: Always find out if someone really needs machine learning solutions before spending time working on it.

I've since settled on a very easy way of determining if someone needs machine learning. These are my rules of thumb

1. Can the problem in this form: "Given X, I want to predict Y"
2. A what-question is generally suspect. A what question looks like this: "I want to know what is our conversion rate for XYZ product"

The general problem solving process

Only if the general rules of thumbs are fulfilled then will I engage to further. The general problem solving process goes as follows for me:

1. Identify clearly the problems.
2. Translate the problems into a more concrete statement.
3. Gather data
4. Perform exploratory data analysis
5. Determine the correct machine learning solution to use
6. Build a model.
7. Train the model.
8. Test the model.

Throughout the chapters in this book, the pattern above will be followed. The exploratory data analysis sections will be only done for the first few chapters. It's implicit that those would have been done in the later chapters.

I have attempted to be clear in the section headings on what exactly are we trying to solve, but writing is a difficult task, so I may miss some.

What is a model?

All models are wrong; but some are useful.

Now it would be very remarkable if any system existing in the real world could be exactly represented by any simple model. However, cunningly chosen parsimonious models often do provide remarkably useful approximations. For example, the law $PV = RT$ relating pressure P, volume V and temperature T of an "ideal" gas via a constant R is not exactly true for any real gas, but it frequently provides a useful approximation and furthermore its structure is informative since it springs from a physical view of the behavior of gas molecules.

For such a model there is no need to ask the question "Is the model true?". If "truth" is to be the "whole truth" the answer must be "No". The only question of interest is "Is the model illuminating and useful?".

- George Box (1978)

Model train are a fairly common hobby, despite being lampooned by the likes of The Big Bang Theory. A model train is not a real train. For one, the sizes are different. Model trains do not work exactly the same way a real train does. There are gradations of model trains, each being more similar to actual trains than the previous.

A model is in that sense a representation of reality. What do we represent it with? By and large, numbers. A model is a bunch of numbers that describes reality, and a bit more.

Every time I try to explain what a model is I inevitably get responses along the lines of "You can't just reduce us to a bunch of numbers!". So what do I mean "numbers"?

Consider the following right angle triangle:

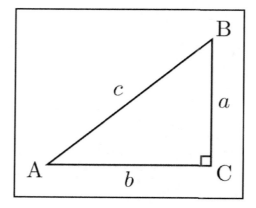

How do we describe *all* right angle triangles? We might say something like this:

$$\angle ABC + \angle BCA + \angle CAB = 180$$
$$\exists \angle = 90$$

This says that the sum of all angles in a right angle adds up to 180 degrees, and there exists an angle that is 90 degrees. This is sufficient to describe *all* right angle triangles in Cartesian space.

But is the description the triangle itself? It is not. This issue has plagued philosophers ever since the days of Aristotle. We shall not enter into a philosophical discussion for such a discussion will only serve to prolong the agony of this chapter.

So for our purposes in this chapter, we'll say that a model is the values that describe reality, *and* the algorithm that produces those values. These values are typically numbers, though they may be of other types as well.

What is a good model?

A model is a bunch of values that describe the world, alongside the program that produces these values. That much, we have concluded from the previous section. Now we have to pass some value judgments on models - whether a model is good or bad.

A good model needs to describe the world accurately. This is said in the most generic way possible. Described thus, this statement about a good model encompasses many notions. We shall have to make this abstract idea a bit more concrete to proceed.

A machine learning algorithm is trained on a bunch of data. To the machine, this bunch of data is the world. But to us, the data that we feed the machine in for training is not the world. To us humans, there is much more to the world than what the machine may know about. So when I say "a good model needs to describe the world accurately", there are two senses to the word "world" that applies - the world as the machine knows, and the world as we know it.

The machine has only seen portions of the world as we know it. There are parts of the world the machine has not seen. So it is then a good machine learning model when it is able to provide the correct outputs for inputs it has not seen yet.

As a concrete example, let's once again suppose that we have a machine learning algorithm that determines if an image is that of a hot dog or not. We feed the model images of hot dogs and hamburgers. To the machine, the world are simply images of hot dogs and hamburgers. What happens when we pass in as input, an image of vegetables? A good model would be able to **generalize** and say it's not a hot dog. A poor model would simply crash.

And thus with this analogy, we have defined a good model to be one that generalizes well to unknown situations.

Often, as part of the process of building machine learning systems, we would want to put this notion to test. So we would have to split our dataset into testing and training datasets. The machine would be trained on the training dataset, and to test how good the model is once the training has completed, we will then feed in the testing dataset to the machine. It's assumed of course that the machine has never seen the testing dataset. A good machine learning model hence would be able to generate the correct output for the testing dataset, despite never having seen it.

On writing and chapter organization

A note on the writing in this book. As you may already have guessed, I have decided to settle upon a more conversational tone. I find this tone to be friendlier to the reader who may be intimidated by machine algorithms. I am also, if you have not yet noticed, quite opinionated in my writing. I strive to make clear, through my writing, what is and what ought to be. Application of Hume's fork is at the discretion at the reader. But as a quick guide, when talking about algorithms and how they work, they are is statements. When talking about what should be done, and organization of code, they are ought statements.

There are two general patterns in the design of the chapters of this book. First, the problems get harder as the chapters go on. Second, one may optionally want to mentally divide the chapters into three different parts. Part 1—Chapters 2, *Linear Regression - House Price Prediction*, Chapter 3, *Classification - Spam Email Detection*, Chapter 4, *Decomposing CO2 Trends Using Time Series Analysis*, Chapter 7, *Convolutional Neural Networks - MNIST Handwriting Recognition*, Chapter 8, *Basic Facial Detection*) correspond to readers who have an urgent ML problem. Part 2—Chapters 5, *Clean Up Your Personal Twitter Timeline by Clustering Tweets*, Chapter 9, *Hot Dog or Not Hot Dog - Using External Services*, Chapter 6, *Neural Networks; MNIST Handwriting Recognition*, Chapter 7, *Convolutional Neural Networks - MNIST Handwriting Recognition*, Chapter 8, *Basic Facial Detection*) are for those who have ML problems akin to the second example. Part 3, the last two chapters, are for people whose machine learning problems are not as urgent, but still require a solution.

Up to Chapter 8, *Basic Facial Detection*, for each chapter there will typically be one or two sections dedicated to the explanation of the algorithm itself. I strongly believe that one cannot write any meaningful program without at least a basic understanding of the algorithms they are using. Sure, you may **use** an algorithm that has been provided by someone else, but, without a proper understanding, it's **meaningless**. Sometimes meaningless programs may produce results, just as sometimes an elephant may appear to know how to do arithmetic, or a pet dog may appear to do a sophisticated feat, like speak.

This also means that I may sound rather dismissive of some ideas. For example, I am dismissive of using ML algorithms to predict stock prices. I do not believe that doing so will be a productive endeavor, because of an understanding of the basic processes that generate prices in a stock market, and the confounding effects of time.

Time, however, will tell if I am right or wrong. It may well be that one day someone will invent a ML algorithm that will work perfectly well on dynamical systems, but not right now, right here. We are at the dawn of a new era of computation, and we must strive to understand things as best as we can. Often you can learn quite a bit from history. Therefore, I also strive to insert important historical anecdotes on how certain things came to be. These are by no means a comprehensive survey. In fact, it is done without much regularity. However, I do rather hope that it adds to the flavor of the book.

Why Go?

This book is a book on ML using Go. Go is a rather opinionated programming language. There's the Go way, or no other way at all. This may sound rather fascist, but it has resulted in a very enjoyable programming experience. It also makes working in teams rather efficient.

Further, Go is a fairly efficient language when compared to Python. I have moved on almost exclusively to using Go to do my ML and data science work.

Go also has the benefit of working well cross-platform. At work, developers may choose to work on different operating systems. Go works well across all of them. The programs that are written in Go can be trivially cross-compiled for other platforms. This makes deployment a lot easier. There's no unnecessary mucking around with Docker or Kubernetes.

Are there drawbacks when using Go for ML? Only as a library author. In general, **using** Go ML libraries is painless. But in order for it to be painless, you must let go of any previous ways you programmed.

Quick start

First install Go, which can be found at `https://golang.org`. It provides comprehensive guides to Go. And now, quick start.

Functions

Functions are the main way that anything is computed in Go.

This is a function:

```
func addInt(a, b int) int { return a + b }
```

We call `func addInt(a, b int) int`, which is the **function signature**. The function signature is composed of the function name, parameters, and return type(s).

The name of the function is `addInt`. Note the formatting being used. The function name is in camelCase—this is the preferred casing of names in Go. The first letter of any name, when capitalized, like `AddInt` indicates that it should be exported. By and large in this book we shan't worry about exported or unexported names, as we will be mostly using functions. But if you are writing a package, then it matters. Exported names are available from outside a package.

Next, note that a and b are parameters, and both have the type int. We'll discuss types in a bit, but the same function can also be written as:

```
func addInt(a int, b int) int { return a + b }
```

Following that, this is what the function returns. This function addInt returns an int. This means when a function is called correctly, like so:

```
z := addInt(1, 2)
```

z will have a type int.

After the return type is defined, { . . . } denotes the body. When { . . . } is written in this book, it means the content of the function body is not as important for the discussion at hand. Some parts of the book may have snippets of function bodies, but without the signature func foo(...). Again those snippets are the snippets under discussion. It's expected that the reader will piece together the function from context in the book.

A Go function may return multiple results. The function signature looks something like this:

```
func divUint(a, b uint) (uint, error) { ... }
func divUint(a, b uint) (retVal uint, err error) { ... }
```

Again, the difference is mainly in naming the return values. In the second example, the return values are named retVal and err respectively. retVal is of type uint and err is of type error.

Variables

This is a variable declaration:

```
var a int
```

It says a is an int. That means a can contain any value that has the type int. Typical int would be like 0, 1, 2, and so on and so forth. It may seem odd to read the previous sentence, but *typically* is used correctly. All values of type int are typically int.

This is a variable declaration, followed by putting a value into the variable:

```
s := "Hello World"
```

Here, we're saying, define s as a `string`, and let the value be `"Hello World"`. The `:=` syntax can only be used within a function body. The main reason for this is not to cause the programmer to have to type `var s string = "Hello World"`.

A note about the use of variables: variables in Go should be thought of as buckets with a name on them, in that they hold values. The names are important insofar as they inform the readers about the values they are supposed to hold. However, names do not necessarily have to cross barriers. I frequently name my return values with `retVal`, but give it a different name elsewhere. A concrete example is shown:

```
func foo(...) (retVal int) { ... return retVal }
func main() {
    something := foo()
    ...
}
```

I have taught programming and ML for a number of years now, and I believe that this is a hump every programmer has got to get over. Frequently students or junior team members may get confused by the difference in naming. They would rather prefer something like this:

```
func foo(...) (something int) { ... return something }
func main() {
    something := foo()
    ...
}
```

This is fine. However again, speaking strictly from experience, this tends to dampen the ability to think abstractly, which is a useful skill to have, especially in ML. My advice is, get used to using different names, it makes you think more abstractly.

In particular, names do not persist past what my friend James Koppel calls an **abstraction barrier**. What is an abstraction barrier? A function is an abstraction barrier. Whatever happens inside the function body, happens inside the function body and cannot be accessed by other things in the language. Therefore if you name a value `fooBar` inside the function body, the meaning of `fooBar` is only valid within the function.

Later we will see another form of abstraction barrier—the package.

Values

A value is what a program deals with. If you wrote a calculator program, then the values of the program are numbers. If you wrote a text search program, then the values are strings.

The programs we deal with nowadays as programmers are much more complicated than calculators. We deal with different types of values, ranging from number types (int, float64, and so on) to text (string).

A variable holds a value:

```
var a int = 1
```

The preceding line indicates that a is a variable that holds an int with the value 1. We've seen previous examples with the "Hello World" string.

Types

Like all major programming languages (yes, including Python and JavaScript), values in Go are typed. Unlike Python or JavaScript however, Go's functions and variables are also typed, and strongly so. What this means is that the following code will cause the program not to compile:

```
var a int
a = "Hello World"
```

This sort of behavior is known outside the academic world as *strongly-typed*. Within academic circles, *strongly-typed* is generally meaningless.

Go allows programmers to define their own types too:

```
type email string
```

Here, we're defining a new type email. The underlying kind of data is a string.

Why would you want to do this? Consider this function:

```
func emailSomeone(address, person string) { ... }
```

If both are string, it would be very easy to make a mistake—we might accidentally do something like this:

```
var address, person string
address = "John Smith"
person = "john@smith.com"
emailSomeone(address, person)
```

In fact, you could even do this: `emailSomeone(person, address)` and the program would still compile correctly!

Imagine, however, if `emailSomeone` is defined thus:

```
func emailSomeone(address email, person string) {...}
```

Then the following will fail to compile:

```
var address email
var person string
person = "John Smith"
address = "john@smith.com"
emailSomeone(person, address)
```

This is a good thing—it prevents bad things from happening. No more shall be said on this matter.

Go also allows programmers to define their own complex types:

```
type Record struct {
    Name string
    Age int
}
```

Here, we defined a new type called `Record`. It's a `struct` that contains two values: `Name` of type `string` and `Age` of type `int`.

What is a `struct`? Simply put, a `struct` is a data structure. The `Name` and `Age` in `Record` are called the **fields of the** `struct`.

A `struct`, if you come from Python, is equivalent to a tuple, but acts as a `NamedTuple`, if you are familiar with those. The closest equivalent in JavaScript is that it's an object. Likewise the closest equivalent in Java is that it's a plain old Java object. The closest equivalent in C# would be a plain old CLR object. In C++, the equivalent would be plain old data.

Note my careful use of the words *closest equivalent* and *equivalent*. The reason why I have delayed introduction to `struct` is because in most modern languages that the reader is likely to come from, it may have some form of Java-esque object orientation. A `struct` is not a class. It's just a definition of how data is arranged in the CPU. Hence the comparison with Python's tuples instead of Python's classes, or even Python's new data classes.

Given a value that is of type `Record`, one might want to extract its inner data. This can be done as so:

```
r := Record {
    Name: "John Smith",
    Age: 20,
}
r.Name
```

The snippet here showcases a few things:

- How to write a struct—kinded value—simply write the name of the type, and then fill in the fields.
- How to read the fields of a struct—the `.Name` syntax is used.

Throughout this book, I shall use `.FIELDNAME` as a notation to get the field name of a particular data structure. It is expected that the reader is able to understand which data structure I am talking about from context. Occasionally I may use a full term, like `r.Name`, to make it clear which fields I am talking about.

Methods

Let's say we wrote these functions, and we have defined `email` as before:

```
type email string

func check(a email) { ... }
func send(a email, msg string) { ... }
```

Observe that `email` is always the first type in the function parameters.

Calling the functions look something like this:

```
e := "john@smith.com"
check(e)
send(e, "Hello World")
```

We may want to make that into a method of the `email` type. We can do so as follows:

```
type email string

func (e email) check() { ... }
func (e email) send(msg string) { ... }
```

`(e email)` is called the **receiver** of the method.

Having defined the methods thus, we may then proceed to call them:

```
e := "john@smith.com"
e.check()
e.send("Hello World")
```

Observe the difference between the functions and methods. `check(e)` becomes `e.check()`. `send(e, "Hello World")` becomes `e.send("Hello World")`. What's the difference other than syntactic difference? The answer is, not much.

A method in Go is exactly the same as a function in Go, with the receiver of the method as the first parameter of the function. It is unlike methods of classes in object-oriented programming languages.

So why bother with methods? For one, it solves the expression problem quite neatly. To see how, we'll look at the feature of Go that ties everything together nicely: interfaces.

Interfaces

An interface is a set of methods. We can define an interface by listing out the methods it's expected to support. For example, consider the following interface:

```
var a interface {
    check()
}
```

Here we are defining `a` to be a variable that has the type `interface{ check() }`. What on earth does that mean?

It means that you can put any value into `a`, as long as the value has a type that has a method called `check()`.

Why is this valuable? It's valuable when considering multiple types that do similar things. Consider the following:

```
type complicatedEmail struct {...}

func (e complicatedEmail) check() {...}
func (e complicatedEmail) send(a string) {...}

type simpleEmail string

func (e simpleEmail) check() {...}
func (e simpleEmail) send(a string) {...}
```

Now we want to write a function do, which does two things:

- Check that an email address is correct
- Send "Hello World" to the email

You would need two do functions:

```
func doC(a complicatedEmail) {
    a.check()
    a.send("Hello World")
}

func doS(a simpleEmail) {
    a.check()
    a.send("Hello World")
}
```

Instead, if that's all the bodies of the functions are, we may opt to do this:

```
func do(a interface{
    check()
    send(a string)
}) {
    a.check()
    a.send("Hello World")
}
```

This is quite hard to read. So let's give the interface a name:

```
type checkSender interface{
    check()
    send(a string)
}
```

Then we can simply redefine `do` to be the following:

```
func do(a checkSender) {
    a.check()
    a.send("Hello World")
}
```

A note on naming interfaces in Go. It is customary to name interfaces with a –er suffix. If a type implements `check()`, then the interface name should be called `checker`. This encourages the interfaces to be small. An interface should only define a small number of methods—larger interfaces are signs of poor program design.

Packages and imports

Finally, we come to the concept of packages and imports. For the majority of the book, the projects described live in something called a `main` package. The `main` package is a special package. Compiling a `main` package will yield an executable file that you can run.

Having said that, it's also often a good idea to organize your code into multiple packages. Packages are a form of abstraction barrier that we discussed previously with regards to variables and names. Exported names are accessible from outside the package. Exported fields of structs are also accessible from outside the package.

To import a package, you need to invoke an import statement at the top of the file:

```
package main
import "PACKAGE LOCATION"
```

Throughout this book I will be explicit in what to import, especially with external libraries that cannot be found in the Go standard library. We will be using a number of those, so I will be explicit.

Go enforces code hygiene. If you import a package and don't use it, your program will not compile. Again, this is a good thing as it makes it less likely to confuse yourself at a later point in time. I personally use a tool called `goimports` to manage my imports for me. Upon saving my file, `goimports` adds the import statements for me, and removes any unused packages from my import statements.

To install `goimports`, run the following command in your Terminal:

```
go get golang.org/x/tools/cmd/goimports
```

Let's Go!

In this chapter we've covered what a problem is and how to model a problem as a machine learning problem. Then we learned the basics of using Go. In the next chapter we will dive into our first problem: linear regression.

I highly encourage you to practice some Go beforehand. But if you already know how to use Go, well, let's Go!

2
Linear Regression - House Price Prediction

Linear regression is one of the world's oldest machine learning concepts. Invented in the early nineteenth century, it is still one of the more vulnerable methods of understanding the relationship between input and output.

The ideas behind linear regression is familiar to us all. We feel that some things are correlated with one another. Sometimes they are causal in nature. There exists a very fine line between correlation and causation. For example, summer sees more sales in ice creams and cold beverages, while winter sees more sales in hot cocoa and coffee. We could say that the seasons themselves cause the amount of sales—they're causal in nature. But are they really?

Without further analysis, the best thing we can say is that they are correlated with one another. The phenomenon of summer is connected to the phenomenon of greater-than the-rest-of-the-year sales of cold drinks and ice cream. The phenomenon of winter is connected, somehow, to the phenomenon of greater-than-the-rest-of-the-year sales of hot beverages.

Understanding the relationship between things is what linear regression, at its core, is all about. There can be many lenses through which linear regression may be viewed, but we will be viewing it through a machine learning lens. That is to say, we wish to build a machine learning model that will accurately predict the results, given some input.

The desire to use correlation for predictive purposes was indeed the very reason why linear regression was invented in the first place. Francis Galton, who was coincidentally Charles Darwin's cousin, hailed from an upper-class family whose lineage included doctors. He had given up his medical studies after a nervous breakdown and began travelling the world as a geologist—this was back when being a geologist was the coolest job (much like being a data scientist today)—however, it was said that Galton hadn't the mettle of Darwin, and soon he gave up the idea of travelling around the world, soured by experiences in Africa. Having inherited his wealth after his father died, Galton dabbled in all things that tickled his fancy, including biology.

The publication of his cousin's magnum opus, *On the Origin of Species*, made Galton double down on his pursuits in biology and ultimately, eugenics. Galton experimented, rather coincidentally in the same manner as Mendel, on peas. He had wanted to predict the characteristics of the offspring plants, when only information about the parent plants' characteristics were available. He realized that the offspring was often somewhere in between the characteristics of the parent plants. When Galton realized that he could derive a mathematical equation that represented inheritance using elliptical curve fitting, he invented regression.

The reasoning behind regression was simple: there was a driving force—a signal of sorts—that led the characteristics of the offspring plants to go towards the curve he had fitted. If that was the case, it meant that the driving force obeyed some mathematical law. And if it did obey the mathematical laws, then it could be used for prediction, Galton reasoned. To further refine his ideas, he sought the help of the mathematician Karl Pearson.

It took Galton and Pearson a few more attempts to refine the concept and quantify the trends. But ultimately they adopted a least-squares methodology for fitting the curves.

Even to this day, when linear regression is mentioned, it can be safely assumed that a least-squares model will be used, which is precisely what we will be doing.

We will be performing exploratory data analysis—this will allow us to understand the data better. Along the way, we will build and use the data structures necessary for a machine learning project. We will rely heavily on Gonum's plotting libraries for that. After that, we will run a linear regression, interpret the results, and identify the strengths and weaknesses of this technique of machine learning.

The project

What we want to do is to create a model of house prices. We will be using this open source dataset of house prices (`https://www.kaggle.com/c/house-prices-advanced-regression-techniques/data`) for our linear regression model. Specifically, the dataset is the data of price of houses that have been sold in the Ames area in Massachusetts, and their associated features.

As with any machine learning project, we start by asking the most basic of questions: what do we want to predict? In this case, I've already indicated that we're going to be predicting house prices, therefore all the other data will be used as signals to predict house prices. In statistical parlance, we call house prices the dependent variable and the other fields the independent variables.

In the following sections, we will build a graph of dependent logical conditions, then with that as a plan, write a program that finds a linear regression model.

Exploratory data analysis

Exploratory data analysis is part and parcel of any model-building process. Understanding the algorithm at play, too, is important. Given that this chapter revolves around linear regression, it might be worth it to explore the data through the lens of understanding linear regression.

But first, let's look at the data. One of the first things I recommend any budding data scientist keen on machine learning to do is to explore the data, or a subset of it, to get a feel for it. I usually do it in a spreadsheet application such as Excel or Google Sheets. I then try to understand, in human ways, the meaning of the data.

This dataset comes with a description of fields, which I can't enumerate in full here. A snapshot, however, would be illuminating for the rest of the discussion in this chapter:

- `SalePrice`: The property's sale price in dollars. This is the dependent variable that we're trying to predict.
- `MSSubClass`: The building class.
- `MSZoning`: The general zoning classification.
- `LotFrontage`: The linear feet of the street connected to the property.
- `LotArea`: The lot size in square feet.

There can be multiple ways of understanding linear regression. However, one of my favorite ways of understanding linear regression directly ties into exploratory data analysis. Specifically, we're interested in looking at linear regression through the lens of the **conditional expectation functions** (**CEFs**) of the independent variable.

The conditional expectation function of a variable is simply the expected value of the variable, dependent upon the value of another variable. This seems like a rather dense subject to get through, so I shall offer three different views of the same topic in an attempt to clarify:

- **Statistical point of view**: The conditional expectation function of a dependent variable Y given a vector of covariates $\bar{X}$ is simply the expected value of Y (the average) when X is fixed to X_i.
- **Programming point of view in pseudo-SQL**: `select avg(Y) from dataset where X = 'Xi'`. When conditioning upon multiple conditions, it's simply this: `select avg(Y) from dataset where X1 = 'Xik' and X2 = 'Xjl'`.
- **Concrete example**: What are the expected house prices if one of the independent variables—say, MSZoning—is RL? The expected house price is the population average, which translates to: of all the houses in Boston, what is the average price of house sold whose zoning type is RL?

As it stands, this is a pretty bastardized version of what the CEF is—there are some subtleties involved in the definition of the CEF, but that is not within the scope of this book, so we shall leave that for later. For now, this rough understanding of CEF is enough to get us started with our exploratory data analysis.

The programming point of view in pseudo-SQL is useful because it informs us about what we would need so that we can quickly calculate the aggregate of data. We would need to create indices. Because our dataset is small, we can be relatively blasé about the data structures used to index the data.

Ingestion and indexing

Perhaps the best way to index the data is to do it at the time of ingestion. We will use the `encoding/csv` package found in the `Go standard` library to ingest the data and build the index.

Before we dive into the code, let's look at the notion of an index, and how one might be built. While indexes are extremely commonly used in databases, they are applicable in any production system as well. The purpose of the index is to allow us to access data quickly.

We want to build an index that will allow us to know at any time which row(s) has the value. In systems with much larger datasets, a more complicated index structure (such as a B-Tree) might be used. In the case of this dataset, however, a map-based index would be more than sufficient.

This is what our index looks like: `[]map[string][]int`—it's a slice of maps. The first slice is indexed by the columns—meaning if we want column 0, we simply get `index[0]`, and get `map[string][]int` in return. The map tells us what values are in the columns (the key of the map), and what rows contain those values (the value of the map).

Now, the question turns to: how do you know which variables associate with which column? A more traditional answer would be to have something like `map[string]int`, where the key represents the variable name and the value represents the column number. While that is a valid strategy, I prefer to have `[]string` as the associative map between the index and column name. Searching is O(N), but for the most part, if you have named variables, N is small. In future chapters, we shall see much much larger Ns.

So, we return the index of column names as `[]string` or, in the case of reading CSVs, it's simply the first row, as shown in the following code snippet:

```go
// ingest is a function that ingests the file and outputs the header, data,
// and index.
func ingest(f io.Reader) (header []string, data [][]string, indices
[]map[string][]int, err error) {
  r := csv.NewReader(f)

  // handle header
  if header, err = r.Read(); err != nil {
    return
  }

  indices = make([]map[string][]int, len(header))
  var rowCount, colCount int = 0, len(header)
  for rec, err := r.Read(); err == nil; rec, err = r.Read() {
    if len(rec) != colCount {
      return nil, nil, nil, errors.Errorf("Expected Columns: %d. Got %d
columns in row %d", colCount, len(rec), rowCount)
    }
    data = append(data, rec)
    for j, val := range rec {
      if indices[j] == nil {
        indices[j] = make(map[string][]int)
      }
      indices[j][val] = append(indices[j][val], rowCount)
    }
    rowCount++
```

```
  }
  return
}
```

Reading this code snippet, a good programmer would have alarm bells going off in their head. Why is everything a string? The answer to that is quite simple: we'll convert the types later. All we need right now is some basic count-based statistics for exploratory data analysis.

The key is in the indexes that are returned by the function. What we have is a column count of unique values. This is how to count them:

```
// cardinality counts the number of unique values in a column.
// This assumes that the index i of indices represents a column.
func cardinality(indices []map[string][]int) []int {
  retVal := make([]int, len(indices))
  for i, m := range indices {
    retVal[i] = len(m)
  }
  return retVal
}
```

With this, we can then analyze the cardinality of each individual column—that is how many distinct values there are. If there are as many distinct values as there are rows in each column, then we can be quite sure that the column is not categorical. Or, if we know that the column is categorical, and there are as many distinct values as there are rows, then we know for sure that the column cannot be used in a linear regression.

Our main function now looks like this:

```
func main() {
  f, err := os.Open("train.csv")
  mHandleErr(err)
  hdr, data, indices, err := ingest(f)
  mHandleErr(err)
  c := cardinality(indices)

  fmt.Printf("Original Data: \nRows: %d, Cols: %d\n========\n", len(data),
len(hdr))
  c := cardinality(indices)
  for i, h := range hdr {
    fmt.Printf("%v: %v\n", h, c[i])
  }
  fmt.Println("")

}
```

For completeness, this is the definition of `mHandleError`:

```
// mHandleErr is the error handler for the main function.
// If an error happens within the main function, it is not
// unexpected for a fatal error to be logged and for the program to
immediately quit.
func mHandleErr(err error){
  if err != nil {
    log.Fatal(err)
  }
}
```

A quick `go run *.go` indicates this result (which has been truncated):

```
$ go run *.go
Rows: 1460
========
Id: 1460
MSSubClass: 15
MSZoning: 5
LotFrontage: 111
LotArea: 1073
SaleCondition: 6
SalePrice: 663
```

Alone, this tells us a lot of interesting facts, chief amongst which is that there is a lot more categorical data than there is continuous data. Additionally, for some columns that are indeed continuous in nature, there are only a few discrete values available. One particular example is the `LowQualSF` column—it's a continuous variable, but there are only 24 unique values.

We'd like to calculate the CEF of the discrete covariates for further analysis. But before that can happen, we would need to clean up the data. While we're at it, we might also want to create a logical grouping of data structures.

Janitorial work

A large part of doing data science work is focused on cleanup. In productionized systems, this data would typically be fetched directly from the database, already relatively clean (high -quality production data science work requires a database of clean data). However, we're not in production mode yet. We're still in the model-building phase. It would be helpful to imagine writing a program solely for cleaning data.

Let's look at our requirements: starting with our data, each column is a variable—most of them are independent variables, except for the last column, which is the dependent variable. Some variables are categorical, and some are continuous. Our task is to write a function that will convert the data, currently `[][]string` to `[][]float64`.

To do that, we would require all the data to be converted into `float64`. For the continuous variables, it's an easy task: simply parse the string into a float. There are oddities that need to be handled, which I hope you had spotted by the time you opened the file in a spreadsheet. But the main pain is in converting categorical data to `float64`.

Fortunately for us, people much smarter than have figured this out decades ago. There exists an encoding scheme that allows categorical data to play nicely with linear regression algorithms.

Encoding categorical data

The trick to encode categorical data is to expand categorical data into multiple columns, each having a 1 or 0 representing whether it's true or false. This of course comes with some caveats and subtle issues that must be navigated with care. For the rest of this subsection, I shall use a real categorical variable to explain further.

Consider the `LandSlope` variable. There are three possible values for `LandSlope`:

- Gtl
- Mod
- Sev

This is one possible encoding scheme (this is commonly known as one-hot encoding):

Slope	Slope_Gtl	Slope_Mod	Slope_Sev
Gtl	1	0	0
Mod	0	1	0
Sev	0	0	1

This would be a terrible encoding scheme. To understand why, we must first understand linear regression by means of ordinary least squares. Without going into too much detail, the meat of OLS-based linear regression is the following formula (which I am so in love with that I have had multiple T-shirts with the formula printed on):

$$\beta = (X'X)^{-1}(X'y)$$

Here, X is an (m x n) matrix and Y is an (m x 1) vector. The multiplications, therefore, are not straightforward multiplications—they are matrix multiplications. When one-hot encoding is used for linear regression, the resulting input matrix $(X'X)$ will typically be singular—in other words, the determinant of the matrix is 0. The problem with singular matrices is that they cannot be inverted.

So, instead, we have this encoding scheme:

Slope	Slope_Mod	Slope_Sev
Gtl	0	0
Mod	1	0
Sev	0	1

Here, we see an application of the Go proverb make the zero value useful for being applied in a data science context. Indeed, clever encoding of categorical variables will yield slightly better results when dealing with previously unseen data.

The topic is far too wide to broach here, but if you have categorical data that can be partially ordered, then when exposed to unseen data, simply encode the unseen data to the closest ordered variable value, and the results will be slightly better than encoding to the zero value or using random encoding. We will cover more of this in the later parts of this chapter.

Handling bad numbers

Another part of the janitorial work is handling bad numbers. A good example is in the LotFrontage variable. From the data description, we know that this is supposed to be a continuous variable. Therefore, all the numbers should be directly convertible to float64. Looking at the data, however, we see that it's not true—there is data that is NA.

LotFrontage, according to the description, is the linear feet of the street connected to property. NA could mean one of two things:

- We have no information on whether there is a street connected to the property
- There is no street connected to the property

In either case, it would be reasonable to replace NA with 0. This is reasonable, because the second lowest value in `LotFrontage` is 21. There are other ways of imputing the data, of course, and often the imputations will lead to better models. But for now, we'll impute it with 0.

We can also do the same with any other continuous variables in this dataset simply because they make sense when you replace the NA with 0. One tip is to use it in a sentence: this house has an Unknown `GarageArea`. If that is the case, then what should be the best guess? Well, it'd be helpful to assume that the house has no garage, so it's OK to replace NA with 0.

Note that this may not be the case in other machine learning projects. Remember—human insight may be fallible, but its often the best solution for a lot of irregularities in the data. If you happen to be a realtor, and you have a lot more domain knowledge, you can infuse said domain knowledge into the imputation phase—you can use variables to calculate and estimate other variables for example.

As for the categorical variables, we can for the most part treat NA as the zero value of the variable, so no change there if there is an NA. There is some categorical data for which NA or None wouldn't make sense. This is where the aforementioned clever encoding of category could come in handy. In the cases of these variables, we'll use the most commonly found value as the zero value:

- `MSZoning`
- `BsmtFullBath`
- `BsmtHalfBath`
- `Utilities`
- `Functional`
- `Electrical`
- `KitchenQual`
- `SaleType`
- `Exterior1st`
- `Exterior2nd`

Furthermore, there are some variables that are categorical, but the data is numerical. An example found in the dataset is the `MSSubclass` variable. It's essentially a categorical variable, but its data is numerical. When encoding these kinds of categorical data, it makes sense to have them sorted numerically, such that the 0 value is indeed the lowest value.

Final requirement

Despite the fact that we're model building right now, we want to build with the future in mind. The future is a production-ready machine learning system that performs linear regression. So whatever functions and methods we write have to take into account other things that may occur in a production environment that may not occur in the model - building phase.

The following are things to consider:

- **Unseen values**: We have to write a function that is able to encode previously unseen values.
- **Unseen variables**: At some point in the future we might pass a different version of the data in that may contain variables that are unknown at model-building time. We would have to handle that.
- **Different imputation strategies**: Different variables will require different strategies for guessing missing data.

Writing the code

Up to this point, we have only done the cleanup in our heads. I personally find this to be a much more rewarding exercise: to mentally clean up the data before actually cleaning up. This is not because I'm highly confident that I will have handled all the irregularities in the data. Instead, I like this process because it clarifies what needs to be done. And that in turn guides the data structures required for the job.

But, once the thinking is done, it's time to validate our thinking with code.

We start with the clean function:

```go
// hints is a slice of bools indicating whether it's a categorical variable
func clean(hdr []string, data [][]string, indices []map[string][]int, hints
[]bool, ignored []string) (int, int, []float64, []float64, []string,
[]bool) {
  modes := mode(indices)
  var Xs, Ys []float64
  var newHints []bool
  var newHdr []string
  var cols int

  for i, row := range data {

    for j, col := range row {
      if hdr[j] == "Id" { // skip id
```

```
        continue
      }
      if hdr[j] == "SalePrice" { // we'll put SalePrice into Ys
        cxx, _ := convert(col, false, nil, hdr[j])
        Ys = append(Ys, cxx...)
        continue
      }

      if inList(hdr[j], ignored) {
        continue
      }

      if hints[j] {
        col = imputeCategorical(col, j, hdr, modes)
      }
      cxx, newHdrs := convert(col, hints[j], indices[j], hdr[j])
      Xs = append(Xs, cxx...)

      if i == 0 {
        h := make([]bool, len(cxx))
        for k := range h {
          h[k] = hints[j]
        }
        newHints = append(newHints, h...)
        newHdr = append(newHdr, newHdrs...)
      }
    }
    // add bias

    if i == 0 {
      cols = len(Xs)
    }
  }
  rows := len(data)
  if len(Ys) == 0 { // it's possible that there are no Ys (i.e. the
test.csv file)
    Ys = make([]float64, len(data))
  }
  return rows, cols, Xs, Ys, newHdr, newHints
}
```

clean takes data (in the form of [][]string), and with the help of the indices built earlier, we want to build a matrix of Xs (which will be float64) and Ys. In Go, it's a simple loop. We'll read over the input data and try to convert that. A hints slice is also passed in to help us figure out if a variable should be considered a categorical or continuous variable.

In particular, the treatment of any year variables is of contention. Some statisticians think it's fine to treat a year variable as a discrete, non-categorical variable, while some statisticians think otherwise. I'm personally of the opinion that it doesn't really matter. If treating a year variable as a categorical variable improves the model score, then by all means use it. It's unlikely, though.

The meat of the preceding code is the conversion of a string into `[]float64`, which is what the convert function does. We will look in that function in a bit, but it's important to note that the data has to be imputed before conversion. This is because Go's slices are well-typed. A `[]float64` can only contain `float64`.

While it's true that we can also replace any unknown data with NaN, that would not be helpful, especially in the case of categorical data, where NA might actually have semantic meaning. So, we impute categorical data before converting them. This is what `imputeCategorical` looks like:

```
// imputeCategorical replaces "NA" with the mode of categorical values
func imputeCategorical(a string, col int, hdr []string, modes []string)
string {
  if a != "NA" || a != "" {
    return a
  }
  switch hdr[col] {
  case "MSZoning", "BsmtFullBath", "BsmtHalfBath", "Utilities",
"Functional", "Electrical", "KitchenQual", "SaleType", "Exterior1st",
"Exterior2nd":
    return modes[col]
  }
  return a
}
```

What this function says is, if the value is not NA and the value is not an empty string, then it's a valid value, hence we return early. Otherwise, we will have to consider whether to return NA as a valid category.

For some specific categories, NAs are not valid categories, and they are replaced by the most-commonly occurring value. This is a logical thing to do—a shed in the middle of nowhere with no electricity, no gas, and no bath is a very rare occurrence. There are techniques to deal with that (such as LASSO regression), but we're not going to do that right now. Instead, we'll just replace them with the mode.

The mode was calculated in the clean function. This is a very simple definition for finding the modes; we simply find the value that has the greatest length and return the value:

```
// mode finds the most common value for each variable
func mode(index []map[string][]int) []string {
  retVal := make([]string, len(index))
  for i, m := range index {
    var max int
    for k, v := range m {
      if len(v) > max {
        max = len(v)
        retVal[i] = k
      }
    }
  }
  return retVal
}
```

After we've imputed the categorical data, we'll convert all the data to `[]float`. For numerical data, that will result in a slice with a single value. But for categorical data, it will result in a slice of 0s and 1s.

For the purposes of this chapter, any NAs found in the numerical data will be converted to 0.0. There are other valid strategies that will improve the results of the model very slightly, but these strategies are not brief.

And so, the conversion code looks simple:

```
// convert converts a string into a slice of floats
func convert(a string, isCat bool, index map[string][]int, varName string)
([]float64, []string) {
  if isCat {
    return convertCategorical(a, index, varName)
  }
  // here we deliberately ignore errors, because the zero value of float64
is well, zero.
  f, _ := strconv.ParseFloat(a, 64)
  return []float64{f}, []string{varName}
}

// convertCategorical is a basic function that encodes a categorical
variable as a slice of floats.
// There are no smarts involved at the moment.
// The encoder takes the first value of the map as the default value,
encoding it as a []float{0,0,0,...}
func convertCategorical(a string, index map[string][]int, varName string)
([]float64, []string) {
```

```
retVal := make([]float64, len(index)-1)

// important: Go actually randomizes access to maps, so we actually need
to sort the keys
// optimization point: this function can be made stateful.
tmp := make([]string, 0, len(index))
for k := range index {
  tmp = append(tmp, k)
}

// numerical "categories" should be sorted numerically
tmp = tryNumCat(a, index, tmp)

// find NAs and swap with 0
var naIndex int
for i, v := range tmp {
  if v == "NA" {
    naIndex = i
    break
  }
}
tmp[0], tmp[naIndex] = tmp[naIndex], tmp[0]

// build the encoding
for i, v := range tmp[1:] {
  if v == a {
    retVal[i] = 1
    break
  }
}
for i, v := range tmp {
  tmp[i] = fmt.Sprintf("%v_%v", varName, v)
}

return retVal, tmp[1:]
}
```

I would like to draw your attention to the `convertCategorical` function. There is some verbosity involved in the code, but the verbosity wills away the magic. Because Go randomizes access to a map, it's important to get a list of keys, and then sort them. This way, all subsequent access will be deterministic.

The function also allows room for optimization—making this function a `stateful` function would optimize it further, but for this project we shan't bother.

This is our main function so far:

```
func main() {
 f, err := os.Open("train.csv")
 mHandleErr(err)
 hdr, data, indices, err := ingest(f)
 mHandleErr(err)
 fmt.Printf("Original Data: nRows: %d, Cols: %dn========n", len(data),
len(hdr))
 c := cardinality(indices)
 for i, h := range hdr {
  fmt.Printf("%v: %vn", h, c[i])
 }
 fmt.Println("")
 fmt.Printf("Building into matricesn=============n")
 rows, cols, XsBack, YsBack, newHdr, _ := clean(hdr, data, indices,
datahints, nil)
 Xs := tensor.New(tensor.WithShape(rows, cols), tensor.WithBacking(XsBack))
 Ys := tensor.New(tensor.WithShape(rows, 1), tensor.WithBacking(YsBack
 fmt.Printf("Xs:\n%+1.1snYs:\n%1.1sn", Xs, Ys)
 fmt.Println("")
}
```

And the output of the code is as follows:

```
Original Data:
Rows: 1460, Cols: 81
========
Id: 1460
MSSubClass: 15
MSZoning: 5
LotFrontage: 111
LotArea: 1073
Street: 2
  ⋮
Building into matrices
==============
Xs:
⌈ 0  0  ⋯  1  0⌉
| 0  0  ⋯  1  0|
  ⋮
| 0  0  ⋯  1  0|
⌊ 0  0  ⋯  1  0⌋
Ys:
C[2e+05 2e+05 ⋯ 1e+05 1e+05]
```

Note that while the original data had 81 variables, by the time we are done with the encoding there are 615 variables. This is what we want to pass into the regression. At this point, the seasoned data scientist may notice a few things that may not sit well with her. For example, the number of variables (615) is too close to the number of observations (1,460) for comfort, so we might run into some issues. We will address those issues later.

Another point to note is that we're converting the data to *tensor.Dense. You can think of the *tensor.Dense data structure as a matrix. It is an efficient data structure with a lot of niceness that we will use later.

Further exploratory work

At this point, it would be very tempting to just take these matrices and run the regression on them. While that could work, it wouldn't necessarily produce the best results.

The conditional expectation functions

Instead, let's do what we originally set out to do: explore the CEFs of the variables. Fortunately, we already have the necessary data structures (in other words, the index), so writing the function to find the CEF is relatively easy.

The following is the code block:

```
func CEF(Ys []float64, col int, index []map[string][]int)
map[string]float64 {
  retVal := make(map[string]float64)
  for k, v := range index[col] {
    var mean float64
    for _, i := range v {
      mean += Ys[i]
    }
    mean /= float64(len(v))
    retVal[k]=mean
  }
  return retVal
}
```

This function finds the conditionally expected house price when a variable is held fixed. We can do an exploration of all the variables, but for the purpose of this chapter, I shall only share the exploration of one –the yearBuilt variable—as an example.

Now, YearBuilt is an interesting variable to dive deep into. It's a categorical variable (1950.5 makes no sense), but it's totally orderable as well (1,945 is smaller than 1,950). And there are many values of YearBuilt. So, instead of printing it out, we shall plot it out with the following function:

```
// plotCEF plots the CEF. This is a simple plot with only the CEF.
// More advanced plots can be also drawn to expose more nuance in
understanding the data.
func plotCEF(m map[string]float64) (*plot.Plot, error) {
  ordered := make([]string, 0, len(m))
  for k := range m {
    ordered = append(ordered, k)
  }
  sort.Strings(ordered)

  p, err := plot.New()
  if err != nil {
    return nil, err
  }

  points := make(plotter.XYs, len(ordered))
  for i, val := range ordered {
    // if val can be converted into a float, we'll use it
    // otherwise, we'll stick with using the index
    points[i].X = float64(i)
    if x, err := strconv.ParseFloat(val, 64); err == nil {
      points[i].X = x
    }

    points[i].Y = m[val]
  }
  if err := plotutil.AddLinePoints(p, "CEF", points); err != nil {
    return nil, err
  }
  return p, nil
}
```

Our ever-growing main function now has this appended to it:

```
ofInterest := 19 // variable of interest is in column 19
cef := CEF(YsBack, ofInterest, indices)
plt, err := plotCEF(cef)
mHandleErr(err)
plt.Title.Text = fmt.Sprintf("CEF for %v", hdr[ofInterest])
plt.X.Label.Text = hdr[ofInterest]
plt.Y.Label.Text = "Conditionally Expected House Price"
mHandleErr(plt.Save(25*vg.Centimeter, 25*vg.Centimeter, "CEF.png"))
```

Running the program yields the following chart:

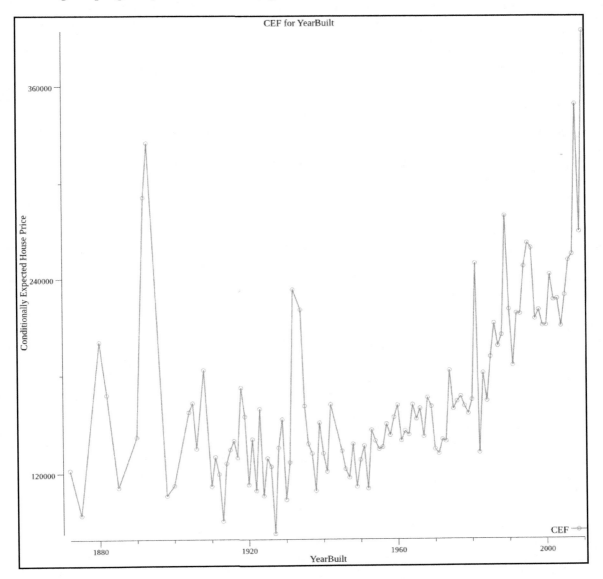

conditional expectation functions for Yearbuilt

Upon inspecting the chart, I must confess that I was a little surprised. I'm not particularly familiar with real estate, but my initial instincts were that older houses would cost more—houses, in my mind, age like fine wine; the older the house, the more expensive it would be. Clearly this is not the case. Oh well, live and learn.

The CEF exploration should be done for as many variables as possible. I am merely eliding for the sake of brevity in this book.

Skews

Now let's look at how the data for the house prices are distributed:

```go
func hist(a []float64) (*plot.Plot, error){
  h, err := plotter.NewHist(plotter.Values(a), 10)
  if err != nil {
    return nil, err
  }
  p, err := plot.New()
  if err != nil {
    return nil, err
  }

  h.Normalize(1)
  p.Add(h)
  return p, nil
}
```

This section is added to the main function:

```go
hist, err := plotHist(YsBack)
mHandleErr(err)
hist.Title.Text = "Histogram of House Prices"
mHandleErr(hist.Save(25*vg.Centimeter, 25*vg.Centimeter, "hist.png"))
```

The following diagram is:

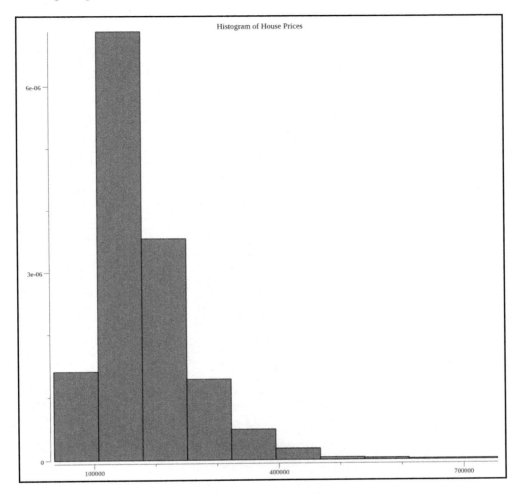

Histogram of House prices

As can be noted, the histogram of the prices is a little skewed. Fortunately, we can fix that by applying a function that performs the logging of the value and then adds 1. The standard library provides a function for this: `math.Log1p`. So, we add the following to our main function:

```
for i := range YsBack {
 YsBack[i] = math.Log1p(YsBack[i])
 }
 hist2, err := plotHist(YsBack)
```

```
mHandleErr(err)
hist2.Title.Text = "Histogram of House Prices (Processed)"
mHandleErr(hist2.Save(25*vg.Centimeter, 25*vg.Centimeter, "hist2.png"))
```

The following diagram is :

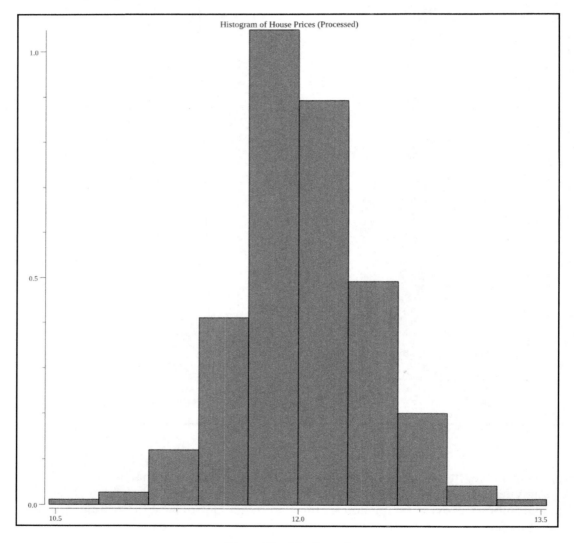

Histogram of House Prices (Processed)

Ahh! This looks better. We did this for all the `Ys`. What about any of the `Xs`? To do that, we will have to iterate through each column of `Xs`, find out if they are skewed, and if they are, we need to apply the transformation function.

This is what we add to the main function:

```
it, err := native.MatrixF64(Xs)
mHandleErr(err)
for i, isCat := range datahints {
  if isCat {
    continue
  }
  skewness := skew(it, i)
  if skewness > 0.75 {
    log1pCol(it, i)
  }
}
```

`native.MatrixF64s` takes a `*tensor.Dense` and converts it into a native Go iterator. The underlying backing data doesn't change, therefore if one were to write `it[0][0] = 1000`, the actual matrix itself would change too. This allows us to perform transformations without additional allocations. For this topic, it may not be as important; however, for larger projects, this will come to be very handy.

This also allows us to write the functions to check and mutate the matrix:

```
// skew returns the skewness of a column/variable
func skew(it [][]float64, col int) float64 {
  a := make([]float64, 0, len(it[0]))
  for _, row := range it {
    for _, col := range row {
      a = append(a, col)
    }
  }
  return stat.Skew(a, nil)
}

// log1pCol applies the log1p transformation on a column
func log1pCol(it [][]float64, col int) {
  for i := range it {
    it[i][col] = math.Log1p(it[i][col])
  }
}
```

Multicollinearity

As mentioned in the opening paragraphs of this section, the number of variables is a little high for comfort. When there is a high number of variables the chances of multicollinearity increases. Multicollinearity is when two or more variables are correlated with each other somehow.

From a cursory glance at the data, we can tell that is in fact true. A simple thing to note is GarageArea is correlated with GarageCars. In real life, this makes sense—a garage that can take two cars would be logically larger in area compared to a garage that can only store one car. Likewise, zoning is highly correlated with the neighborhood.

A good way to think about the variables is in terms of information included in the variables. Sometimes, the variables have information that overlaps. For example, when GarageArea is 0, that overlaps with the GarageType of NA—after all, if you have no garage, the area of your garage is zero.

The difficult part is going through the list of variables, and deciding which to keep. It's something of an art that has help from algorithms. In fact, the first thing we're going to do is to find out how correlated a variable is with another variable. We do this by calculating the correlation matrix, then plotting out a heatmap.

To calculate the correlation matrix, we simply use the function in Gonum with this snippet:

```
m64, err := tensor.ToMat64(Xs, tensor.UseUnsafe())
mHandleErr(err)
corr := stat.CorrelationMatrix(nil, m64, nil)
hm, err := plotHeatMap(corr, newHdr)
mHandleErr(err)
hm.Save(60*vg.Centimeter, 60*vg.Centimeter, "heatmap.png")
```

Let's go through this line by line:

`m64, err := tensor.ToMat64(Xs, tensor.UseUnsafe())` performs the conversion from `*tensor.Dense` to `mat.Mat64`. Because we don't want to allocate an additional chunk of memory, and we've determined that it's safe to actually reuse the data in the matrix, we pass in a `tensor.UseUnsafe()` function option that tells Gorgonia to reuse the underlying memory in the Gonum matrix.

`stat.CorrelationMatrix(nil, m64, nil)` calculates the correlation matrix. The correlation matrix is a triangular matrix—a particularly useful data structure that the Gonum package provides. It is a clever little data structure for this use case because the matrix is mirrored along the diagonal.

Next, we plot `heatmap` using the following snippet of code:

```
type heatmap struct {
  x mat.Matrix
}

func (m heatmap) Dims() (c, r int) { r, c = m.x.Dims(); return c, r }
func (m heatmap) Z(c, r int) float64 { return m.x.At(r, c) }
func (m heatmap) X(c int) float64 { return float64(c) }
func (m heatmap) Y(r int) float64 { return float64(r) }

type ticks []string

func (t ticks) Ticks(min, max float64) []plot.Tick {
  var retVal []plot.Tick
  for i := math.Trunc(min); i <= max; i++ {
    retVal = append(retVal, plot.Tick{Value: i, Label: t[int(i)]})
  }
  return retVal
}


func plotHeatMap(corr mat.Matrix, labels []string) (p *plot.Plot, err
error) {
  pal := palette.Heat(48, 1)
  m := heatmap{corr}
  hm := plotter.NewHeatMap(m, pal)
  if p, err = plot.New(); err != nil {
    return
  }
  hm.NaN = color.RGBA{0, 0, 0, 0} // black

  // add and adjust the prettiness of the chart
  p.Add(hm)
  p.X.Tick.Label.Rotation = 1.5
  p.Y.Tick.Label.Font.Size = 6
  p.X.Tick.Label.Font.Size = 6
  p.X.Tick.Label.XAlign = draw.XRight
  p.X.Tick.Marker = ticks(labels)
  p.Y.Tick.Marker = ticks(labels)

  // add legend
  l, err := plot.NewLegend()
  if err != nil {
    return p, err
  }

  thumbs := plotter.PaletteThumbnailers(pal)
```

```go
  for i := len(thumbs) - 1; i >= 0; i-- {
    t := thumbs[i]
    if i != 0 && i != len(thumbs)-1 {
      l.Add("", t)
      continue
    }
    var val float64
    switch i {
    case 0:
      val = hm.Min
    case len(thumbs) - 1:
      val = hm.Max
    }
    l.Add(fmt.Sprintf("%.2g", val), t)
  }

  // this is a hack. I place the legends between the axis and the actual
heatmap
  // because if the legend is on the right, we'd need to create a custom
canvas to take
  // into account the additional width of the legend.
  //
  // So instead, we shrink the legend width to fit snugly within the
margins of the plot and the axes.
  l.Left = true
  l.XOffs = -5
  l.ThumbnailWidth = 5
  l.Font.Size = 5

  p.Legend = l
  return
}
```

The `plotter.NewHeatMap` function expects an interface, which is why I wrapped `mat.Mat` in the heatmap data structure, which provides the interface for the plotter to draw a heatmap. This pattern will become more and more common in the coming chapters—wrapping a data structure just to provide an additional interface to other functions. They are cheap and readily available and should be used to the fullest extent.

A large portion of this code involves a hack for the labels. The way Gonum plots work, is that when the canvas size is calculated, the label is considered to be inside the plot. To be able to draw the labels outside the plot, a lot of extra code would have to be written. So, instead, I shrunk the labels to fit into the gutter between the axis and the plot itself as to not overlay into important areas of the plot:

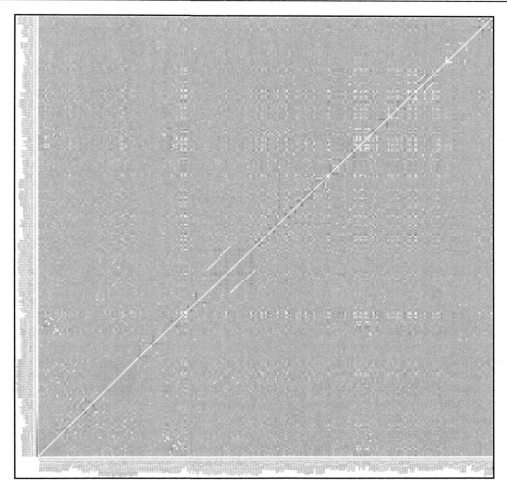

Heatmap

Of particular note in this heatmap are the white streaks. We expect a variable to correlate with itself completely. But if you notice, there are areas of white lines that are somewhat parallel to the diagonal white line. These are total correlations. We will need to remove them.

Heatmaps are nice to look at but are quite silly. The human eye isn't great at telling hues apart. So what we're going to do is also report back the numbers. The correlation between variables is between -1 and 1. We're particularly interested in correlations that are close to either end.

This snippet prints the results:

```
// heatmaps are nice to look at, but are quite ridiculous.
var tba []struct {
  h1, h2 string
  corr float64
}
for i, h1 := range newHdr {
  for j, h2 := range newHdr {
    if c := corr.At(i, j); math.Abs(c) >= 0.5 && h1 != h2 {
      tba = append(tba, struct {
        h1, h2 string
        corr float64
      }{h1: h1, h2: h2, corr: c})
    }
  }
}
fmt.Println("High Correlations:")
for _, a := range tba {
  fmt.Printf("\t%v-%v: %v\n", a.h1, a.h2, a.corr)
}
```

Here I use an anonymous struct, instead of a named struct, because we're not going to reuse the data—it's solely for printing. An anonymous tuple would suffice. This is not the best practice in most cases.

This correlation plot shows only the correlation of the independent variables. To truly understand multicollinearity, we would have to find the correlation of each variable to each other, and to the dependent variable. This will be left as an exercise for the reader.

If you were to plot the correlation matrix, it'd look the same as the one we have right here, but with an additional row and column for the dependent variable.

Ultimately, multicollinearity can only be detected after running a regression. The correlation plot is simply a shorthand way of guiding the inclusion and exclusion of variables. The actual process of removing multicollinearity is an iterative one, often with other statistics such as the variance inflation factor to lend a hand in deciding what to include and what not to include.

For the purpose of this chapter, I've identified multiple variables to be included—and the majority of variables are excluded. This can be found in the `const.go` file. The commented out lines in the ignored list are what was included in the final model.

As mentioned in the opening paragraph of this section, it's really a bit of an art, aided by algorithms.

Standardization

As a last bit of transformation, we would need to standardize our input data. This allow us to compare models to see if one model is better than another. To do so, I wrote two different scaling algorithms:

```go
func scale(a [][]float64, j int) {
    l, m, h := iqr(a, 0.25, 0.75, j)
    s := h - l
    if s == 0 {
        s = 1
    }

    for _, row := range a {
        row[j] = (row[j] - m) / s
    }
}

func scaleStd(a [][]float64, j int) {
    var mean, variance, n float64
    for _, row := range a {
        mean += row[j]
        n++
    }
    mean /= n
    for _, row := range a {
        variance += (row[j] - mean) * (row[j] - mean)
    }
    variance /= (n-1)

    for _, row := range a {
        row[j] = (row[j] - mean) / variance
    }
}
```

If you come from the Python world of data science, the first scale function is essentially what scikits-learn's `RobustScaler` does. The second function is essentially `StdScaler`, but with the variance adapted to work for sample data.

This function takes the values in a given column (j) and scales them in such a way that all the values are constrained to within a certain value. Also, note that the input to both scaling functions is `[][]float64`. This is where the benefits of the `tensor` package comes in handy. A `*tensor.Dense` can be converted to `[][]float64` without any extra allocations. An additional beneficial side effect is that you can mutate `a` and the tensor values will change as well. Essentially, `[][]float64` will act as an iterator to the underlying tensor data.

Our transform function now looks like this:

```
func transform(it [][]float64, hdr []string, hints []bool) []int {
  var transformed []int
  for i, isCat := range hints {
    if isCat {
      continue
    }
    skewness := skew(it, i)
    if skewness > 0.75 {
      transformed = append(transformed, i)
      log1pCol(it, i)
    }
  }
  for i, h := range hints {
    if !h {
      scale(it, i)
    }
  }
  return transformed
}
```

Note that we only want to scale the numerical variables. The categorical variables can be scaled, but there isn't really much difference.

Linear regression

Now that that's all done, let's do some linear regression! But first, let's clean up our code. We'll move our exploratory work so far into a function called `exploration()`. Then we will reread the file, split the dataset into training and testing dataset, and perform all the transformations before finally running the regression. For that, we will use `github.com/sajari/regression` and apply the regression.

The first part looks like this:

```
func main() {
  // exploratory() // commented out because we're done with exploratory
work.

  f, err := os.Open("train.csv")
  mHandleErr(err)
  defer f.Close()
  hdr, data, indices, err := ingest(f)
  rows, cols, XsBack, YsBack, newHdr, newHints := clean(hdr, data, indices,
datahints, ignored)
  Xs := tensor.New(tensor.WithShape(rows, cols),
tensor.WithBacking(XsBack))
  it, err := native.MatrixF64(Xs)
  mHandleErr(err)

  // transform the Ys
  for i := range YsBack {
    YsBack[i] = math.Log1p(YsBack[i])
  }
  // transform the Xs
  transform(it, newHdr, newHints)

  // partition the data
  shuffle(it, YsBack)
  testingRows := int(float64(rows) * 0.2)
  trainingRows := rows - testingRows
  testingSet := it[trainingRows:]
  testingYs := YsBack[trainingRows:]
  it = it[:trainingRows]
  YsBack = YsBack[:trainingRows]
  log.Printf("len(it): %d || %d", len(it), len(YsBack))
  ...
```

We first ingest and clean the data, then we create an iterator for the matrix of Xs for easier access. We then transform both the Xs and the Ys. Finally, we shuffle the Xs, and partition them into a training dataset and a testing dataset.

Recall from the first chapter on knowing whether a model is good. A good model must be able to generalize to previously unseen combinations of values. To prevent overfitting, we must cross-validate our model.

In order to achieve that, we must only train on a limited subset of data, then use the model to predict on the test set of data. We can then get a score of how well it did when being run on the testing set.

Ideally, this should be done before the parsing of the data into the Xs and Ys. But we'd like to reuse the functions we wrote earlier, so we shan't do that. The separate functions of ingest and clean, however, allows you to do that. And if you visit the repository on GitHub, you will find that all the functions for such an act can easily be done.

For now, we simply take out 20% of the dataset, and set it aside. A shuffle is used to resample the rows so that we don't train on the same 80% every time.

Also, note that now the clean function takes ignored, while in the exploratory mode, it took nil. This, along with the shuffle, are important for cross-validation later on.

The regression

And so, now we're ready to build the regression model. Bear in mind that this section is highly iterative in real life. I will describe the iterations, but will only share the model that I chose to settle on.

The github.com/sajari/regression package does an admirable job. But we want to extend the package a little to be able to compare models and the coefficients of the parameters. So I wrote this function:

```
func runRegression(Xs [][]float64, Ys []float64, hdr []string) (r
*regression.Regression, stdErr []float64) {
  r = new(regression.Regression)
  dp := make(regression.DataPoints, 0, len(Xs))
  for i, h := range hdr {
    r.SetVar(i, h)
  }
  for i, row := range Xs {
    if i < 3 {
      log.Printf("Y %v Row %v", Ys[i], row)
    }
    dp = append(dp, regression.DataPoint(Ys[i], row))
  }
  r.Train(dp...)
  r.Run()

  // calculate StdErr
  var sseY float64
  sseX := make([]float64, len(hdr)+1)
  meanX := make([]float64, len(hdr)+1)
  for i, row := range Xs {
    pred, _ := r.Predict(row)
    sseY += (Ys[i] - pred) * (Ys[i] - pred)
    for j, c := range row {
```

```
      meanX[j+1] += c
    }
  }
  sseY /= float64(len(Xs) - len(hdr) - 1) // n - df ; df = len(hdr) + 1
  vecf64.ScaleInv(meanX, float64(len(Xs)))
  sseX[0] = 1
  for _, row := range Xs {
    for j, c := range row {
      sseX[j+1] += (c - meanX[j+1]) * (c - meanX[j+1])
    }
  }
  sseY = math.Sqrt(sseY)
  vecf64.Sqrt(sseX)
  vecf64.ScaleInvR(sseX, sseY)

  return r, sseX
}
```

`runRegression` will perform the regression analysis, and print the outputs of the standard errors of the coefficients. It is an estimate of the standard deviation of the coefficients—imagine this model being run many many times: each time the coefficients might be slightly different. The standard error simply reports amount of variation in the coefficients.

The standard errors are calculated with the help of the `gorgonia.org/vecf64` package, which performs in-place operations for vectors. Optionally, you may choose to write them as loops.

This function also introduces us to the API for the `github.com/sajari/regression` package—to predict, simply use `r.Predict(vars)`. This will be useful in cases where one would like to use this model for production.

For now, let us focus on the other half of the main function:

```
// do the regessions
r, stdErr := runRegression(it, YsBack, newHdr)
tdist := distuv.StudentsT{Mu: 0, Sigma: 1, Nu: float64(len(it) -
len(newHdr) - 1), Src:
rand.New(rand.NewSource(uint64(time.Now().UnixNano())))}
fmt.Printf("R^2: %1.3f\n", r.R2)
fmt.Printf("\tVariable \tCoefficient \tStdErr \tt-stat\tp-value\n")
fmt.Printf("\tIntercept: \t%1.5f \t%1.5f \t%1.5f \t%1.5f\n", r.Coeff(0),
stdErr[0], r.Coeff(0)/stdErr[0], tdist.Prob(r.Coeff(0)/stdErr[0]))
for i, h := range newHdr {
  b := r.Coeff(i + 1)
  e := stdErr[i+1]
  t := b / e
```

```
    p := tdist.Prob(t)
    fmt.Printf("\t%v: \t%1.5f \t%1.5f \t%1.5f \t%1.5f\n", h, b, e, t, p)
}
...
```

Here, we run the regression, and then we print the results. We don't just want to output the regression coefficients. We also want to output the standard errors, the t-statistic, and the P-value. This would give us some confidence over the estimated coefficients.

```
tdist := distuv.StudentsT{Mu: 0, Sigma: 1, Nu: float64(len(it) -
len(newHdr) - 1), Src:
rand.New(rand.NewSource(uint64(time.Now().UnixNano())))}
```
creates a Student's t-distribution, which we will compare against our data. The t-statistic is very simply calculated by dividing the coefficient by the standard error.

Cross-validation

And now we come to the final part—in order to compare models, we would like to cross-validate the model. We've already set aside a portion of the data. Now, we will have to test the model on the data that was set aside, and compute a score.

The score we'll be using is a Root Mean Square Error. It's used because it's simple and straightforward to understand:

```
// VERY simple cross validation
var MSE float64
for i, row := range testingSet {
  pred, err := r.Predict(row)
  mHandleErr(err)
  correct := testingYs[i]
  eStar := correct - pred
  e2 := eStar * eStar
  MSE += e2
}
MSE /= float64(len(testingSet))
fmt.Printf("RMSE: %v\n", math.Sqrt(MSE))
```

With this, now we're really ready to run the regression analysis.

Running the regression

Simply run the program. If the program is run with an empty ignored list, the result will show up as a bunch of NaNs. Do you recall that earlier we have done some correlation analysis on how some variables are correlated with one another?

We'll start by adding those into our ignored list, and then run the regression. Once we have a score that is no longer NaN, we can start comparing models.

The final model I have prints the following output:

```
R^2: 0.871
  Variable Coefficient StdErr t-stat p-value
  Intercept: 12.38352 0.14768 83.85454 0.00000
  MSSubClass_30: -0.06466 0.02135 -3.02913 0.00412
  MSSubClass_40: -0.03771 0.08537 -0.44172 0.36175
  MSSubClass_45: -0.12998 0.04942 -2.63027 0.01264
  MSSubClass_50: -0.01901 0.01486 -1.27946 0.17590
  MSSubClass_60: -0.06634 0.01061 -6.25069 0.00000
  MSSubClass_70: 0.04089 0.02269 1.80156 0.07878
  MSSubClass_75: 0.04604 0.03838 1.19960 0.19420
  MSSubClass_80: -0.01971 0.02177 -0.90562 0.26462
  MSSubClass_85: -0.02167 0.03838 -0.56458 0.34005
  MSSubClass_90: -0.05748 0.02222 -2.58741 0.01413
  MSSubClass_120: -0.06537 0.01763 -3.70858 0.00043
  MSSubClass_160: -0.15650 0.02135 -7.33109 0.00000
  MSSubClass_180: -0.01552 0.05599 -0.27726 0.38380
  MSSubClass_190: -0.04344 0.02986 -1.45500 0.13840
  LotFrontage: -0.00015 0.00265 -0.05811 0.39818
  LotArea: 0.00799 0.00090 8.83264 0.00000
  Neighborhood_Blueste: 0.02080 0.10451 0.19903 0.39102
  Neighborhood_BrDale: -0.06919 0.04285 -1.61467 0.10835
  Neighborhood_BrkSide: -0.06680 0.02177 -3.06894 0.00365
  Neighborhood_ClearCr: -0.04217 0.03110 -1.35601 0.15904
  Neighborhood_CollgCr: -0.06036 0.01403 -4.30270 0.00004
  Neighborhood_Crawfor: 0.08813 0.02500 3.52515 0.00082
  Neighborhood_Edwards: -0.18718 0.01820 -10.28179 0.00000
  Neighborhood_Gilbert: -0.09673 0.01858 -5.20545 0.00000
  Neighborhood_IDOTRR: -0.18867 0.02825 -6.67878 0.00000
  Neighborhood_MeadowV: -0.24387 0.03971 -6.14163 0.00000
  Neighborhood_Mitchel: -0.15112 0.02348 -6.43650 0.00000
  Neighborhood_NAmes: -0.11880 0.01211 -9.81203 0.00000
  Neighborhood_NPkVill: -0.05093 0.05599 -0.90968 0.26364
  Neighborhood_NWAmes: -0.12200 0.01913 -6.37776 0.00000
  Neighborhood_NoRidge: 0.13126 0.02688 4.88253 0.00000
  Neighborhood_NridgHt: 0.16263 0.01899 8.56507 0.00000
  Neighborhood_OldTown: -0.15781 0.01588 -9.93456 0.00000
```

```
Neighborhood_SWISU: -0.12722 0.03252 -3.91199 0.00020
Neighborhood_Sawyer: -0.17758 0.02040 -8.70518 0.00000
Neighborhood_SawyerW: -0.11027 0.02115 -5.21481 0.00000
Neighborhood_Somerst: 0.05793 0.01845 3.13903 0.00294
Neighborhood_StoneBr: 0.21206 0.03252 6.52102 0.00000
Neighborhood_Timber: -0.00449 0.02825 -0.15891 0.39384
Neighborhood_Veenker: 0.04530 0.04474 1.01249 0.23884
HouseStyle_1.5Unf: 0.16961 0.04474 3.79130 0.00031
HouseStyle_1Story: -0.03547 0.00864 -4.10428 0.00009
HouseStyle_2.5Fin: 0.16478 0.05599 2.94334 0.00531
HouseStyle_2.5Unf: 0.04816 0.04690 1.02676 0.23539
HouseStyle_2Story: 0.03271 0.00937 3.49038 0.00093
HouseStyle_SFoyer: 0.02498 0.02777 0.89968 0.26604
HouseStyle_SLvl: -0.02233 0.02076 -1.07547 0.22364
YearBuilt: 0.01403 0.00151 9.28853 0.00000
YearRemodAdd: 5.06512 0.41586 12.17991 0.00000
MasVnrArea: 0.00215 0.00164 1.30935 0.16923
Foundation_CBlock: -0.01183 0.00873 -1.35570 0.15910
Foundation_PConc: 0.01978 0.00869 2.27607 0.03003
Foundation_Slab: 0.01795 0.03416 0.52548 0.34738
Foundation_Stone: 0.03423 0.08537 0.40094 0.36802
Foundation_Wood: -0.08163 0.08537 -0.95620 0.25245
BsmtFinSF1: 0.01223 0.00145 8.44620 0.00000
BsmtFinSF2: -0.00148 0.00236 -0.62695 0.32764
BsmtUnfSF: -0.00737 0.00229 -3.21186 0.00234
TotalBsmtSF: 0.02759 0.00375 7.36536 0.00000
Heating_GasA: 0.02397 0.02825 0.84858 0.27820
Heating_GasW: 0.06687 0.03838 1.74239 0.08747
Heating_Grav: -0.15081 0.06044 -2.49506 0.01785
Heating_OthW: -0.00467 0.10451 -0.04465 0.39845
Heating_Wall: 0.06265 0.07397 0.84695 0.27858
CentralAir_Y: 0.10319 0.01752 5.89008 0.00000
1stFlrSF: 0.01854 0.00071 26.15440 0.00000
2ndFlrSF: 0.01769 0.00131 13.46733 0.00000
FullBath: 0.10586 0.01360 7.78368 0.00000
HalfBath: 0.09048 0.01271 7.11693 0.00000
Fireplaces: 0.07432 0.01096 6.77947 0.00000
GarageType_Attchd: -0.37539 0.00884 -42.44613 0.00000
GarageType_Basment: -0.47446 0.03718 -12.76278 0.00000
GarageType_BuiltIn: -0.33740 0.01899 -17.76959 0.00000
GarageType_CarPort: -0.60816 0.06044 -10.06143 0.00000
GarageType_Detchd: -0.39468 0.00983 -40.16266 0.00000
GarageType_2Types: -0.54960 0.06619 -8.30394 0.00000
GarageArea: 0.07987 0.00301 26.56053 0.00000
PavedDrive_P: 0.01773 0.03046 0.58214 0.33664
PavedDrive_Y: 0.02663 0.01637 1.62690 0.10623
WoodDeckSF: 0.00448 0.00166 2.69397 0.01068
OpenPorchSF: 0.00640 0.00201 3.18224 0.00257
```

```
PoolArea: -0.00075 0.00882 -0.08469 0.39742
MoSold: 0.00839 0.01020 0.82262 0.28430
YrSold: -4.27193 6.55001 -0.65220 0.32239
RMSE: 0.1428929042451045
```

The cross-validation results (a RMSE of 0.143) are decent—not the best, but not the worst either. This was done through careful elimination of variables. A seasoned econometrician may come into this, read the results, and decide that further feature engineering may be done.

Indeed, looking at these results, off the top of my head I could think of several other feature engineering that could be done—subtracting the year remodeled from the year sold (recency of remodeling/renovations). Another form of feature engineering is to run a PCA-whitening process on the dataset.

For linear regression models, I tend to stay away from complicated feature engineering. This is because the key benefit of a linear regression is that it's explainable in natural language.

For example, we can say this: for every unit increase in lot area size, if everything else is held constant, we can expect a 0.07103 times increment in house price.

A particularly counter intuitive result from this regression is the `PoolArea` variable. Interpreting the results, we would say: for every unit increase in pool area, we can expect a -0.00075 times increment in price, *ceteris paribus*. Granted, the p-value of the coefficient is 0.397, meaning that this coefficient could have been gotten by sheer random chance. Hence, we must be quite careful in saying this—having a pool decreases the value of your property in Ames, Massachusetts.

Discussion and further work

This model is now ready to be used to predict things. Is this the best model? No, it's not. Finding the best model is a never ending quest. To be sure, there are indefinite ways of improving this model. One can use LASSO methods to determine the importance of variables before using them.

The model is not only the linear regression, but also the data cleaning functions and ingestion functions that come with it. This leads to a very high number of tweakable parameters. Maybe if you didn't like the way I imputed data, you can always write your own method!

Furthermore the code in this chapter can be cleaned up further. Instead of returning so many values in the clean function, a new tuple type can be created to hold the Xs and Ys—a data frame of sorts. In fact, that's what we're going to build in the upcoming chapters. Several functions can be made more efficient using a state-holder struct.

If you will note, there are not very many statistical packages like Pandas for Go. This is not for the lack of trying. Go as a language is all about solving problems, not about building generic packages. There are definitely dataframe-like packages in Go, but in my experience, using them tends to blind one to the most obvious and efficient solutions. Often, it's better to build your own data structures that are specific to the problem at hand.

For the most part in Go, the model building is an iterative process, while productionizing the model is a process that happens after the model has been built. This chapter shows that with a little awkwardness, it is possible to build a model using an iterative process that immediately translates to a production-ready system.

Summary

In this chapter, we have learned how to explore data (with some awkwardness) using Go. We plotted some charts and used them as a guiding rod to select variables for the regression. Following that, we implemented a regression model that came with reporting of errors which enabled us to compare models. Lastly, to ensure we were not over fitting, we used a RMSE score to cross-validate our model and came out with a fairly decent score.

This is just a taste of what is to come. The ideas in abstract are repeated over the next chapters—we will be cleaning data, then writing the machine learning model, which will be cross-validated. The only difference will generally be the data, and the models.

In the next chapter, we'll learn a simple way to determine if an email is spam or not.

3
Classification - Spam Email Detection

What makes you you? I have dark hair, pale skin, and Asiatic features. I wear glasses. My facial structure is vaguely round, with extra subcutaneous fat in my cheeks compared to my peers. What I have done is describe the features of my face. Each of these features described can be thought of as a point within a probability continuum. What is the probability of having dark hair? Among my friends, dark hair is a very common feature, and so are glasses (a remarkable statistic is out of the 300 people or so I polled on my Facebook page, 281 of them require prescription glasses). The epicanthic folds of my eyes are probably less common, as is the extra subcutaneous fat in my cheeks.

Why am I bringing up my facial features in a chapter about spam classification? It's because the principles are the same. If I show you a photo of a human face, what is the probability that the photo is of me? We can say that the probability that the photo is a photo of my face is a combination of the probability of having dark hair, the probability of having pale skin, the probability of having an epicanthic fold, and so on, and so forth. From a Naive point of view, we can think of each of the features independently contributing to the probability that the photo is me—the fact that I have an epicanthic fold in my eyes is independent from the fact that my skin is of a yellow pallor. But, of course, with recent advancements in genetics, this has been shown to be patently untrue. These features are, in real life, correlated with one another. We will explore this in a future chapter.

Despite a real-life dependence of probability, we can still assume the Naive position and think of these probabilities as independent contributions to the probability that the photo is one of my face.

In this chapter, we will build a email spam classification system using a Naive Bayes algorithm, which can be used beyond email spam classification. Along the way, we will explore the very basics of natural language processing, and how probability is inherently tied to the very language we use. A probabilistic understanding of language will be built up from the ground with the introduction of the **term frequency-inverse document frequency (TF-IDF)**, which will then be translated into Bayesian probabilities, which is used to classify the emails.

The project

What we want to do is simple: given an email, is it kosher (which we call ham), or is it a spam email? We will be using the `LingSpam` database. The emails from that database are a little dated—spammers update their techniques and words all the time. However, I chose the `LingSpam` corpus for a good reason: it is already nicely preprocessed. The original scope of this chapter was to introduce the preprocessing of emails; however, the topic of preprocessing options for natural language is itself a topic for an entire book, so we will use a dataset that has already been preprocessed. This allows us to focus more on the mechanics of a very elegant algorithm.

Fear not, though, as I will actually walk through the brief basics of preprocessing. Be warned, however, that the level of complexity jumps up in a very steep curve, so be prepared to be sucked into a black hole of many hours on preprocessing natural language. At the end of this chapter, I will also recommend some libraries that will be useful for preprocessing.

Exploratory data analysis

Let's jump into the data. The `LingSpam` corpus comes with four variants of the same corpus: `bare`, `lemm`, `lemm_stop`, and `stop`. In each variant, there are ten parts and each part contains multiple files. Each file represents an email. Files with a `spmsg` prefix in its name are spam, while the rest are ham. An example email looks as follows (from the `bare` variant):

```
Subject: re : 2 . 882 s - > np np
> date : sun , 15 dec 91 02 : 25 : 02 est > from : michael < mmorse @ vm1 .
yorku . ca > > subject : re : 2 . 864 queries > > wlodek zadrozny asks if
there is " anything interesting " to be said > about the construction " s >
np np " . . . second , > and very much related : might we consider the
construction to be a form > of what has been discussed on this list of late
as reduplication ? the > logical sense of " john mcnamara the name " is
```

```
tautologous and thus , at > that level , indistinguishable from " well ,
well now , what have we here ? " . to say that ' john mcnamara the name '
is tautologous is to give support to those who say that a logic-based
semantics is irrelevant to natural language . in what sense is it
tautologous ? it supplies the value of an attribute followed by the
attribute of which it is the value . if in fact the value of the name-
attribute for the relevant entity were ' chaim shmendrik ' , ' john
mcnamara the name ' would be false . no tautology , this . ( and no
reduplication , either . )
```

Here are some things to note about this particular email:

- This is an email about linguistics—specifically, about the parsing of a natural sentence into multiple **noun phrases (np)**. This is a largely irrelevant fact to the project at hand. I do, however, think it's a good idea to go through the topics, if only to provide a sanity check on manual occasions.
- There is an email and a person attached to this email—the dataset is not particularly anonymized. This has some implications in the future of machine learning, which I will explore in the final chapter of this book.
- The email is very nicely split into fields (that is, space separated for each word).
- The email has a `Subject` line.

The first two points are particularly noteworthy. Sometimes, the subject matter actually matters in machine learning. In our case, we can build our algorithms to be blind—they can be used generically across all emails. But there are times where being context-sensitive will bring new heights to your machine-learning algorithms. The second thing to note is anonymity. We live in an age where software flaws are often the downfall of companies. Doing machine learning on non-anonymous datasets are often fraught with biases. We should try to anonymize data as much as possible.

Tokenization

When dealing with natural language sentences, the first activity is typically to tokenize the sentence. Given a sentence that reads such as `The child was learning a new word and was using it excessively. "Shan't!", she cried`. We need to split the sentence into the components that make up the sentence. We call each component a token, hence the name of the process is **tokenization**. Here's one possible tokenization method, in which we do a simple `strings.Split(a, " ")`.

Here's a simple program:

```
func main() {
  a := "The child was learning a new word and was using it excessively.
\"shan't!\", she cried"
  dict := make(map[string]struct{})
  words := strings.Split(a, " ")
  for _, word := range words{
    fmt.Println(word)
    dict[word] = struct{}{} // add the word to the set of words already
seen before.
  }
}
```

This is the output we will get:

```
The
child
was
learning
a
new
word
and
was
using
it
excessively.
"shan't!",
she
cried
```

Now think about this in the context of adding words to a dictionary to learn. Let's say we want to use the same set of English words to form a new sentence: she shan't be learning excessively. (Forgive the poor implications in the sentence). We add it to our program, and see if it shows up in the dictionary:

```
func main() {
  a := "The child was learning a new word and was using it excessively.
\"shan't!\", she cried"
  dict := make(map[string]struct{})
  words := strings.Split(a, " ")
  for _, word := range words{
    dict[word] = struct{}{} // add the word to the set of words already
seen before.
  }

  b := "she shan't be learning excessively."
```

```
    words = strings.Split(b, " ")
    for _, word := range words {
        _, ok := dict[word]
        fmt.Printf("Word: %v - %v\n", word, ok)
    }
}
```

This leads to the following result:

```
Word: she - true
Word: shan't - false
Word: be - false
Word: learning - true
Word: excessively. - true
```

A superior tokenization algorithm would yield a result as follows:

```
The
child
was
learning
a
new
word
and
was
using
it
excessively
.
"
sha
n't
!
"
,
she
cried
```

A particular thing to note is that the symbols and punctuation are now tokens. Another particular thing to note is `shan't` is now split into two tokens: `sha` and `n't`. The word `shan't` is a contraction of *shall* and *not*; therefore, it is tokenized into two words. This is a tokenization strategy that is unique to English. Another unique point of English is that words are separated by a boundary marker—the humble space. In languages where there are no word boundary markers, such as Chinese or Japanese, the process of tokenization becomes significantly more complicated. Add to that languages such as Vietnamese, where there are markers for boundaries of syllables, but not words, and you have a very complicated tokenizer at hand.

The details of a good tokenization algorithm are fairly complicated, and tokenization is worthy of a book to itself, so we `shan't` cover it here.

The best part about the `LingSpam` corpus is that the tokenization has already been done. Some notes such as compound words and contractions are not tokenized into different tokens such as the example of `shan't`. They are treated as a single word. For the purposes of a spam classifier, this is fine. However, when working with different types of NLP projects, the reader might want to consider better tokenization strategies.

Here is a final note about tokenization strategies: English is not a particularly regular language. Despite this, regular expressions are useful for small datasets. For this project, you may get away with the following regular expression:

```
const re = `([A-Z])(\.[A-Z])+\.?|\w+(-
\w+)*|\$?\d+(\.\d+)?%?|\.\.\.|[][.,;"'?():-_` + "`]"
```

Normalizing and lemmatizing

In the previous section, I wrote that all the words in the second example, `she shan't be excessively learned`, are already in the dictionary from the first sentence. The observant reader might note the word `be` isn't actually in the dictionary. From a linguistics point of view, that isn't necessarily false. The word `be` is the root word of `is`, of which `was` is the past tense. Here, there is a notion that instead of just adding the words directly, we should add the root word. This is called **lemmatization**. Continuing from the previous example, the following are the lemmatized words from the first sentence:

```
the
child
be
learn
a
new
```

```
word
and
be
use
it
excessively
shall
not
she
cry
```

Again, here I would like to point out some inconsistencies that will be immediately obvious to the observant reader. Specifically, the word `excessively` has the root word of `excess`. So why was `excessively` listed? Again, the task of lemmatization isn't exactly a straightforward lookup of the root word in a dictionary. Often, in complex NLP related tasks, the words have to be lemmatized according to the context they are in. That's beyond the scope of this chapter because, as before, it's a fairly involved topic that could span an entire chapter of a book on NLP preprocessing.

So, let's go back to the topic of adding a word to a dictionary. Another useful thing to do is to normalize the words. In English, this typically means lowercasing the text, replacing unicode combination characters and the like. In the Go ecosystem, there is an extended standard library package that does just this: `golang.org/x/text/unicode/norm`. In particular, if we are going to work on real datasets, I personally prefer a NFC normalization schema. A good resource on string normalization is on the Go blog post as well: `https://blog.golang.org/normalization`. The content is not specific to Go, and is a good guide to string normalization in general.

The `LingSpam` corpus comes with variants that are normalized (by lowercasing and NFC) and lemmatized. They can be found in the `lemm` and `lemm_stop` variants of the corpus.

Stopwords

By reading this, I would assume the reader is familiar with English. And you may have noticed that some words are used more often than others. Words such as `the`, `there`, `from`, and so on. The task of classifying whether an email is spam or ham is inherently statistical in nature. When certain words are used often in a document (such as an email), it conveys more weight about what that document is about. For example, I received an email today about cats (I am a patron of the Cat Protection Society). The word `cat` or `cats` occurred eleven times out of the 120 or so words. It would not be difficult to assume that the email is about cats.

However, the word `the` showed up 19 times. If we were to classify the topic of the email by a count of words, the email would be classified under the topic `the`. Connective words such as these are useful in understanding the specific context of the sentences, but for a Naïve statistical analysis, they often add nothing more than noise. So, we have to remove them.

Stopwords are often specific to projects, and I'm not a particular fan of removing them outright. However, the `LingSpam` corpus has two variants: `stop` and `lemm_stop`, which has the stopwords list applied, and the stopwords removed.

Ingesting the data

Now, without much further ado, let's write some code to ingest the data. First, we need a data structure of a training example:

```
// Example is a tuple representing a classification example
type Example struct {
    Document []string
    Class
}
```

The reason for this is so that we can parse our files into a list of `Example`. The function is shown here:

```
func ingest(typ string) (examples []Example, err error) {
  switch typ {
  case "bare", "lemm", "lemm_stop", "stop":
  default:
    return nil, errors.Errorf("Expected only \"bare\", \"lemm\",
\"lemm_stop\" or \"stop\"")
  }

  var errs errList
  start, end := 0, 11

  for i := start; i < end; i++ { // hold 30% for crossval
    matches, err :=
filepath.Glob(fmt.Sprintf("data/lingspam_public/%s/part%d/*.txt", typ, i))
    if err != nil {
      errs = append(errs, err)
      continue
    }

    for _, match := range matches {
      str, err := ingestOneFile(match)
      if err != nil {
```

```
        errs = append(errs, errors.WithMessage(err, match))
        continue
    }

    if strings.Contains(match, "spmsg") {
        // is spam
        examples = append(examples, Example{str, Spam})
    } else {
        // is ham
        examples = append(examples, Example{str, Ham})
    }
  }
}
if errs != nil {
  err = errs
}
return
}
```

Here, I used `filepath.Glob` to find a list of files that matches the pattern within the specific directory, which is hardcoded. It doesn't have to be hardcoded in your actual code, but hardcoding the path makes for simpler demo programs. For each of the matching filenames, we parse the file using the `ingestOneFile` function. Then we check whether the filename contains `spmsg` as a prefix. If it does, we create an `Example` that has `Spam` as its class. Otherwise, it will be marked as `Ham`. In the later sections of this chapter, I will walk through the `Class` type and the rationale for choosing it. For now, here's the `ingestOneFile` function. Take note of its simplicity:

```
func ingestOneFile(abspath string) ([]string, error) {
  bs, err := ioutil.ReadFile(abspath)
  if err != nil {
    return nil, err
  }
  return strings.Split(string(bs), " "), nil
}
```

Handling errors

There is a central thesis in some programming language theories that errors in most programs happen at the boundary. While there are many interpretations of this thesis (boundaries of what? Some scholars think it's at the boundaries of functions; some think it's at the boundaries of computation), what is certainly true from experience is that boundaries of I/O are where the most errors happen. Hence, we have to be extra careful when dealing with input and output.

For the purposes of ingesting the files, we define an `errList` type as follows:

```
type errList []error

func (err errList) Error() string {
  var buf bytes.Buffer
  fmt.Fprintf(&buf, "Errors Found:\n")
  for _, e := range err {
    fmt.Fprintf(&buf, "\t%v\n", e)
  }
  return buf.String()
}
```

That way we can continue, even if an error happens while reading a file. The error will be bubbled back all the way to the top without causing any panic.

The classifier

Before we continue to build our classifier, let's imagine what the main function will look as follows. It will look something similar to this:

```
unc main() {
  examples, err := ingest("bare")
  log.Printf("Examples loaded: %d, Errors: %v", len(examples), err)
  shuffle(examples)

  if len(examples) == 0 {
    log.Fatal("Cannot proceed: no training examples")
  }

  // create new classifier
  c := New()

  // train new classifier
  c.Train(examples)

  // predict
  predicted := c.Predict(aDocument)
  fmt.Printf("Predicted %v", predicted)
}
```

The use of `Train` and `Predict` as exported methods are useful in guiding us on what to build next. From the sketch in the preceding code block, we need a `Classifier` type, that has `Train` and `Predict` at the very least. So we'll start by doing that:

```
type Classifier {}

func (c *Classifier) Train(examples []Example) {}

func (c *Classifier) Predict(document []string) Class { ... }
```

So, now, it becomes a question of how the classifier works.

Naive Bayes

The classifier is a Naive Bayes classifier. To break it down, Naive in the phrase Naive Bayes means that we are assuming that all the input features are independent. To understand how the classifier works, an additional component needs to be introduced first: the **term frequency-inverse frequency (TF-IF)** pair of statistics.

TF-IDF

TF-IDF, per its namesake, is comprised of two statistics: **term frequency (TF)** and **inverse document frequency (IDF)**.

The central thesis to TF is that if a word (called a **term**) occurs many times in a document, it means that the document revolves more around that word. It makes sense; look at your emails. The keywords typically revolve around a central topic. But TF is a lot more simplistic than that. There is no notion of topics. It's just a count of how many times a word happens in a document.

IDF, on the other hand, is a statistic that determines how important a term is to a document. In the examples we've seen, do note that the word `Subject`, with a capital `S` occurs once in both types of documents: spam and ham. In broad strokes, IDF is calculated by the following:

$$IDF \propto \frac{Documents}{Number\ of\ Documents\ where\ "Subject"\ occurs}.$$

The exact formula varies and there are subtleties to each variation, but all adhere to the notion of dividing the total number of documents over the frequency of the term.

For the purposes of our project, we will be using the `tf-idf` library from `go-nlp`, which is a repository of NLP-related libraries for Go. To install it, simply run the following command:

```
go get -u github.com/go-nlp/tfidf
```

It is an extremely well, tested library, with 100% test coverage.

When used together, $tf \times idf$ represents a useful weighting scheme for calculating the importance of a word in a document. It may seem simple, but it is very powerful, especially when used in the context of probability.

 Do note that TF-IDF cannot strictly be interpreted as a probability. There are some theoretical nastiness that presents itself when strictly interpreting IDF as a probability. Hence, in the context of this project, we will be treating TF-IDF as a sort of weighting scheme to a probability.

Now we are ready to talk about the basics of the Naive Bayes algorithm. But first I'd like to further emphasize certain intuitions of Bayes' theorem.

Conditional probability

We'll start with the notion of conditional probability. To set a scene, we'll consider several fruit types:

- Apple
- Avocado
- Banana
- Pineapple
- Nectarine
- Mango
- Strawberry

For each fruit type, we will have several instances of those fruits—so we could have a green Granny Smith and a red Red Delicious in the class of apples. Likewise, we could have ripe and unripe fruits—mangoes and bananas could be yellow (ripe) or green (unripe), for example. Lastly, we can also classify these fruits by what kind of fruit it is—tropical (avocado, banana, pineapple, and mango) versus non-tropical fruits:

Fruit	Can be green	Can be yellow	Can be red	Is tropical
Apple	yes	no	yes	no
Avocado	yes	no	no	yes
Banana	yes	yes	no	yes
Lychee	yes	no	yes	yes
Mango	yes	yes	no	yes
Nectarine	no	yes	yes	no
Pineapple	yes	yes	no	yes
Strawberry	yes	no	yes	no

I would like you to now imagine you're blindfolded and you pick a fruit. I will then describe a feature of the fruit, and you would guess the fruit.

Let's say the fruit you picked has a yellow outside. What are the possible fruits? Nectarines, bananas, pineapples, and mangoes come to mind. If you pick one of the options you would have a one in four chance of being correct. We call this the probability of yellow $P(can\ be\ yellow) = \frac{4}{8}$. The numerator is the number of yeses along the `Can be yellow` column, and the denominator is the total number of rows.

If I give you another feature about the fruit, you can improve your odds. Let's say I tell you that the fruit is tropical. Now you have a one in three chance of being right—nectarines has been eliminated from the possible choices.

We can ask this question: If we know a fruit is tropical, what is the probability that the fruit is yellow? The answer is 3/5. From the preceding table, we can see that there are five tropical fruits and three of them are yellow. This is called a **conditional probability**. We write it in a formula such as this (for the more mathematically inclined, this is the Kolmogorov definition of conditional probability):

$$P(A|B) = \frac{P(A \cap B)}{P(B)}$$

This is how you read the formula: the probability of *A* given *B* is known, and we will need to get the probability of *A AND B* happening at the same time and the probability of *B* itself.

The conditional probability of a fruit being yellow, given that it's tropical is three in five; there are actually a lot of tropical fruits that are yellow—tropical conditions allow for greater depositions of carotinoids and vitamin C during the growth of the fruit.

Looking at a tabulated result can yield an easier understanding of conditional probability. However, it must be noted that the conditional probability *can* be calculated. Specifically, to calculate the conditional probability, this is the formula:

$$P(Yellow|Tropical) = \frac{P(Yellow \cap Tropical)}{P(Tropical)}$$

The probability of a fruit being yellow *and* tropical ($P(Yellow \cap Tropical)$) is three in eight; there are three such fruits, out of a total of eight. The probability of a fruit being tropical ($P(Tropical)$) is five in eight; there are five topical fruits out of the eight listed.

And now, we are finally ready to figure out how we got to that one in three number. The probability of each class of fruits is uniform. If you had to choose randomly, you would get it right one in eight of the time. We can rephrase the question to this: What is the probability of a fruit being a banana given that it's yellow and tropical?

Let's rewrite this as a formula:

$$P(Banana|(Yellow \cap Tropical)) = \frac{P(Banana \cap (Yellow \cap Tropical))}{P(Yellow \cap Tropical)}$$

$$= \frac{\frac{1}{8}}{\frac{3}{8}}$$

$$= \frac{1}{3}$$

It is important that we relied on a special trick to perform the analysis of the preceding probabilities. Specifically, we acted as though each *yes* represents a singular example existing, while a *no* indicates that there are no examples, or, in short, this table:

Fruit	Is Green	Is Yellow	Is Red	Is Tropical
Apple	1	0	1	0
Avocado	1	0	0	1

Banana	1	1	0	1
Lychee	1	0	1	1
Mango	1	1	0	1
Nectarine	0	1	1	0
Pineapple	1	1	0	1
Strawberry	1	0	1	0

This will be important for analysis for the spam detection project. The numbers in each would be the number of occurrences within the dataset.

Features

We've seen from the previous examples, that we need features, such as whether a fruit can be green, yellow, or red, or whether it's tropical. We're now focused on the project at hand. What should the features be?:

Class	???	???	???
Spam			
Ham			

What makes up an email? Words make an email. So, it would be appropriate to consider the appearance of each word feature. We can take it further, and take the intuition that we have developed previously with TF-IDF and instead use the frequency of the words among the document types. Instead of counting 1 for the existence, we count the total number of times a word exists in the document types.

The table would look something as follows:

Class	Has XXX	Has Site	Has Free	Has Linguistics	...
Spam	200	189	70	2	...
Ham	1	2	55	120	...

That also means that there are many features. We can certainly try to enumerate all possible calculations. But doing so would be tedious and quite computationally intensive. Instead, we can try to be clever about it. Specifically, we will use another definition of conditional probability to do the trick to reduce the amount of computations that needs to be done.

Bayes' theorem

A conditional probability formula can also be written as Bayes' theorem:

$$P(A|B) = \frac{P(B|A)P(A)}{P(B)}$$

We call $P(A)$ the prior probability. $P(B|A)$ is called the **likelihood**. These are the things we're interested in, as $P(B)$ is essentially a constant anyway.

The theory at this point is a little dry. How does this relate to our project?

For one, we can rewrite the generic Bayes' theorem to one that fits our project:

$$P(Class|Document) = \frac{P(Class)P(Document|Class)}{P(Document)}$$

This formula perfectly encapsulates our project; given a document made up of words, what is the probability that it's Ham or Spam? In the next section, I will show you how to translate this formula into a very powerful classifier, in fewer than 100 lines of code.

Implementating the classifier

In the earlier parts of the chapter, we sketched out a dummy Classifier type that does nothing. Let's make it do something now:

```
type Classifier struct {
  corpus *corpus.Corpus

  tfidfs [MAXCLASS]*tfidf.TFIDF
  totals [MAXCLASS]float64

  ready bool
  sync.Mutex
}
```

Here, there are introductions to a few things. Let's walk them through one by one:

- We'll start with the corpus.Corpus type.
- This is a type imported from the corpus package, which is a subpackage of the NLP library for Go, lingo.

- To install `lingo`, simply run `go get -u github.com/chewxy/lingo/....`
- To use the `corpus` package, simply import it like so: `import "github.com/chewxy/lingo/corpus"`.

 Bear in mind that in the near future, the package will change to `github.com/go-nlp/lingo`. If you are reading this after January 2019, use the new address.

A `corpus.Corpus` object simply maps from a word to an integer. The reason for doing this is twofold:

- **It saves on memory**: A `[]int` uses considerably less memory than `[]string`. Once a corpus has been converted to be IDs, the memory for the strings can be freed. The purpose of this is to provide an alternative to string interning.
- **String interning is fickle**: String interning is a procedure where for the entire program's memory, only exactly one copy of the string exists. This turns out to be harder than expected for most tasks. Integers provide a more stable interning procedure.

Next, we are faced with two fields which are arrays. Specifically, `tfidfs [MAXCLASS]*tfidf.TFIDF` and `totals [MAXCLASS]float64`. At this point, it might be a good idea to talk about the `Class` type.

Class

We were introduced to the `Class` type when we were writing the ingestion code. This is the definition of `Class`:

```
type Class byte

const (
  Ham Class = iota
  Spam
  MAXCLASS
)
```

In other words, `Ham` is 0, `Spam` is 1, and `MAXCLASS` is 2. They're all constant values and can't be changed at runtime.

It would be prudent to note upfront, that there are limitations to this approach. In particular, it means that you have to know before running the program how many classes there will be. In our case, we know that there will be at most two classes: Spam or Ham. If we know there is a third class, say Prosciutto, for example, then we can code it as a value before MAXCLASS. There are many reasons for using a constant numerical value typed as a Class. Two of the primary reasons would be correctness and performance.

Imagine we have a function that takes Class as an input:

```
func ExportedFn(a Class) error {
  // does some decision making with a
}
```

Someone who uses this function outside this library may pass in 3 as the class: ExportedFn(Class(3)). We can instantly tell if the value is valid if we have a validation function that looks something as follows:

```
func (c Class) isValid() bool { return c < MAXCLASS }
```

Granted, this is not as nice as other languages, such as Haskell, where you could just do this:

```
data Class = Ham
           | Spam
```

And let the compiler check for you if that is at the call site, whether the value passed in was valid or not. We still want the correctness, so we defer the checks to the runtime. ExportedFn now reads as follows:

```
func ExportedFn(a Class) error {
  if !a.isValid() {
    return errors.New("Invalid class")
  }
  // does some decision making with a
  }
}
```

The notion of data types with ranges of valid value is not a revolutionary notion. Ada for example, has bounded ranges since the 1990s. And the best part about using a constant value as a range with MAXCLASS is that we can fake the range checks and do them at runtime. In this respect, Go is more or less the same as Python, Java, or other unsafe languages. Where this truly shines however, is in performance.

A tip for good software engineering practice is to make your program as knowable by the human as possible without sacrificing understanding or neatness. Using constant numerical values (or enums) generally allows the human programmer to understand the constrains that the value is allowed to have. Having constant string values, as we will see in the next section, exposes the programmer to unconstrained values. This is where bugs usually happen.

Note that in the `Classifier` struct, both `tfidfs` and `totals` are arrays. Unlike slices, arrays in Go do not require an extra layer of indirection when accessing values. This makes things a tiny bit faster. But in order to truly understand the tradeoffs of this design, we need to look at alternative designs for `Class` and with them the alternative designs of the fields, `tfidfs` and `totals`.

Alternative class design

Here, we imagine an alternative design of `Class`:

```
type Class string

const (
    Ham Class = "Ham"
    Spam Class = "Spam"
)
```

With this change, we will have to update the definition of `Classifier`:

```
type Classifier struct {
    corpus *corpus.Corpus

    tfidfs map[Class]*tfidf.TFIDF
    totals map[Class]float64

    ready bool
    sync.Mutex
}
```

Consider now the steps required to get the totals of class `Ham`:

1. The string has to be hashed
2. The hash will be used to look up the bucket where the data for `totals` is stored
3. An indirection is made to the bucket and the data is retrieved and returned to the user

Consider now the steps required to get the totals of class `Ham` if the class design was the original:

- Since `Ham` is a number, we can directly compute the location of the data for retrieval and return to the user.

By using a constant value and a numeric definition of the type `Class`, and an array type for `totals`, we are able to skip two steps. This yields very slight performance improvements. In this project, they're mostly negligible, until your data gets to a certain size.

The aim of this section on the `Class` design is to instill a sense of mechanical sympathy. If you understand how the machine works, you can design very fast machine learning algorithms.

All this said and done, there is one assumption that underpins this entire exercise. This is a `main` package. If you're designing a package that will be reused on different datasets, the tradeoff considerations are significantly different. In the context of software engineering, overgeneralizing your package often leads to leaky abstractions that are hard to debug. Better to write slightly more concrete and specific data structures that are purpose built.

Classifier part II

One of the main considerations is that a Naive Bayes classifier is a very simple program, and very difficult to get wrong. The entire program is in fact fewer than 100 lines. Let's look at it further.

We have sketched out so far the method `Train`, which will train the classifier on a given set of inputs. Here's how it looks:

```
func (c *Classifier) Train(examples []Example) {
  for _, ex := range examples {
    c.trainOne(ex)
  }
}

func (c *Classifier) trainOne(example Example) {
  d := make(doc, len(example.Document))
  for i, word := range example.Document {
    id := c.corpus.Add(word)
    d[i] = id
  }
  c.tfidfs[example.Class].Add(d)
  c.totals[example.Class]++
}
```

So here it's very clear that `Train` is an $O(NM)$ operation. But the function is structured in such a way that it would be trivial to parallelize the calls to `c.trainOne`. Within the context of this project, this wasn't necessary because the program was able to complete in under a second. However, if you are adapting this program for larger and more varied datasets, it may be instructive to parallelize the calls. The `Classifier` and `tfidf.TFIDF` structs have mutexes in them to allow for these sorts of extensions.

But what's more interesting is the `trainOne` example. Looking at it, all it seems to do is to add each word to the corpus, get its ID, and then add the ID to the `doc` type. `doc`, incidentally, is defined as such:

```
type doc []int

func (d doc) IDs() []int { return []int(d) }
```

This definition is done to fit into the interface that `tfidf.TFIDF.Add` accepts.

Let's look closer at the `trainOne` method. After making the `doc`, the words from the example are added to the corpus, while the IDs are then put into the `doc`. The `doc` is then added to the `tfidf.TFIDF` of the relevant class.

At first glance, there isn't much training here; we're just adding to the TF statistic.

The real magic happens in the `Predict` and `Score` methods.

`Score` is defined as such:

```
func (c *Classifier) Score(sentence []string) (scores [MAXCLASS]float64) {
  if !c.ready {
    c.Postprocess()
  }

  d := make(doc, len(sentence))
  for i, word := range sentence {
    id := c.corpus.Add(word)
    d[i] = id
  }

  priors := c.priors()

  // score per class
  for i := range c.tfidfs {
    score := math.Log(priors[i])
    // likelihood
    for _, word := range sentence {
      prob := c.prob(word, Class(i))
```

```
      score += math.Log(prob)
    }

    scores[i] = score
  }
  return
}
```

Given a tokenized sentence, we want to return the `scores` of each class. The idea is so that we can then look through the `scores` and find the class with the highest score:

```
func (c *Classifier) Predict(sentence []string) Class {
  scores := c.Score(sentence)
  return argmax(scores)
}
```

The `Score` function is worth a deeper look because that's where all the magic happens. First, we check the classifier is ready to score. An online machine learning system learns as new data comes in. This design means that the classifier cannot be used in an online fashion. All the training needs to be done up front. Once that training is done, the classifier will be locked, and won't train any further. Any new data will have to be part of a different run.

The `Postprocess` method is quite simple. Having recorded all the TF statistics, we now want to calculate the relative importance of each term to the documents. The `tfidf` package comes with a simple `Log`-based calculation of the IDF, but you can use any other IDF calculating function, as follows:

```
func (c *Classifier) Postprocess() {
  c.Lock()
  if c.ready {
    c.Unlock()
    return
  }

  var docs int
  for _, t := range c.tfidfs {
    docs += t.Docs
  }
  for _, t := range c.tfidfs {
    t.Docs = docs
    // t.CalculateIDF()
    for k, v := range t.TF {
      t.IDF[k] = math.Log1p(float64(t.Docs) / v)
    }
  }
  c.ready = true
```

```
    c.Unlock()
  }
```

It is important to note that there is an update to the document count of each class: t.Docs = docs to the sum of all the documents seen. This was because as we were adding to the term frequency of each class, the tfidf.TFIDF struct wouldn't be aware of documents in other classes.

The reason we would want to calculate the IDF is to control the values a bit more.

Recall that the conditional probability can be written in the Bayes' theorem form:

$$P(Class|Document) = \frac{P(Class)P(Document|Class)}{P(Document)}$$

Let's familiarize ourselves with the formula, once again by restating it in English, first by familiarizing ourselves with the terms:

- $P(Class)$: This is the **prior probability** of a class. If we have a pool of email messages and we randomly pick one out, what is the probability that the email is Ham or Spam? This largely corresponds to the dataset that we have. From the exploratory analysis, we know that the ratio between Ham and Spam is around 80:20.
- $P(Document|Class)$: This is the **likelihood** of any random document belongs to a class. Because a document is comprised of individual words, we simply make a Naïve assumption that these words are independent of one another. So we want the probability of $P("\,hello\,"\,|Ham) \cdot P("\,sir\,"\,|Ham)\cdots$. Assuming the words are independent gives us the ability to simply multiply the probabilities.

So, to put it in English:

The conditional probability of a class being Ham given a document is the result of multiplying the prior probability of a document being ham and the likelihood that the document is Ham.

The observant reader may note that I have elided explanation of $P(Document)$. The reason is simple. Consider what the probability of the document is. It's simply the multiplication of all the probabilities of a word in the corpus. It doesn't in anyway interact with the Class. It could well be a constant.

Furthermore, we run into another problem if we do use probabilities multiplied. Multiplying probabilities tend to yield smaller and smaller numbers. Computers do not have true rational numbers. `float64` is a neat trick to mask the fundamental limitations that a computer has. You will frequently run into edge cases where the numbers become too small or too big when working on machine learning problems.

Fortunately, for this case, we have an elegant solution: We can elect to work in the log domain. Instead of considering the likelihood, we would consider the log likelihood. Upon taking logs, multiplication becomes addition. This allows us to keep it out of sight, and out of mind. For most cases, this project included, this is a fine choice. There may be cases where you wish to normalize the probabilities. Then, ignoring the denominator wouldn't work well.

Let's look at some code on how to write `priors`:

```go
func (c *Classifier) priors() (priors []float64) {
  priors = make([]float64, MAXCLASS)
  var sum float64
  for i, total := range c.totals {
    priors[i] = total
    sum += total
  }
  for i := Ham; i < MAXCLASS; i++ {
    priors[int(i)] /= sum
  }
  return
}
```

The priors are essentially the proportion of `Ham` or `Spam` to the sum of all documents. This is fairly simple. To compute the likelihood, let's look at the loop in `Score`:

```go
// likelihood
for _, word := range sentence {
  prob := c.prob(word, Class(i))
  score += math.Log(prob)
}
```

We incorporate the likelihood function into the scoring function simply for ease of understanding. But the important takeaway of the likelihood function is that we're summing the probabilities of the word given the class. How do you calculate $P(Word_i|Class_j)$? such as the following:

```go
func (c *Classifier) prob(word string, class Class) float64 {
  id, ok := c.corpus.Id(word)
  if !ok {
    return tiny
```

```
}

freq := c.tfidfs[class].TF[id]
idf := c.tfidfs[class].IDF[id]
// idf := 1.0

// a word may not appear at all in a class.
if freq == 0 {
  return tiny
}

return freq * idf / c.totals[class]
}
```

First, we check whether the word has been seen. If the word hasn't been seen before, then we return a default value `tiny`—a small non-zero value that won't cause a division-by-zero error.

The probability of a word occurring in a class is simply its frequency divided by the number of words seen by the class. But we want to go a bit further; we want to control for frequent words being too important a factor in deciding the probability of the class, so we multiply it by the IDF that we had calculated earlier. And that's how you'd get the probabilities of the word given a class.

After we have the probability, we take the log of it, and then add it to the score.

Putting it all together

Now we have all the pieces. Let's look at how to put it all together:

1. We first `ingest` the dataset and then split the data out into training and cross validation sets. The dataset is split into ten parts for a k-fold cross-validation. We won't do that. Instead, we'll do a single fold cross-validation by holding out 30% of the data for cross-validation:

```
typ := "bare"
examples, err := ingest(typ)
log.Printf("errs %v", err)
log.Printf("Examples loaded: %d", len(examples))
shuffle(examples)
cvStart := len(examples) - len(examples)/3
cv := examples[cvStart:]
examples = examples[:cvStart]
```

2. We then train the classifier and then check to see whether the classifier can predict its own dataset well:

```
c := New()
c.Train(examples)

var corrects, totals float64
for _, ex := range examples {
  // log.Printf("%v", c.Score(ham.Document))
  class := c.Predict(ex.Document)
  if class == ex.Class {
    corrects++
  }
  totals++
}
log.Printf("Corrects: %v, Totals: %v. Accuracy %v", corrects,
totals, corrects/totals)
```

3. After training the classifier, we perform a cross-validation on the data:

```
log.Printf("Start Cross Validation (this classifier)")
corrects, totals = 0, 0
hams, spams := 0.0, 0.0
var unseen, totalWords int
for _, ex := range cv {
  totalWords += len(ex.Document)
  unseen += c.unseens(ex.Document)
  class := c.Predict(ex.Document)
  if class == ex.Class {
    corrects++
  }
  switch ex.Class {
  case Ham:
    hams++
  case Spam:
    spams++
  }
  totals++
}
```

4. Here, I also added an `unseen` and `totalWords` count, as a simple statistic to see how well the classifier can generalize when encountering previously unseen words.

Additionally, because we know ahead of time that the dataset comprises roughly 80% `Ham` and 20% `Spam`, we have a baseline to beat. Simply put, we could write a classifier that does this:

```
type Classifier struct{}
func (c Classifier) Predict(sentence []string) Class { return Ham }
```

Imagine we have such a classifier. Then it would be right 80% of the time! For us to know that our classifier is good, it would have to beat a baseline. For the purposes of this chapter, we simply print out the statistics and tweak accordingly:

```
    fmt.Printf("Dataset: %q. Corrects: %v, Totals: %v. Accuracy %v\n", typ,
corrects, totals, corrects/totals)
    fmt.Printf("Hams: %v, Spams: %v. Ratio to beat: %v\n", hams, spams,
hams/(hams+spams))
    fmt.Printf("Previously unseen %d. Total Words %d\n", unseen, totalWords)
```

So, this is what the final `main` function looks as follows:

```
func main() {
  typ := "bare"
  examples, err := ingest(typ)
  if err != nil {
    log.Fatal(err)
  }

  fmt.Printf("Examples loaded: %d\n", len(examples))
  shuffle(examples)
  cvStart := len(examples) - len(examples)/3
  cv := examples[cvStart:]
  examples = examples[:cvStart]

  c := New()
  c.Train(examples)

  var corrects, totals float64
  for _, ex := range examples {
    // fmt.Printf("%v", c.Score(ham.Document))
    class := c.Predict(ex.Document)
    if class == ex.Class {
      corrects++
    }
    totals++
  }
  fmt.Printf("Dataset: %q. Corrects: %v, Totals: %v. Accuracy %v\n", typ,
corrects, totals, corrects/totals)

  fmt.Println("Start Cross Validation (this classifier)")
```

```
corrects, totals = 0, 0
hams, spams := 0.0, 0.0
var unseen, totalWords int
for _, ex := range cv {
  totalWords += len(ex.Document)
  unseen += c.unseens(ex.Document)
  class := c.Predict(ex.Document)
  if class == ex.Class {
    corrects++
  }
  switch ex.Class {
  case Ham:
    hams++
  case Spam:
    spams++
  }
  totals++
}

fmt.Printf("Dataset: %q. Corrects: %v, Totals: %v. Accuracy %v\n", typ,
corrects, totals, corrects/totals)
  fmt.Printf("Hams: %v, Spams: %v. Ratio to beat: %v\n", hams, spams,
hams/(hams+spams))
  fmt.Printf("Previously unseen %d. Total Words %d\n", unseen, totalWords)
}
```

Running it on `bare`, this is the result I get the following:

```
Examples loaded: 2893
Dataset: "bare". Corrects: 1917, Totals: 1929. Accuracy 0.9937791601866252
Start Cross Validation (this classifier)
Dataset: "bare". Corrects: 946, Totals: 964. Accuracy 0.9813278008298755
Hams: 810, Spams: 154. Ratio to beat: 0.8402489626556017
Previously unseen 17593. Total Words 658105
```

To see the effects of removing stopwords and lemmatization, we simply switch to using the `lemm_stop` dataset, and this is the result I get the following:

```
Dataset: "lemm_stop". Corrects: 1920, Totals: 1929. Accuracy
0.995334370139969
Start Cross Validation (this classifier)
Dataset: "lemm_stop". Corrects: 948, Totals: 964. Accuracy
0.983402489626556
Hams: 810, Spams: 154. Ratio to beat: 0.8402489626556017
Previously unseen 16361. Total Words 489255
```

Either way, the classifier is brutally effective.

Summary

In this chapter, I have shown the basics of what a Naive Bayes classifier looks like—a classifier written with the fundamental understanding of statistics will trump any publicly available library any day.

The classifier itself is fewer than 100 lines of code, but with it comes a great deal of power. Being able to perform classification with 98% or greater accuracy is no mean feat.

A note on the 98% figure: This is not state of the art. State of the art is in the high 99.xx%. The main reason why there is a race for that final percent is because of scale. Imagine you're Google and you're running Gmail. A 0.01% error means millions of emails being misclassified. That means many unhappy customers.

For the most part, in machine learning, the case of whether to go for newer untested methods really depends on the scale of your problems. In my experience from the past 10 years doing machine learning, most companies do not reach that scale of data. As such, the humble Naive Bayes classifier would serve very well.

In the next chapter, we shall look at one of the most vexing issues that humans face: time.

4
Decomposing CO2 Trends Using Time Series Analysis

If you are reading this book in the year 2055—assuming you're still using a year system based on the Common Era (a year is the time taken by the planet you're on to go around the sun once)—congratulations! You have survived. This book is written in the year 2018, and we as humans have much to worry about in terms of the survival of our species.

By and large, we have managed to work our way into a relatively stable peace, but the future of our species as a whole is somewhat at risk from various threats. Most of these threats have been caused by our own actions in the past. I'd like to emphasize a point here: I'm not assigning blame to anyone in the past for causing these threats. Our ancestors were busy optimizing to different goals, and the threats are typically an unforeseen/unforeseeable side-effect of the actions at that time.

A compounding factor is that humans are, biologically speaking, not very well suited to thinking about the future. Our brains simply do not see our future selves as a continuity of our current selves [0],[1]. As a result, we often think of things that may happen to us in the future as things that happen to someone else, or that the future is exaggerated. This has led to decisions made today without consideration to the effect in the future. This has led to many threats that arise from past actions of our species.

One of those threats is runaway climate change that could ruin our entire way of living, and potentially threaten the entire human species with extinction. It is very real and very unexaggerated. Human-induced climate change is a very wide topic with many niches. The primary gist of the major cause of human-induced climate change is the increased rates release of **carbon dioxide (CO_2)** into the air.

In this chapter, we will perform a time series analysis on CO_2 in the air. The main goal of this chapter is to serve as an introduction to time series analysis. On the technical end, you will learn the finer side of plotting using **Gonum**. Also, we'll learn how to deal with non-conventional data formats.

Exploratory data analysis

The amount of CO_2 in the air can be measured. The **National Oceanic and Atmospheric Administration (NOAA)** department has been collecting data on the amount of CO_2 in the air since the early 1950s. The data we'll be using can be found at `https://www.esrl.noaa.gov/gmd/ccgg/trends/data.html`. We'll specifically be using that Mauna Loa monthly mean data.

The data, after removing the comments, looks something like this:

```
# decimal average interpolated trend #days
# date (season corr)
1958  3 1958.208 315.71 315.71 314.62 -1
1958  4 1958.292 317.45 317.45 315.29 -1
1958  5 1958.375 317.50 317.50 314.71 -1
1958  6 1958.458 -99.99 317.10 314.85 -1
1958  7 1958.542 315.86 315.86 314.98 -1
1958  8 1958.625 314.93 314.93 315.94 -1
```

In particular, we are interested in the `interpolated` column.

Because this is a particularly interesting dataset, it might be worth looking at how to download and preprocess the data directly in Go.

Downloading from non-HTTP sources

We'll start by writing the function that will download the data, as follows:

```
func download() io.Reader {
  client, err := ftp.Dial("aftp.cmdl.noaa.gov:21")
  dieIfErr(err)
  dieIfErr(client.Login("anonymous", "anonymous"))
  reader, err := client.Retr("products/trends/co2/co2_mm_mlo.txt")
  dieIfErr(err)
  return reader
}
```

The NOAA data sits on a publicly accessible FTP server: `ftp://aftp.cmdl.noaa.gov/products/trends/co2/co2_mm_mlo.txt`. If you visit the URI via a web browser, you would see the data immediately. To access the data programmatically is a little tricky, as this is not a typical HTTP URL.

To handle FTP connections, we will be using the `github.com/jlaffaye/ftp` package. The package can be installed using the standard `go get` method: `go get -u github.com/jlaffaye/ftp`. The documentation for the package is a little sparse and somewhat requires you to understand the FTP standards. But, fear not, using FTP to acquire the file is relatively simple.

First we need to dial in to the server (you would need to do the same if you were working with HTTP endpoints—`net/http` merely abstracts out the dialing in so you wouldn't necessarily see what's happening in the background). Because dialing in is a fairly low-level procedure, we would need to supply the ports as well. Just like the convention for HTTP is for the server to listen on port `80`, the convention for an FTP server is to listen to port `21`, so we'd have to connect to a server specifying that we want to connect on port `21`.

An additional oddity to those not used to working with FTP is that FTP requires a login to the server. For servers with anonymous read-only access, the convention is typically to use "anonymous" as the username and password.

After successfully logging in, we retrieve the requested resource (the file that we want) and download the file. The `fttp` library at `github.com/jlaffaye/ftp` returns `io.Reader`. Think of it as a file that contains the data.

Handling non-standard data

Parsing the data is a piece of cake with only the standard library:

```
func parse(l loader) (dates []string, co2s []float64) {
  s := bufio.NewScanner(l())
  for s.Scan() {
    row := s.Text()
    if strings.HasPrefix(row, "#") {
      continue
    }
    fields := strings.Fields(row)
    dates = append(dates, fields[2])
    co2, err := strconv.ParseFloat(fields[4], 64)
    dieIfErr(err)
    co2s = append(co2s, co2)
  }
  return
}
```

The parsing function takes a `loader`, which when called, returns a `io.Reader`. We then wrap the `io.Reader` in a `bufio.Scanner`. Recall that the format is not standard. There are some things that we want and some things we don't. The data however is in a fairly consistent format—we can use the standard library functions to filter the ones we want and the ones we don't.

The `s.Scan()` method scans `io.Reader` until it encounters a newline. We can retrieve the string using `s.Text()`. If the string starts with #, we skip the line.

Otherwise, we use `strings.Fields` to split the string into fields. The reason why we use `strings.Fields` instead of `strings.Split` is because the latter does not handle multiple spaces well.

Following the splitting of the row into fields, we parse things that are necessary:

```
type loader func() io.Reader
```

Why do we need a `loader` type?

The reason is simple: we want to be good citizens— we should not be repeatedly requesting data from the FTP server while we are developing the program. Rather, we would cache the file and work with that single file while in development mode. This way, we wouldn't have to download from the internet all the time.

The corresponding `loader` type that reads from the file looks something like this, and is rather self-explanatory:

```
func readFromFile() io.Reader {
  reader, err := os.Open("data.txt")
  dieIfErr(err)
  return reader
}
```

Dealing with decimal dates

One of the more interesting custom formats used in this data is dates. It's a format known as **decimal dates**. They look like as follows:

```
2018.5
```

What this means is that this date represents the halfway point of the year 2018. There are 365 days in 2018. The 50% mark would be 183 days into the year: July 3 2018.

We can translate this logic into the following code:

```
// parseDecimalDate takes a string in format of a decimal date
// "2018.05" and converts it into a date.
//
func parseDecimalDate(a string, loc *time.Location) (time.Time, error) {
  split := strings.Split(a, ".")
  if len(split) != 2 {
    return time.Time{}, errors.Errorf("Unable to split %q into a year
followed by a decimal", a)
  }
  year, err := strconv.Atoi(split[0])
  if err != nil {
    return time.Time{}, err
  }
  dec, err := strconv.ParseFloat("0."+split[1], 64) // bugs can happen if
you forget to add "0."
  if err != nil {
    return time.Time{}, err
  }

  // handle leap years
  var days float64 = 365
  if year%400 == 0 || year%4 == 0 && year%100 != 0 {
    days = 366
  }

  start := time.Date(year, time.January, 1, 0, 0, 0, 0, loc)
  daysIntoYear := int(dec * days)
  retVal := start.AddDate(0, 0, daysIntoYear)
  return retVal, nil
}
```

The first step is to split the string into the year and the decimal portion. The year is parsed as an int datatype, while the decimal part is parsed as a floating point number to ensure we can perform math. Here, it's important to note that a bug can happen if you're not careful about it: after splitting the string, "0." needs to be prepended to the string.

A cleaner alternative would be to parse the string as float64, and then use math.Modf to split the float into the integer component and the decimal component.

Either way, once we have the decimal component, we can use it to figure out how many days into the year it is. But first we'd have to figure out if the year is a leap year.

We can calculate the number of days into the years simply by multiplying the decimal number by the number of days in the year. Following from that, we simply add the number of dates, and return the date.

 One thing to note is that we pass in a `*time.Location`—in this specific instance, we know that the observatory is in Hawaii, and therefore we set it to `"Pacific/Honolulu"`. Although in this case, we could set the location to any other location in the world, and it wouldn't change the results of the data. But this is unique to this project—in other time series data, time zones may be important as the data collection method may involve time data from different time zones.

Plotting

Now that we've finished with getting the file and parsing it, let's plot the data. Again, as in `Chapter 2`, *Linear Regression-House Price Prediction,*we will be using Gonum's excellent plotting library. This time around, we're going to be exploring more of it in detail. We'll learn the following:

- How to plot a time series
- How a plot breaks down into its elements and how we can manipulate those elements to style a chart
- How to create plotters for chart types that Gonum does not provide for

We'll start by writing a function to plot a time series:

```
func newTSPlot(xs []time.Time, ys []float64, seriesName string) *plot.Plot
{
  p, err := plot.New()
  dieIfErr(err)
  xys := make(plotter.XYs, len(ys))
  for i := range ys {
    xys[i].X = float64(xs[i].Unix())
    xys[i].Y = ys[i]
  }
  l, err := plotter.NewLine(xys)
  dieIfErr(err)
  l.LineStyle.Color = color.RGBA{A: 255} // black
  p.Add(l)
  p.Legend.Add(seriesName, l)
  p.Legend.TextStyle.Font = defaultFont

  // dieIfErr(plotutil.AddLines(p, seriesName, xys))
```

```
p.X.Tick.Marker = plot.TimeTicks{Format: "2006-01-01"}
p.Y.Label.TextStyle.Font = defaultFont
p.X.Label.TextStyle.Font = defaultFont
p.X.Tick.Label.Font = defaultFont
p.Y.Tick.Label.Font = defaultFont
p.Title.Font = defaultFont
p.Title.Font.Size = 16

return p
}
```

Here, we use the already familiar `plotter.XYs` (which you would have been acquainted with in the first chapter). Instead of using `plotutil.AddLines` as we did the last time, we shall do it manually, which allows us to control the styling of the lines a bit better.

We simply create a new `*Line` object with `plotter.NewLine`. The `*Line` object is primarily `plot.Plotter`, which is any type that can draw itself onto a canvas. In the later part of this chapter, we shall explore how to create our own `plot.Plotter` interface and other associated types to draw a custom type.

Styling

But, for now, having access to the `*Line` object allows us to play around with the styling a bit more. To set the right mood with the rather gloomy nature of this chapter, I have chosen a stark black line (in fact, I have grown rather fond of the stark black line charts and have started using them in my daily plots as well). A point to note is that I did this:

```
l.LineStyle.Color = color.RGBA{A: 255}
```

`l.LineStyle.Color` takes `color.Color`—`color.RGBA` is a struct found in the `color` library in the standard library. It's a struct that has four fields representing a color, such as `Red`, `Green`, `Blue`, and `Alpha`. Here I take advantage of Go's default values—0s. But having an `Alpha` value of 0 would mean that it's invisible. Hence, I only set the `A` field to 255—the rest of the fields are defaulted to 0, which gives it a stark black color.

After we set the line style, we add the line to the plot with `p.Add(l)`. Because we're not using `plotutil.AddLines`, which abstracts away some of the manual work, we may find that if we run the function there isn't a legend in the plot. A plot without legends is generally useless. So, we also need to add a legend by using `p.Legend.Add(seriesName, l)`.

Aside from color, width, and the like, I also want to set a more brutal feel to the plots I make for this chapter—after all, this chapter is rather doom and gloom. I feel that the default font, which is Times New Roman is a little too humanist. So, we'd need to change fonts. Luckily, the extended Go standard library comes with a font-processing library. While usually I'd choose to go with slab serif style fonts for the brutal look, Go itself comes with a font that works well—the Go family of fonts.

How do we change fonts in a `*plot.Plot`? Most components of `*plot.Plot` take a `draw.TextStyle`, which is a data structure that configures the styling of text, including fonts. So, we can set those fields to indicate we want to use the font we chose.

As I mentioned, in the extended standard library, Go comes with fonts and font-processing utilities. We'll be using it here. First, we'd have to install the packages: `go get -u golang.org/x/image/font/gofont/gomono` and `go get -u github.com/golang/freetype/truetype`. The former is the official **Monospace Type** of the Go family of typefaces. The latter is a library to handle TrueType fonts.

Here, a caveat must be mentioned—while `draw.TextStyle` does allow for the configuration of fonts, the fonts are in a `vg.Font` type, which wraps a `*truetype.Font` type. If we use `truetype.Parse(gomono.TTF)`, we will get `*truetype.Font`. The `vg` package provides a function to make those fonts—`vg.MakeFont`. The reason why this is necessary instead of just using `*truetype.Font` is because `vg` has plenty of backends—some that could render fonts would require information about the font size.

So, to avoid having many calls to parse the font and making a vg.Font type, we can safely put it in a global variable, given we've already decided ahead that all fonts will be of the same brutal style:

```
var defaultFont vg.Font

func init() {
  font, err := truetype.Parse(gomono.TTF)
  if err != nil {
    panic(err)
  }
  vg.AddFont("gomono", font)
  defaultFont, err = vg.MakeFont("gomono", 12)
  if err != nil {
    panic(err)
  }
}
```

Once that's done, we can set all draw.TextStyle.Font to be defaultFont. Setting a default font size of 12 does not, however, mean that you're stuck with the size for everything. Because vg.Font is a struct, not a pointer to a struct, once set in an object, you are free to change the font size of that particular field, as I have shown in the following two lines:

```
p.Title.Font = defaultFont
p.Title.Font.Size = 16
```

With our main function we can execute the following code:

```
func main() {
  dateStrings, co2s := parse(readFromFile)
  dates := parseDates(dateStrings)
  plt := newTSPlot(dates, co2s, "CO2 Level")
  plt.X.Label.Text = "Time"
  plt.Y.Label.Text = "CO2 in the atmosphere (ppm)"
  plt.Title.Text = "CO2 in the atmosphere (ppm) over time\nTaken over the
Mauna-Loa observatory"
  dieIfErr(plt.Save(25*vg.Centimeter, 25*vg.Centimeter, "Moana-Loa.png"))
}
```

The result is stark , as shown in the following screenshot:

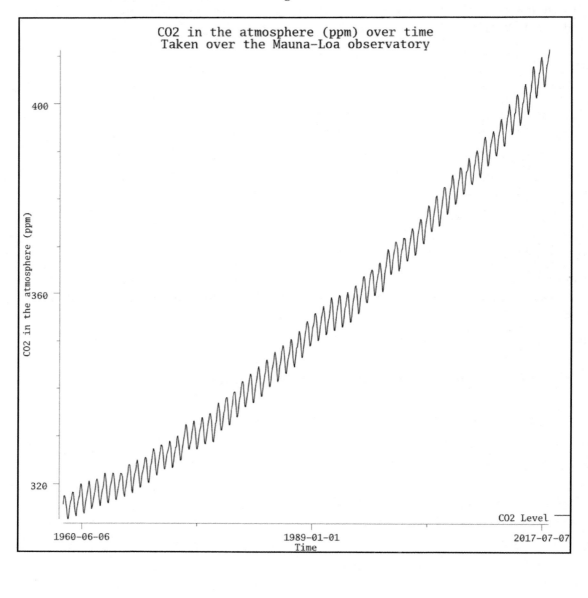

Decomposition

There are two things to note about the previous screenshot:

- CO_2 levels in the air are steadily rising over time.
- There are dips and then bumps in the levels of CO_2, but the result still ends up rising overall. These dips and bumps happen on a regular pattern.

The first point is what is known to statisticians as a **trend**. You may already be familiar with the notion of a Trend Line from Microsoft Excel. A trend is a kind of pattern that describes gradual change over time. In our case, it is quite clear that the trend is upward.

The second point is called **seasonality**—for very apt reasons, as it may turn out. Seasonality describes the pattern of variance that happens regularly. If you carefully look at the chart, typically at around August to October of each year, the CO_2 levels drop to the lowest point of the year. After which, they rise steadily again until around May, where they peak. Here's a good hint as to why this happens: plants suck CO_2 from the air through a process called **photosynthesis**. Photosynthesis requires a organelle in a plant's cell called a **chloroplast**, which contains a green pigment called **chlorophyll**. If you live in the Northern Hemisphere, you would be well aware that trees are greenest from Spring till Autumn. This largely coincides with the period from May till October. The changing of seasons cause a change in atmospheric carbon dioxide levels. You can certainly see why the term "seasonality" is quite apt.

A good question to ask might be this: Can we separate the trend out from the seasonality so that we may be able to work on each component individually? The answer is yes, we can. In fact, in the remaining parts of this section, I'll show how to do so.

Now, as to why you would want to do that, well, in our project so far, we've seen seasonalities that are affected by real-life calendar seasons. Imagine you were doing statistical analysis for a toy company in a Western country. You'd see a yearly spike around Christmas time. Often seasonality adds noise to our analysis—it's hard to tell whether a bump in sales was due to Christmas time or an actual increase in sales. Furthermore, there are some cycles that don't necessarily follow the calendar year. If you are dealing with sales in a largely Chinese/Vietnamese community, you'd see spikes in sales before Chinese New Year/Tet. Those do not follow our calendar year. Ditto, if you were in the dates industry—you'd see spikes around Ramadan as demand for dates increases sharply during the Muslim fasting period.

While it's true that most time series would have some kind of trend and seasonality component, it would be remiss for me to mention that not all trends and seasonalities are particularly useful. You might be tempted to take what you learn in this chapter and apply it on the stock markets but buyer beware! Analyzing complex market places is quite different from analyzing trends of CO_2 in the air or sales from a business. The fundamental properties of time series in markets are somewhat different—it's a process that has the Markov property, which is best described as **past performance does not indicate future performance**. By contrast, we shall see, for this project, that the past is quite well correlated with the present and the future.

But back to the topic at hand—decomposition. If you read the comments on the data file (the lines we skipped from importing), the following is mentioned:

> *"First, we compute for each month the average seasonal cycle in a 7-year window around each monthly value. In this way, the seasonal cycle is allowed to change slowly over time. We then determine the "trend" value for each month by removing the seasonal cycle; this result is shown in the "trend" column."*

STL

But how does one calculate a seasonal cycle? In this section, we'll be using an algorithm invented in the late 1980s called **Seasonal and Trend Decomposition (STL)** by LOESS by Cleveland et al. I wrote a library that implements that. You can install it by running `go get -u github.com/chewxy/stl`.

The library is really small—there is only one `main` function to call (`stl.Dcompose`), and the library comes with a litany of features to aid with decomposition of data.

Despite that, I think it would be a good idea to have a rough understanding of the STL algorithm before using it, as usage requires knowledge.

LOESS

The thing that powers STL is the notion of local regression—LOESS itself is a terrible acronym formed from **LO**cal regr**ESS**ion—whatever drugs the statisticians were on in the 1990s, sign me up for them. We're already familiar with the idea of linear regression from `Chapter 1`, *How to Solve All Machine Learning*.

Recall that the role of linear regression is that given a straight line function: $y = mx + c$.
We want to estimate m and c. Instead of trying to fit the whole dataset at once, what if we broke the dataset up into many small **local** components, and ran a regression on each small dataset? Here's an example of what I mean:

```
| X | Y |
|:--:|:--|
| -1 | 1 |
| -0.9 | 0.81 |
| -0.8 | 0.64 |
| -0.7 | 0.49 |
| -0.6 | 0.36 |
| -0.5 | 0.25 |
| -0.4 | 0.16 |
| -0.3 | 0.09 |
| -0.2 | 0.04 |
| -0.1 | 0.01 |
| 0 | 0 |
| 0.1 | 0.01 |
| 0.2 | 0.04 |
| 0.3 | 0.09 |
| 0.4 | 0.16 |
| 0.5 | 0.25 |
| 0.6 | 0.36 |
| 0.7 | 0.49 |
| 0.8 | 0.64 |
| 0.9 | 0.81 |
```

The preceding table is a function representing $y = x^2$. Instead of pulling in the entire dataset for a regression, what if we did a running regression of every three rows? We'd start with row 2 (x = -0.9). And the data points under consideration are 1 before it and 1 after it (*x* = -1 and *x* = -0.8). And for row 3, we'd do a linear regression using row 2, 3, 4 as data points. At this point, we're not particularly interested in the errors of the local regression. We just want an estimate of the gradient and the crossings. Here's the resulting table:

```
| X | Y | m | c
|:--:|:--:|:--:|:--:|
| -0.9 | 0.81 | -1.8 | -0.803333333333333 |
| -0.8 | 0.64 | -1.6 | -0.633333333333334 |
| -0.7 | 0.49 | -1.4 | -0.483333333333334 |
| -0.6 | 0.36 | -1.2 | -0.353333333333333 |
| -0.5 | 0.25 | -1 | -0.243333333333333 |
| -0.4 | 0.16 | -0.8 | -0.153333333333333 |
| -0.3 | 0.09 | -0.6 | -0.083333333333333 |
| -0.2 | 0.04 | -0.4 | -0.033333333333333 |
```

```
| -0.1 | 0.01 | -0.2 | -0.003333333333333 |
| 0 | 0 | -2.71050543121376E-17 | 0.006666666666667 |
| 0.1 | 0.01 | 0.2 | -0.003333333333333 |
| 0.2 | 0.04 | 0.4 | -0.033333333333333 |
| 0.3 | 0.09 | 0.6 | -0.083333333333333 |
| 0.4 | 0.16 | 0.8 | -0.153333333333333 |
| 0.5 | 0.25 | 1 | -0.243333333333333 |
| 0.6 | 0.36 | 1.2 | -0.353333333333333 |
| 0.7 | 0.49 | 1.4 | -0.483333333333334 |
| 0.8 | 0.64 | 1.6 | -0.633333333333333 |
| 0.9 | 0.81 | 1.8 | -0.803333333333333 |
```

In fact, we can show that if you plot each line individually, you will have a somewhat "curved" shape. So, here's a side program I wrote to plot this out:

```go
// +build sidenote

package main

import (
  "image/color"

  "github.com/golang/freetype/truetype"
  "golang.org/x/image/font/gofont/gomono"
  "gonum.org/v1/plot"
  "gonum.org/v1/plot/plotter"
  "gonum.org/v1/plot/vg"
  "gonum.org/v1/plot/vg/draw"
)

var defaultFont vg.Font

func init() {
  font, err := truetype.Parse(gomono.TTF)
  if err != nil {
    panic(err)
  }
  vg.AddFont("gomono", font)
  defaultFont, err = vg.MakeFont("gomono", 12)
  if err != nil {
    panic(err)
  }
}

var table = []struct {
  x, m, c float64
}{
  {-0.9, -1.8, -0.803333333333333},
```

```
   {-0.8, -1.6, -0.633333333333334},
   {-0.7, -1.4, -0.483333333333334},
   {-0.6, -1.2, -0.353333333333333},
   {-0.5, -1, -0.243333333333333},
   {-0.4, -0.8, -0.153333333333333},
   {-0.3, -0.6, -0.083333333333333},
   {-0.2, -0.4, -0.033333333333333},
   {-0.1, -0.2, -0.003333333333333},
   {0, -2.71050543121376E-17, 0.006666666666667},
   {0.1, 0.2, -0.003333333333333},
   {0.2, 0.4, -0.033333333333333},
   {0.3, 0.6, -0.083333333333333},
   {0.4, 0.8, -0.153333333333333},
   {0.5, 1, -0.243333333333333},
   {0.6, 1.2, -0.353333333333333},
   {0.7, 1.4, -0.483333333333334},
   {0.8, 1.6, -0.633333333333333},
   {0.9, 1.8, -0.803333333333333},
}

type estimates []struct{ x, m, c float64 }

func (es estimates) Plot(c draw.Canvas, p *plot.Plot) {
  trX, trY := p.Transforms(&c)
  lineStyle := plotter.DefaultLineStyle
  lineStyle.Dashes = []vg.Length{vg.Points(2), vg.Points(2)}
  lineStyle.Color = color.RGBA{A: 255}
  for i, e := range es {
    if i == 0 || i == len(es)-1 {
      continue
    }
    strokeStartX := es[i-1].x
    strokeStartY := e.m*strokeStartX + e.c
    strokeEndX := es[i+1].x
    strokeEndY := e.m*strokeEndX + e.c
    x1 := trX(strokeStartX)
    y1 := trY(strokeStartY)
    x2 := trX(strokeEndX)
    y2 := trY(strokeEndY)
    x := trX(e.x)
    y := trY(e.x*e.m + e.c)

    c.DrawGlyph(plotter.DefaultGlyphStyle, vg.Point{X: x, Y: y})
    c.StrokeLine2(lineStyle, x1, y1, x2, y2)
  }
}

func main() {
```

```
p, err := plot.New()
if err != nil {
  panic(err)
}
p.Title.Text = "X^2 Function and Its Estimates"
p.X.Label.Text = "X"
p.Y.Label.Text = "Y"
p.X.Min = -1.1
p.X.Max = 1.1
p.Y.Min = -0.1
p.Y.Max = 1.1
p.Y.Label.TextStyle.Font = defaultFont
p.X.Label.TextStyle.Font = defaultFont
p.X.Tick.Label.Font = defaultFont
p.Y.Tick.Label.Font = defaultFont
p.Title.Font = defaultFont
p.Title.Font.Size = 16
```

Now, we will see how to plot the original function:

```
// Original function
original := plotter.NewFunction(func(x float64) float64 { return x * x })
original.Color = color.RGBA{A: 16}
original.Width = 10
p.Add(original)

// Plot estimates
est := estimates(table)
p.Add(est)

if err := p.Save(25*vg.Centimeter, 25*vg.Centimeter, "functions.png");
err != nil {
  panic(err)
}
}
```

The preceding code yields a chart, as shown in the following screenshot:

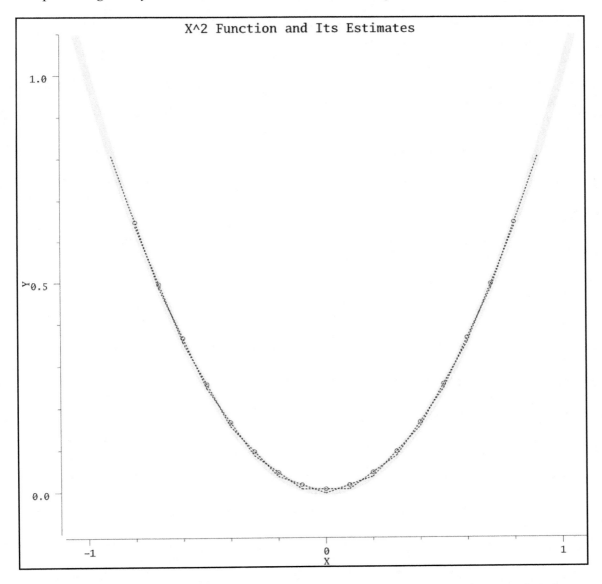

Most of the code will be explained in the latter parts of this chapter, but, for now, let's focus on the fact that you can indeed run many small linear regressions on "local" subsets of the data to plot a curve.

LOESS brings this idea further, by stating that if you have a window of values (in the toy example, we used 3), then the values should be weighted. The logic is simple: the closer a value is to the row in consideration, the higher the weight. If we had used a window size of 5, then when considering row 3, 2, and 4 would be weighted more heavily than rows 1 and 5. This **width**, it turns out, is important to our smoothing.

The subpackage, `"github.com/chewxy/stl/loess"`, implements LOESS as a smoothing algorithm. Do read through the code if you're interested in knowing more about the details.

The algorithm

Recall that our goal is to split a time series into seasonality and trend. Obviously, once we've removed the seasonality and trend, there will be some remaining parts. We call those **residuals**. So, how do we do it?

The algorithm has a lot of fine tuning for the sake of robustness. I will elide on explaining on the various robustness optimizations performed, but I think it is important to have a rough idea of how the algorithm works in general.

The following is a rough overview of the algorithm:

1. Calculate trend (on the first loop, the trend is all 0s).
2. Subtract the trend from the input data. This is called **detrending**.
3. Cycle subseries smoothing: the data is partitioned into N subcycles. Each subcycle corresponds to a period. The data is then smoothed using LOESS. The result is a temporary seasonal dataset.
4. For each temporary seasonal dataset (one per period), we perform a low pass filter—we keep the values with a low frequency.
5. The low pass filtered values are subtracted from temporary seasonal dataset. This is the seasonal data.
6. Subtract the seasonal data from the input data. This is the new trend data.
7. Iterate step 1 to step 6 until the number of iterations is desired. This is typically 1 or 2.

As you can see, the algorithm is iterative—each iteration improves on the trend, which is then used to find the new seasonal data, which is then used to update the trend, and so on and so forth. But there is a very important blink-and-you-miss-it "magic" that STL relies on.

And so we come to the second important reason to understand the algorithm: **STL is dependent upon the definition of how many periods the dataset has.**

Using STL

To recap, there are two important parts that are fundamental to the STL algorithm:

- The **width** used for smoothing
- The **periods** in the dataset

When we look at the CO_2 dataset, we can count the periods by counting the number of peaks in the chart. I counted 60 peaks. This corresponds to the fact that the observatory has been collecting data for the past 60 years.

From here, we move from the hard sciences of statistics into the softer realms of interpretation. This is often true in data science and machine learning—we often have to use our intuition to guide us.

In this case, we have a hard starting point: there has been 60 years so we expect at least 60 periods. Another starting point can be found in the notes of the dataset itself: the NOAA uses a seven-year window to calculate the seasonal component. I don't see any reason to not use those values. So, let's decompose our time series into the **trend**, **seasonal**, and **residual** components.

But before we begin, there is an additional note to make: we want to decompose the time series into three components, but how do these three components recompose to become whole again? In general, there are two methods: additive or multiplicative. Simply put, we can decompose the data as either one of the following equations:

$$Data = Trend + Seasonal + Residual$$

This can also be stated as follows:

$$Data = Trend \times Seasonal \times Residual$$

The `github.com/chewxy/stl` package supports both models, and even supports custom models that fall "in-between" additive and multiplicative models.

When to use an additive model: Use an additive model when the seasonality does not vary with the level of the time series. Most standard business case time series fall in this category.

When to use a multiplicative model: Use a multiplicative model when the seasonality or trend does vary with the level of the time series. Most econometric models fall in this category.

For the purpose of this project, we will be using an additive model. Here's the `main` function again:

```
func main() {
  dateStrings, co2s := parse(readFromFile)
  dates := parseDates(dateStrings)
  plt := newTSPlot(dates, co2s, "CO2 Level")
  plt.X.Label.Text = "Time"
  plt.Y.Label.Text = "CO2 in the atmosphere (ppm)"
  plt.Title.Text = "CO2 in the atmosphere (ppm) over time\nTaken over the
Mauna-Loa observatory"
  dieIfErr(plt.Save(25*vg.Centimeter, 25*vg.Centimeter, "Moana-Loa.png"))

  decomposed := stl.Decompose(co2s, 12, 84, stl.Additive(),
stl.WithIter(1))
  dieIfErr(decomposed.Err)
  plts := plotDecomposed(dates, decomposed)
  writeToPng(plts, "decomposed.png", 25, 25)
}
```

Let's break this down; in particular, the parameters:

```
decomposed := stl.Decompose(co2s, 12, 84, stl.Additive(), stl.WithIter(1))
```

Take a look at the following terms from the preceding code:

- `12`: We counted 60 periods. The data is monthly data; therefore, it would make sense that a period takes 12 months, or as we know it—a year.
- `84`: We use the smoothing window as specified by the NOAA. Seven years is 84 months.
- `stl.Additive()`: We want to use an additive model.
- `stl.WithIter(1)`: STL is fairly sensitive to the number of iterations run. The default is 2. But if you run it too many times, everything gets iteratively "smoothed" out. So, instead, we stick with 1.

In the following sections, I'll show examples of misuse and why despite everything, 1 and 2 are still pretty good iteration counts.

You may note that instead of specifying the number of periods, we specified the length of a period. The package expects the data to be evenly spaced—the distance between any two rows should be the same.

Running this yields the following plot:

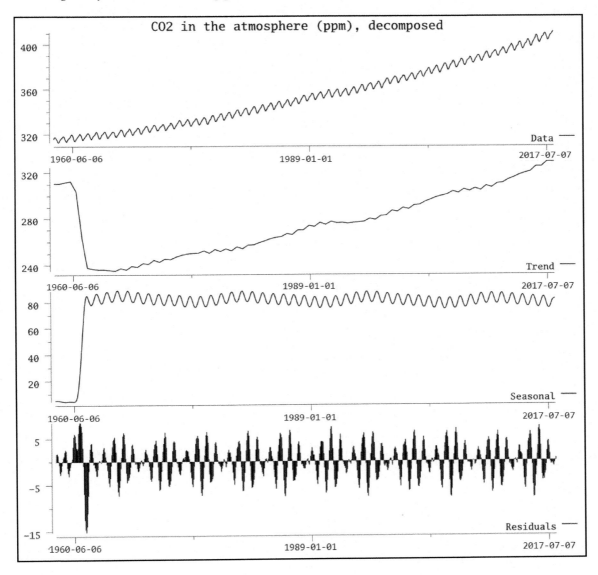

The first chart is the original data, followed by the extracted trend and seasonality, and, finally, the residuals. There remains some weirdness with regards to the beginning of the graph, but that artifact is solely due to the fact that the github.com/chewxy/stl library does not "backcast". Hence, it's always a good idea to start with at least one extra period.

How to interpret the plot? Well, since this is an additive model, interpretation is a lot simpler—the Y values indicate the ppm of carbon dioxide in the air that each component contributes to the actual data, so the first chart is literally the result of adding the bottom charts together.

How to lie with statistics

It is important to note that these parameters essentially control how much to attribute the CO_2 in the atmosphere to each component. And these controls are rather subjective. The stl package offers a lot of control over how a time series is decomposed, and I think it's up to the data scientist or statistician reading this book (that is you), to do statistics responsibly.

What if we said that a period was five years? Keeping everything the same, we can use the following code and find out:

```
lies := stl.Decompose(co2s, 60, 84, stl.Additive(), stl.WithIter(1))
dieIfErr(lies.Err)
plts2 := plotDecomposed(dates, lies)
writeToPng(plts2, "CO2 in the atmosphere (ppm), decomposed (Liar Edition)",
"lies.png", 25, 25)
```

The following chart is produced:

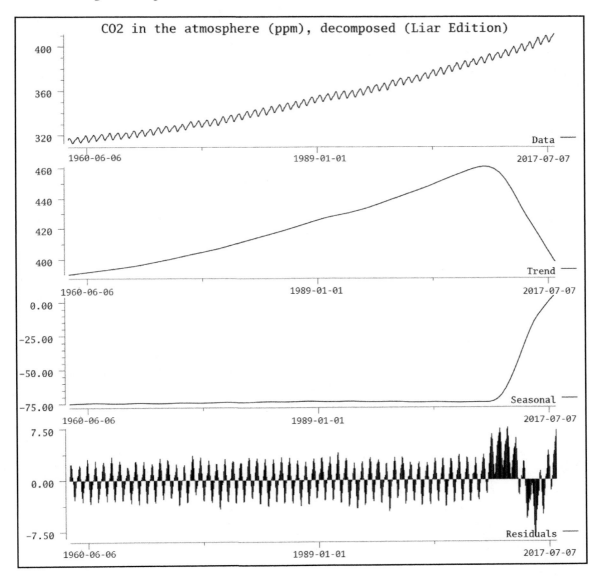

We could then take this chart and parade the top two sections and say "Look! Statistics tells us that despite the data looking like it's going up, it's in fact trending down. Hashtag science."

You're of course free to do so. But I know you're not a dishonest person. Instead, I hope that you are reading this book with good intentions of saving the world.

But knowing the correct parameters to use is difficult. One suggestion I have is to go to extremes and then come back down. This is what I mean—we have a rough idea of how the STL algorithm works. A known controlling factor is the iteration count, which defaults to 2. Here's the original correct version, with 1, 2, 5, 10, 20, and 100 iterations:

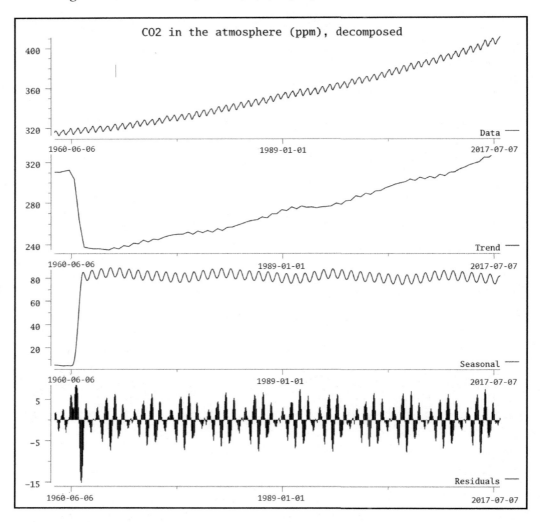

Interations:

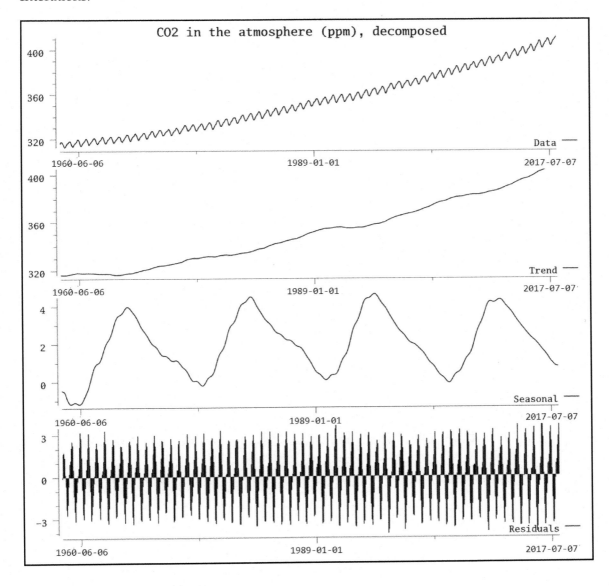

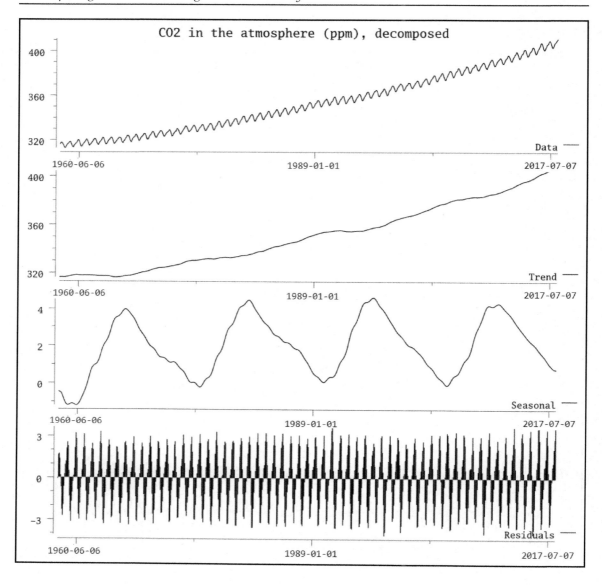

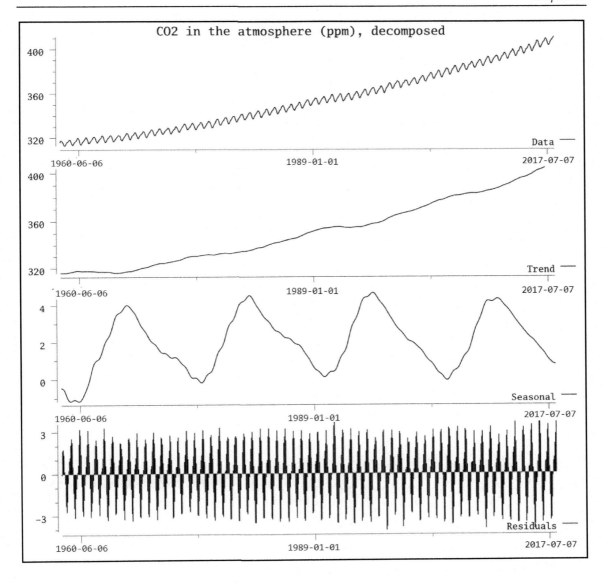

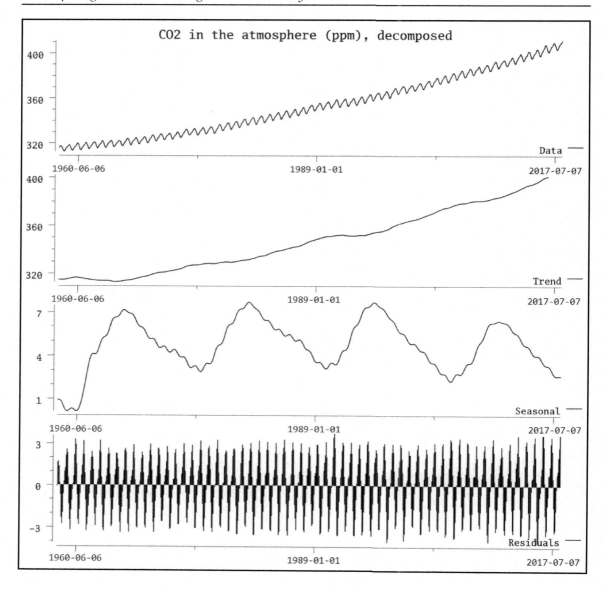

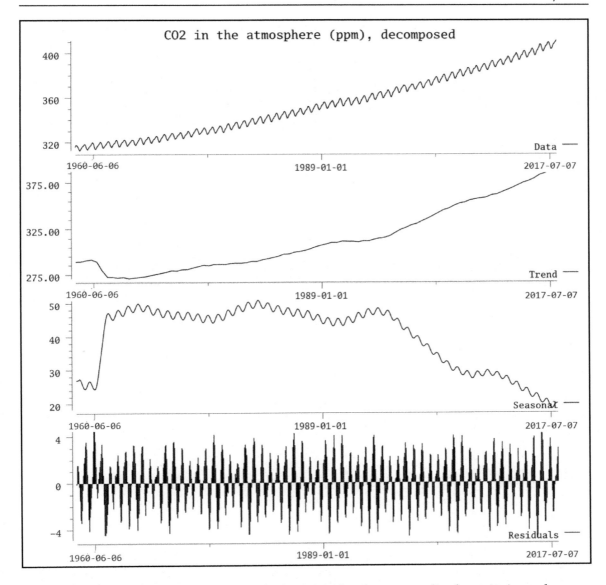

Over the iterations, having been smoothed iteratively, the seasonality loses its jaggedness. Nonetheless, the shape of the trend stays the same. Therefore, in this case, increasing the iteration counts merely shifts the seasonal contribution to the trend component. This implies that the trend component is the stronger "signal" of sorts.

By contrast, if we run the "lies" version, we see that at two iterations, the shape of the trend changes, and by the 10th iteration onward, the shape of the trend stays the same. This gives us a clue as to what the "real" trend is.

With STL, the thing that we're really controlling is the seasonality. What we're saying to the algorithm is that we believe that a period is 12 months; therefore, please find a seasonality that fits. If we say to the algorithm that we believe that a period is five years (60 months), the algorithm will try its best to find a seasonality and trend that fits that pattern.

I wish to be clear—the notion of a seasonality that happens every five years is **not wrong**. In fact, it is common for business-related forecasting to work on multiple levels of seasonalities. But knowing how many iterations to run, that comes with experience and wisdom.

Check the units! If the units don't make sense, like in the "lies" chart, then it probably isn't real.

More plotting

A major theme in this chapter other than time series analysis is plotting. You may have also noticed a few new functions in the main function earlier. Now it's time to revisit them.

We start with the output of stl.Decompose. This is the definition:

```
type Result struct {
  Data []float64
  Trend []float64
  Seasonal []float64
  Resid []float64
  Err error
}
```

There is no notion of time in the result. It's assumed that when you pass in data into stl.Decompose, the data is ordered by the time series. The result also follows this notion.

We've already defined newTSPlot previously, which works fine for the data, trend, and seasonal, but not the residuals. The reason why we don't want to plot residuals as a line chart is because if done right, the residuals should be more or less random. Having a line plot run through random points would be rather messy.

Typical residual plots are simply scatter plots of the residuals. However, that too is relatively uninterpretable when squashed into a multiplot image.

Instead, we want to draw a straight vertical line for each residual value.

To recap, this is what we want to do:

1. Plot a time series chart for each of `Data`, `Trend`, and `Seasonal`.
2. Plot a residuals chart for `Resid`.
3. Combine all the preceding plots into one image.

Step 1 is easy, as we simply call `newTSPlot` with the parsed dates from earlier for each of the components. Step 2 is a little trickier. Gonum doesn't have the residuals plots that we want by default.

To plot it, we'd need to create a new `plot.Plotter` interface. Here's the definition:

```go
type residChart struct {
  plotter.XYs
  draw.LineStyle
}

func (r *residChart) Plot(c draw.Canvas, p *plot.Plot) {
  xmin, xmax, ymin, ymax := r.DataRange()
  p.Y.Min = ymin
  p.Y.Max = ymax
  p.X.Min = xmin
  p.X.Max = xmax

  trX, trY := p.Transforms(&c)
  zero := trY(0)
  lineStyle := r.LineStyle
  for _, xy := range r.XYs {
    x := trX(xy.X)
    y := trY(xy.Y)
    c.StrokeLine2(lineStyle, x, zero, x, y)
  }
}

func (r *residChart) DataRange() (xmin, xmax, ymin, ymax float64) {
  xmin = math.Inf(1)
  xmax = math.Inf(-1)
  ymin = math.Inf(1)
  ymax = math.Inf(-1)
  for _, xy := range r.XYs {
    xmin = math.Min(xmin, xy.X)
```

```
    xmax = math.Max(xmax, xy.X)
    ymin = math.Min(ymin, xy.Y)
    ymax = math.Max(ymax, xy.Y)
  }
  return
}
```

Despite the fact that Gonum doesn't have the chart type that we want, as you can see it doesn't take very many lines of code for us to define our own chart type. This is part of the power of Gonum's `plot` library—it's abstract enough to enable you to write your own chart type, and at the same time, it provides all the helper functions necessary to make it work without much code.

A primer on Gonum plots

Before we go further, I think it might be worth it to have an understanding of Gonum's plotting library in general. We've so far been using Gonum's `plot` library in rather ad hoc ways. This was to familiarize you with how to use the library. Now that you're somewhat familiar, it's time to learn more about the internals in order to plot better in the future.

A `*plot.Plot` object holds the metadata of a plot. A plot consists of the following features:

- A title
- `X` and `Y` axes
- A legend
- A list of `plot.Plotter`

A `plot.Plotter` interface is simply anything that can take a `*plot.Plot` object and draw it on to `draw.Canvas`, defined as follows:

```
type Plotter interface {
 Plot(draw.Canvas, *Plot)
}
```

By separating the notions of a `plot` object and the canvas upon which the plot will be drawn, this opens Gonum's plots to a variety of different plotting backend options. To see what I mean about backend options, we need to take a closer look at `draw.Canvas`.

The `draw.Canvas` is a tuple of `vg.Canvas` and `vg.Rectangle`. So what exactly is `vg`? `vg`, it turns out, stands for **vector graphics**. In it, the `Canvas` type is defined as an interface with a bunch of methods. This allows for the rich variety of backends that `vg` has:

- `vg/vgimg`: This is the primary package we've been using so far; it writes to an image file.
- `vg/vgpdf`: This package writes to a PDF file.
- `vg/vgsvg`: This package writes to a SVG file.
- `vg/vgeps`: This package writes to a EPS file.
- `vg/vgtex`: This package writes to a TEX file.

Each of these canvas implementations has a coordinate system that begins with (0, 0) at the bottom left.

The residuals plotter

A deeper look at the canvasing system will be explored later in the chapter. For now, let's return to the `Plot` method that satisfies the `plot.Plotter` interface.

Most interesting are the following lines:

```
trX, trY := p.Transforms(&c)
zero := trY(0)
lineStyle := r.LineStyle
for _, xy := range r.XYs {
  x := trX(xy.X)
  y := trY(xy.Y)
  c.StrokeLine2(lineStyle, x, zero, x, y)
}
```

`p.Transforms(&c)` returns two functions, which will transform the coordinate of our data point to the coordinate of the backend. This way we wouldn't have to worry about the absolute location of each point. Instead, it will be treated in relation to the absolute location in the final image.

Having gotten the transformation functions, we then loop through the residuals that we have, and transform each to the coordinate (`x := trX(xy.X)` and `y := trY(xy.Y)`) within the canvas.

Finally, we tell the canvas to draw a straight line between two points: $(x, 0)$ and (x, y). This draws a straight line up or down from the `X` axis.

Thus, we have created our own `plot.Plotter` interface, which we can now add to the `plot` object. But adding to a `*plot.Plot` object directly requires a lot of tinkering. So, here's a function to nicely wrap all that up:

```
func newResidPlot(xs []time.Time, ys []float64) *plot.Plot {
  p, err := plot.New()
  dieIfErr(err)
  xys := make(plotter.XYs, len(ys))
  for i := range ys {
    xys[i].X = float64(xs[i].Unix())
    xys[i].Y = ys[i]
  }
  r := &residChart{XYs: xys, LineStyle: plotter.DefaultLineStyle}
  r.LineStyle.Color = color.RGBA{A: 255}
  p.Add(r)
  p.Legend.Add("Residuals", r)

  p.Legend.TextStyle.Font = defaultFont
  p.X.Tick.Marker = plot.TimeTicks{Format: "2006-01-01"}
  p.Y.Label.TextStyle.Font = defaultFont
  p.X.Label.TextStyle.Font = defaultFont
  p.X.Tick.Label.Font = defaultFont
  p.Y.Tick.Label.Font = defaultFont
  p.Title.Font.Size = 16
  return p
}
```

This function is reminiscent of `newTSPlot`—you provide it the X and Y values, and get a `*plot.Plot` object back out, with everything properly styled and formatted.

You may note that we're also adding the plotter object as a legend. To do this without an error, the `residChart` type needs to implement `plot.Thumbnailer`. Again, that's fairly straightforward:

```
func (r *residChart) Thumbnail(c *draw.Canvas) {
  y := c.Center().Y
  c.StrokeLine2(r.LineStyle, c.Min.X, y, c.Max.X, y)
}
```

At this point, you may be wondering about the `canvas` object. If we are to draw a line between the canvas's minimum X to maximum X, wouldn't that just cause a horizontal line across the entire canvas?

The answer is not really. Recall earlier that the canvas is provided in the backend, and `draw.Canvas` is simply a tuple of a canvas backend and a rectangle? The rectangle actually serves to subset and constrain the canvas upon which it is being drawn.

We shall see this in action. Now that we've finished, we can turn our attention to the next section, which depicts a combination of all the plots into one image.

Combining plots

A key function that allows us to do this is the `plot.Align` function. For us to see this in action, we need to write a that allows us to plot any number of plots to a file, as follows:

```
func writeToPng(a interface{}, title, filename string, width, height
vg.Length) {
  switch at := a.(type) {
  case *plot.Plot:
    dieIfErr(at.Save(width*vg.Centimeter, height*vg.Centimeter, filename))
    return
  case [][]*plot.Plot:
    rows := len(at)
    cols := len(at[0])
    t := draw.Tiles{
      Rows: rows,
      Cols: cols,
    }
    img := vgimg.New(width*vg.Centimeter, height*vg.Centimeter)
    dc := draw.New(img)

    if title != "" {
      at[0][0].Title.Text = title
    }

    canvases := plot.Align(at, t, dc)
    for i := 0; i < t.Rows; i++ {
      for j := 0; j < t.Cols; j++ {
        at[i][j].Draw(canvases[i][j])
      }
    }

    w, err := os.Create(filename)
    dieIfErr(err)

    png := vgimg.PngCanvas{Canvas: img}
    _, err = png.WriteTo(w)
    dieIfErr(err)
    return
```

```
    }
    panic("Unreachable")
}
```

We'll skip the part where if `a` is `plot.Plot`, we simply call the `.Save` method. Instead, we'll look at the second case, where `a` is `[][]*plot.Plot`.

At first this may seem rather strange—why have a slice of slice of plots when all we want to do is to combine them in quick succession. The key to understanding this is that Gonum supports the tiling of charts so if you want four charts arranged in 2x2 fashion, it can be done. Having four charts in a row is simply a special case of a 4x1 layout.

We can arrange the layouts using a function, as follows:

```
func plotDecomposed(xs []time.Time, a stl.Result) [][]*plot.Plot {
    plots := make([][]*plot.Plot, 4)
    plots[0] = []*plot.Plot{newTSPlot(xs, a.Data, "Data")}
    plots[1] = []*plot.Plot{newTSPlot(xs, a.Trend, "Trend")}
    plots[2] = []*plot.Plot{newTSPlot(xs, a.Seasonal, "Seasonal")}
    plots[3] = []*plot.Plot{newResidPlot(xs, a.Resid, "Residuals")}

    return plots
}
```

Having acquired `[][]*plot.Plot`, we need to tell Gonum the tiling format that we're interested in, so the following code snippet defines the tiling format:

```
t := draw.Tiles{
    Rows: rows,
    Cols: cols,
}
```

If you're following along with the code, you will realize that `rows` is 3 and `cols` is 1.

Next, we have to provide a canvas to draw on:

```
img := vgimg.New(width*vg.Centimeter, height*vg.Centimeter)
dc := draw.New(img)
```

Here, we use the `vgimg` backend because we want to write to a PNG image. If, for example, you want to set the DPI of the image, you may use `vgimg.NewWith` instead, and pass in the DPI option.

dc is draw.Canvas initiated from the large piece of canvas img. Now comes the magic: canvases := plot.Align(at, t, dc) basically splits the big canvas (img) into various smaller canvases—they're still part of the big canvas, but now, each *plot.Plot object gets allocated a smaller piece of the canvas, each with their own coordinate systems that are relative to the bigger canvas.

The following code simply draws the plots onto their respective mini-canvases:

```
for i := 0; i < t.Rows; i++ {
  for j := 0; j < t.Cols; j++ {
    at[i][j].Draw(canvases[i][j])
  }
}
```

Naturally, this process can be recursively repeated. A Legend object in *plot.Plot simply gets a smaller chunk of the canvas, and drawing a straight line from minimum X to maximum X simply draws a horizontal line across the entire mini canvas.

And this is how plots are made.

Forecasting

We're decomposing a time series here with the STL algorithm. There are other methods of decomposing time series—you may be familiar with one: the discrete Fourier transform. If your data is a time-based signal (like electrical pulses or music), a Fourier transform essentially allows you to decompose a time series into various parts. Bear in mind that they are no longer seasonality and trend, but rather decompositions of different time and frequency domains.

This begs the question: what is the point of decomposing a time series?

A primary reason why we do any machine learning at all is to be able to predict values based on an input. When done on time series, this is called **forecasting**.

Think about this for a bit: if a time series is made up of multiple components, wouldn't it be better to be able to predict per component? If we are able to break a time series up into its components, be it by STL or by Fourier transforms, we would get better results if we predict per component and then recombine the data at the end.

Since we work on STL, we already have our series decomposed. A very simple exponential smoothing algorithm invented by Holt in 1957 allows us to use the trend and seasonal components, along with the original data, to forecast.

Holt-Winters

In this section, I shall explain a modified form of the Holt-Winters exponential smoothing algorithm, which is quite useful for forecasting. Holt-Winters is a fairly simple algorithm. Here it is:

```
func hw(a stl.Result, periodicity, forward int, alpha, beta, gamma float64)
[]float64 {
  level := make([]float64, len(a.Data))
  trend := make([]float64, len(a.Trend))
  seasonal := make([]float64, len(a.Seasonal))
  forecast := make([]float64, len(a.Data)+forward)
  copy(seasonal, a.Seasonal)

  for i := range a.Data {
    if i == 0 {
      continue
    }
    level[i] = alpha*a.Data[i] + (1-alpha)*(level[i-1]+trend[i-1])
    trend[i] = beta*(level[i]-level[i-1]) + (1-beta)*(trend[i-1])
    if i-periodicity < 0 {
      continue
    }
    seasonal[i] = gamma*(a.Data[i]-level[i-1]-trend[i-1]) + (1-
gamma)*(seasonal[i-periodicity])
  }

  hplus := ((periodicity - 1) % forward) + 1
  for i := 0; i+forward < len(forecast); i++ {
    forecast[i+forward] = level[i] + float64(forward)*trend[i] +
seasonal[i-periodicity+hplus]
  }
  copy(forecast, a.Data)

  return forecast
}
```

Calling it is rather easy. We would wind up with a time series with a number of additional periods. Hence, we would also need to extend our dates range before we call `newTSPlot`. Again, it's a rather simple matter:

```
func forecastTime(dates []time.Time, forwards int) []time.Time {
  retVal := append(dates, make([]time.Time, forwards)...)
  lastDate := dates[len(dates)-1]
  for i := len(dates); i < len(retVal); i++ {
    retVal[i] = lastDate.AddDate(0, 1, 0)
    lastDate = retVal[i]
```

```
  }
  return retVal
}
```

Ideally, we would also like to draw a gray background indicating that the values in the area are forecasts. Putting it all together, it looks rather like this:

```
fwd := 120
forecast := hw(decomposed, 12, fwd, 0.1, 0.05, 0.1)
datesplus := forecastTime(dates, fwd)
forecastPlot := newTSPlot(datesplus, forecast, "")
maxY := math.Inf(-1)
minY := math.Inf(1)
for i := range forecast {
  if forecast[i] > maxY {
    maxY = forecast[i]
  }
  if forecast[i] < minY {
    minY = forecast[i]
  }
}
// extend the range a little
minY--
maxY++
maxX := float64(datesplus[len(datesplus)-1].Unix())
minX := float64(datesplus[len(dates)-1].Unix())

shadePoly := plotter.XYs{
  {X: minX, Y: minY},
  {X: maxX, Y: minY},
  {X: maxX, Y: maxY},
  {X: minX, Y: maxY},
}
poly, err := plotter.NewPolygon(shadePoly)
dieIfErr(err)
poly.Color = color.RGBA{A: 16}
poly.LineStyle.Color = color.RGBA{}
forecastPlot.Add(poly)

writeToPng(forecastPlot, "Forecasted CO2 levels\n(10 years)",
"forecast.png", 25, 25)
```

This would yield the following plot:

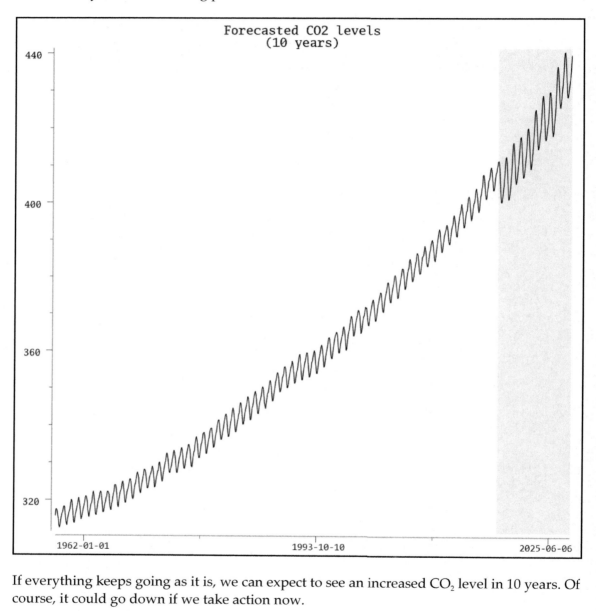

If everything keeps going as it is, we can expect to see an increased CO_2 level in 10 years. Of course, it could go down if we take action now.

Summary

This has been a rather hard chapter to write. The primary subject matter, without exaggeration, is one of existential threat. The methods used in the science at large are far more sophisticated than what I have covered in this chapter.

The techniques I covered is a small part of a large field of statistics known as time series analysis, where we've yet to even scratch the surface of it with this composition technique.

References

The following are the references:

- *[0] Hershfield, Hal. (2011). Future self-continuity*: How conceptions of the future self transform intertemporal choice. Annals of the New York Academy of Sciences. 1235. 30-43. 10.1111/j.1749-6632.2011.06201.x.
- *[1] Qin, P. and Northoff, G. (2011)*: How is our self related to midline regions and the default-mode network?. NeuroImage, 57(3), pp.1221-1233.

5

Clean Up Your Personal Twitter Timeline by Clustering Tweets

Here's a little bit of gossip for you: The original project for this title had to do with detecting foreign influence on US elections in social media. At about the same time, I was also applying for a visa to the United States, to give a series of talks. It later transpired that I hadn't needed the visa after all; ESTA covered all the things I had wanted to do in the United States. But as I was preparing for the visa, an attorney gave me a very stern talking-to about writing a book on the politics of the United States. The general advice is this—if I don't want trouble with US Customs and Border Patrol, I should not write or say anything on social media about American politics, and especially not write a chapter of a book on it. So, I had to hastily rewrite this chapter. The majority of methods used in this chapter can be used for the original purpose, but the content is a lot milder.

I use Twitter a lot. I mainly tweet and read Twitter in my downtime. I follow many people who share similar interests, among other things, machine learning, artificial intelligence, Go, linguistics, and programming languages. These people not only share interests with me; they also share interests with one another. As such, sometimes, multiple people may be tweeting about the same topic.

As may be obvious from the fact that I use Twitter a lot, I am a novelty junkie. I like new things. Multiple people tweeting about the same topic is nice if I am interested in the differing viewpoints, but I don't use Twitter like that. I use Twitter as a sort of summary of interesting topics. Events X, Y, and Z happened. It's good enough that I know they happened. For most topics, there is no benefit for me to go deep and learn what the finer points are, and 140 characters is not a lot of characters for nuance anyway. Therefore, a shallow overview is enough to keep my general knowledge abreast with the rest of the population.

Thus, when multiple people tweet about the same topic, that's repetition in my newsfeed. That's annoying. What if, instead of that, my feed could just be one instance of each topic?

I think of my Twitter-reading habit as happening in sessions. Each session is typically five minutes. I really only read about 100 tweets each session. If out of 100 tweets I read, 30% of the people I follow overlap on topics, then I really only have read 30 tweets of real content. That's not efficient at all! Efficiency means being able to cover more topics per session.

So, how do you increase efficiency in reading tweets? Well, remove the tweets that cover the same topic of course! There is the secondary matter of choosing the best tweet that summarizes the topic, but that's a subject for another day.

The project

What we're going to do is to cluster tweets on Twitter. We will be using two different clustering techniques, K-means and DBSCAN. For this chapter, we're going to rely on some skills we built up in Chapter 2, *Linear Regression – House Price Prediction*. We will also be using the same libraries used in Chapter 2, *Linear Regression – House Price Prediction*. On top of that, we will also be using the clusters library by mpraski.

By the end of the project, we will be able to clean up any collection of tweets from Twitter, and cluster them into groups. The main body of code that fulfills the objective is very simple, it's only about 150 lines of code in total. The rest of the code is for fetching and preprocessing data.

K-means

K-means is a method of clustering data. The problem is posed as this—given a dataset of N items, we wish to partition the data into K groups. How do you do so?

Allow me to take a side bar and explore the wonderful world of coordinates. No, no, don't run! It's very visual.

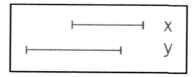

Which line is longer? How do you know?

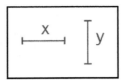

You know which line is longer because you can measure each line from points a, b, c, and d. Now, let's try something different:

Which dot is closest to X? How do you know?

You know because again, you can measure the distance between the dots. And now, for our final exercise:

Consider the distance between the following:

- **A and X**
- **A and Y**
- **A and Z**
- **B and X**
- **B and Y**
- **B and Z**
- **C and X**
- **C and Y**
- **C and Z**

What is the average distance between **A** and **X**, **B** and **X**, and **C** and **X**? What is the average distance between **A** and **Y**, **B** and **Y** and **C** and **Y**? What is the average distance between **A** and **Z**, **B** and **Z**, and **C** and **Z**?

If you had to choose one point between **X**, **Y**, and **Z** to represent the **A**, **B**, and **C**, which would you choose?

Congratulations! You just did a very simple and abbreviated version of K-means clustering. Specifically, you did a variant where *k = 1*. If you had to pick two points between **X**, **Y**, and **Z**, then that's *k = 2*. A cluster is therefore the set of points that make it such that the average distance of the group is minimal.

That's a mouthful, but think back to what you just did. Now, instead of just three points, **A**, **B**, and **C**, you have many points. And you aren't given **X**, **Y**, or **Z**; you'd have to generate your own **X**, **Y**, and **Z** points. Then, you have to find the groups that minimize the distance to each possible points of **X**, **Y**, and **Z**.

That is, in a nutshell, K-means. It's easy to understand, but hard to implement it well. It turns out K-means is NP-hard; it may not be solved in polynomial time.

DBSCAN

DBSCAN inherits the idea that data can be represented as multidimensional points. Again, sticking with a two-dimensional example, this is in rough steps how DBSCAN works:

1. Pick a point that has not been visited before.
2. Draw a circle with the point as the center. The radius of the circle is epsilon.
3. Count how many other points fall into the circle. If there are more than a specified threshold, we mark all the points as being part of the same cluster.
4. Recursively do the same for each point in this cluster. Doing so expands the cluster.
5. Repeat these steps.

I highly encourage you to do this on dotted paper and try to draw this out yourself. Start by plotting random points, and use pencils to draw circles on paper. This will give you an intuition of how DBSCAN works. The picture shows my working that enhanced my intuition about how DBSCAN works. I found this intuition to be very useful.

Data acquisition

In the earlier exercises, I asked you to look at the dots and figure out the distance. This gives a hint as to how we need to think of our data. We need to think of our data as coordinates in some imaginary coordinate space. Now, our data won't be just two-dimensional, because it's textual. Instead, it'll be multidimensional. This gives us hints as to how our data will look—slices of numbers representing a coordinate in some arbitrarily large N-dimensional space.

But, first, we'll need to get the data.

To acquire the tweets from the feed, we'll be using Aditya Mukherjee's excellent Anaconda library. To install it, simply run `go get -u github.com/ChimeraCoder/Anaconda`.

Of course, one can't just grab data from Twitter willy-nilly. We will need to acquire data via the Twitter API. The documentation of Twitter's API is the best source to get started: `https://developer.twitter.com/en/docs/basics/getting-started`.

You will need to first apply for a Twitter developer account (if you don't already have it): `https://developer.twitter.com/en/apply/user`. The process is rather lengthy and requires human approval for a developer account. Despite this, you don't need developer access to develop this project. I thought I had access to Twitter's API when I started, but it turns out I didn't. The good news is, the Twitter API documentation page does provide enough examples to get started with developing the necessary data structures.

The specific end point that we're interested in is this: `https://developer.twitter.com/en/docs/tweets/timelines/api-reference/get-statuses-home_timeline.html`.

Exploratory data analysis

Let's look at the JSON acquired from the Twitter API endpoint. A single tweet looks something like this (from the Twitter API documentation example):

```
{
"coordinates": null,
"truncated": false,
"created_at": "Tue Aug 28 19:59:34 +0000 2012",
"favorited": false,
"id_str": "240539141056638977",
"in_reply_to_user_id_str": null,
"entities": {
"urls": [
],
```

```
  "hashtags":
],
  "user_mentions": [
]
 },
 "text": "You'd be right more often if you thought you were wrong.",
 "contributors": null,
 "id": 240539141056638977,
 "retweet_count": 1,
 "in_reply_to_status_id_str": null,
 "geo": null,
 "retweeted": false,
 "in_reply_to_user_id": null,
 "place": null,
 "source": "web",
 "user": {
 "name": "Taylor Singletary",
 "profile_sidebar_fill_color": "FBFBFB",
 "profile_background_tile": true,
 "profile_sidebar_border_color": "000000",
 "profile_image_url":
"http://a0.twimg.com/profile_images/2546730059/f6a8zq58mg1hn0ha8vie_normal.
jpeg",
 "created_at": "Wed Mar 07 22:23:19 +0000 2007",
 "location": "San Francisco, CA",
 "follow_request_sent": false,
 "id_str": "819797",
 "is_translator": false,
 "profile_link_color": "c71818",
 "entities": {
 "url": {
 "urls": [
 {
 "expanded_url": "http://www.rebelmouse.com/episod/",
 "url": "http://t.co/Lxw7upbN",
 "indices": [
 0,
 20
 ],
 "display_url": "rebelmouse.com/episod/"
 }
 ]
 },
 "description": {
 "urls": [
 ]
 }
 },
```

```
"default_profile": false,
"url": "http://t.co/Lxw7upbN",
"contributors_enabled": false,
"favourites_count": 15990,
"utc_offset": -28800,
"profile_image_url_https":
"https://si0.twimg.com/profile_images/2546730059/f6a8zq58mg1hn0ha8vie_norma
l.jpeg",
"id": 819797,
"listed_count": 340,
"profile_use_background_image": true,
"profile_text_color": "D20909",
"followers_count": 7126,
"lang": "en",
"protected": false,
"geo_enabled": true,
"notifications": false,
"description": "Reality Technician, Twitter API team, synthesizer
enthusiast; a most excellent adventure in timelines. I know it's hard to
believe in something you can't see.",
"profile_background_color": "000000",
"verified": false,
"time_zone": "Pacific Time (US & Canada)",
"profile_background_image_url_https":
"https://si0.twimg.com/profile_background_images/643655842/hzfv12wini4q60zz
rthg.png",
"statuses_count": 18076,
"profile_background_image_url":
"http://a0.twimg.com/profile_background_images/643655842/hzfv12wini4q60zzrt
hg.png",
"default_profile_image": false,
"friends_count": 5444,
"following": true,
"show_all_inline_media": true,
"screen_name": "episod"
},
"in_reply_to_screen_name": null,
"in_reply_to_status_id": null
}
```

We will be representing each individual tweet in a data structure that looks like this:

```
type processedTweet struct {
anaconda.Tweet
// post processed stuff
ids []int // to implement Document
textVec []float64
normTextVec []float64
```

```
location []float64
isRT bool
}
```

Note that we embed `anaconda.Tweet`, which is given as such in the Anaconda package:

```
type Tweet struct {
Contributors []int64 `json:"contributors"`
Coordinates *Coordinates `json:"coordinates"`
CreatedAt string `json:"created_at"`
DisplayTextRange []int `json:"display_text_range"`
Entities Entities `json:"entities"`
ExtendedEntities Entities `json:"extended_entities"`
ExtendedTweet ExtendedTweet `json:"extended_tweet"`
FavoriteCount int `json:"favorite_count"`
Favorited bool `json:"favorited"`
FilterLevel string `json:"filter_level"`
FullText string `json:"full_text"`
HasExtendedProfile bool `json:"has_extended_profile"`
Id int64 `json:"id"`
IdStr string `json:"id_str"`
InReplyToScreenName string `json:"in_reply_to_screen_name"`
InReplyToStatusID int64 `json:"in_reply_to_status_id"`
InReplyToStatusIdStr string `json:"in_reply_to_status_id_str"`
InReplyToUserID int64 `json:"in_reply_to_user_id"`
InReplyToUserIdStr string `json:"in_reply_to_user_id_str"`
IsTranslationEnabled bool `json:"is_translation_enabled"`
Lang string `json:"lang"`
Place Place `json:"place"`
QuotedStatusID int64 `json:"quoted_status_id"`
QuotedStatusIdStr string `json:"quoted_status_id_str"`
QuotedStatus *Tweet `json:"quoted_status"`
PossiblySensitive bool `json:"possibly_sensitive"`
PossiblySensitiveAppealable bool `json:"possibly_sensitive_appealable"`
RetweetCount int `json:"retweet_count"`
Retweeted bool `json:"retweeted"`
RetweetedStatus *Tweet `json:"retweeted_status"`
Source string `json:"source"`
Scopes map[string]interface{} `json:"scopes"`
Text string `json:"text"`
User User `json:"user"`
WithheldCopyright bool `json:"withheld_copyright"`
WithheldInCountries []string `json:"withheld_in_countries"`
WithheldScope string `json:"withheld_scope"`
}
```

In the interest of building the program, we'll use the example tweets supplied by Twitter. I saved the example responses into a file called `example.json` and then a `mock` function is created to mock calling the API:

```
func mock() []*processedTweet {
f, err := os.Open("example.json")
dieIfErr(err)
return load(f)
}
func load(r io.Reader) (retVal []*processedTweet) {
dec := json.NewDecoder(r)
dieIfErr(dec.Decode(&retVal))
return retVal
}
```

The utility function `dieIfErr` is defined as usual:

```
func dieIfErr(err error) {
if err != nil {
log.Fatal(err)
}
}
```

Note that in `mock`, no API calls to Twitter were made. In the future, we will be creating a function with a similar API so we can just replace the mock version of this function with the real one, which acquires the timeline from the API.

For now, we can test that this works by the following program:

```
func main(){
tweets := mock()
for _, tweet := range tweets {
fmt.Printf("%q\n", tweet.FullText)
}
}
```

This is the output I got:

```
$ go run *.go
"just another test"
"lecturing at the \"analyzing big data with twitter\" class at @cal with
@othman http://t.co/bfj7zkDJ"
"You'd be right more often if you thought you were wrong."
```

Data massage

When we tested that the data structure made sense, we printed the `FullText` field. We wish to cluster based on the content of the tweet. What matters to us is that content. This can be found in the `FullText` field of the struct. Later on in the chapter, we will see how we may use the metadata of the tweets, such as location, to help cluster the tweets better.

As mentioned in the previous sections, each individual tweet needs to be represented as a coordinate in some higher-dimensional space. Thus, our goal is to take all the tweets in a timeline and preprocess them in such a way that we can get this output table:

Tweet ID	twitter	test	right	wrong
1	0	1	0	0
2	1	0	0	0
3	0	0	1	1

Each row in the table represents a tweet, indexed by the tweet ID. The columns that follow are words that exist in the tweet, indexed by its header. So, in the first row, `test` appears in the tweet, while `twitter`, `right`, and `wrong` do not. The slice of numbers `[0 1 0 0]` in the first row is the input we require for the clustering algorithms.

Of course, binary numbers indicating the presence of a word in a tweet isn't the best. It'd be more interesting if the relative importance of the word is used instead. Again, we turn to the familiar TF-IDF, first introduced in `Chapter 2`, *Linear Regression – House Price Prediction*, for this. More advanced techniques such as using word embeddings exist. But you'd be surprised how well something as simple as TF-IDF can perform.

By now, the process should be familiar—we want to represent the text as a slice of numbers, not as a slice of bytes. In order to do so, we would have to require some sort of dictionary to convert the words in the text into IDs. From there, we can built the table.

Again, like in `Chapter 2`, *Linear Regression – House Price* Prediction, we shall approach this with a simple tokenization strategy. More advanced tokenizers are nice, but not necessary for our purpose. Instead, we'll rely on good old `strings.Field`.

The processor

Having laid out our requirements, we can combine them into a single data structure that contains the things we need. Here's how the processor data structure looks:

```
type processor struct {
tfidf *tfidf.TFIDF
corpus *corpus.Corpus
locations map[string]int
t transform.Transformer
locCount int
}
```

For now, ignore the `locations` field. We shall look into how metadata might be useful in clustering.

To create a new `processor`, the following function is defined:

```
func newProcessor() *processor {
c, err := corpus.Construct(corpus.WithWords([]string{mention, hashtag,
retweet, url}))
dieIfErr(err)
return &processor{
tfidf: tfidf.New(),
corpus: c,
locations: make(map[string]int),
}
}
```

Here, we see some interesting decisions. The corpus is constructed with a number of special strings—`mention`, `hashtag`, `retweet`, and `url`. These are defined as follows:

```
const (
mention = "<@MENTION>"
hashtag = "<#HASHTAG>"
retweet = "<RETWEET>"
url = "<URL>"
)
```

Some of the designs of this is for historical reasons. A long time ago, before Twitter supported retweets as an action, people manually retweeted tweets by prepending RT on to tweets. If we are to analyze data far into the past (which we won't for this chapter), then we'd have to be aware of the historical designs of Twitter as well. So, you must design for that.

But having constructed a corpus with special keywords implies something. It implies that when converting the text of a tweet into a bunch of IDs and numbers, mentions, hashtags, retweets, and URLs are all treated as the same. It implies we don't really want to care what the URL is, or who is mentioned. However, when it comes to hashtags, that's the interesting case.

A hashtag is typically used to denote the topic of the tweet. Think #MeToo or #TimesUp. A hashtag contains information. Compressing all hashtags into one single ID may not be useful. This is a point to note when we experiment later on.

Having said all that, here's how a list of *processedTweet is processed. We will be revisiting and revising the function as the chapter goes on:

```
func (p *processor) process(a []*processedTweet) {
for _, tt := range a {
for _, word := range strings.Fields(tt.FullText) {
wordID, ok := p.single(word)
if ok {
tt.ids = append(tt.ids, wordID)
}
if isRT(word) {
tt.isRT = true
}
}
p.tfidf.Add(tt)
}
p.tfidf.CalculateIDF()
// calculate scores
for _, tt := range a {
tt.textVec = p.tfidf.Score(tt)
}
// normalize text vector
size := p.corpus.Size()
for _, tt := range a {
tt.normTextVec = make([]float64, size)
for i := range tt.ids {
tt.normTextVec[tt.ids[i]] = tt.textVec[i]
}
}
}
```

Let's go through this function line by line.

We start by ranging over all the `*processedTweets`. `a` is `[]*processedTweet` for a good reason—we want to modify the structure as we go along. If `a` were `[]processedTweet`, then we would have to either allocate a lot more, or have complicated modification schemes.

Each tweet is comprised of its `FullText`. We want to extract each word from the text, and then give each word its own ID. To do that, this is the loop:

```
for _, word := range strings.Fields(tt.FullText) {
wordID, ok := p.single(word)
if ok {
tt.ids = append(tt.ids, wordID)
}
}
```

Preprocessing a single word

The `p.single` processes a single word. It returns the ID of the word, and whether to add it to the list of words that make up the tweet. It is defined as follows:

```
func (p *processor) single(a string) (wordID int, ok bool) {
word := strings.ToLower(a)
if _, ok = stopwords[word]; ok {
return -1, false
}
if strings.HasPrefix(word, "#") {
return p.corpus.Add(hashtag), true
}
if strings.HasPrefix(word, "@") {
return p.corpus.Add(mention), true
}
if strings.HasPrefix(word, "http://") {
return p.corpus.Add(url), true
}
if isRT(word) {
return p.corpus.Add(retweet), false
}
return p.corpus.Add(word), true
}
```

We start by making the word lowercase. This makes words such as café and Café equivalent.

Speaking of café, what would happen if there are two tweets mentioning a café, but one user writes café and the other writes cafe? Assume, of course, they both refer to the same thing. We'd need some form of normalization to tell us that they're the same.

Normalizing a string

First, the word is to be normalized into NFKC form. In Chapter 2, *Linear Regression–House Price Prediction*, this was introduced, but I then mentioned that LingSpam basically provides normalized datasets. In real-world data, which Twitter is, data is often dirty. Hence, we need to be able to compare them on an apples-to-apples basis.

To show this, let's write a side program:

```
package main
import (
 "fmt"
 "unicode"
"golang.org/x/text/transform"
 "golang.org/x/text/unicode/norm"
 )
func isMn(r rune) bool { return unicode.Is(unicode.Mn, r) }
func main() {
 str1 := "cafe"
 str2 := "café"
 str3 := "cafe\u0301"
 fmt.Println(str1 == str2)
 fmt.Println(str2 == str3)
t := transform.Chain(norm.NFD, transform.RemoveFunc(isMn), norm.NFKC)
 str1a, _, _ := transform.String(t, str1)
 str2a, _, _ := transform.String(t, str2)
 str3a, _, _ := transform.String(t, str3)
fmt.Println(str1a == str2a)
 fmt.Println(str2a == str3a)
 }
```

The first thing to note is that there are at least three ways of writing the word café, which for the purposes of this demonstration means coffee shop. It's clear from the first two comparisons that the words are not the same. But since they mean the same thing, a comparison should return true.

To do that, we will need to transform all the text to one form, and then comapare it. To do so, we would need to define a transformer:

```
t := transform.Chain(norm.NFD, transform.RemoveFunc(isMn), norm.NFKC)
```

This transformer is a chain of text transformers, applied one after another.

First, we convert all the text to its decomposing form, NFD. This would turn `café` into `cafe\u0301`.

Then, we remove any non-spacing mark. This turns `cafe\u0301` into `cafe`. This removal function is done with the `isMn` function, defined as follows:

```
func isMn(r rune) bool { return unicode.Is(unicode.Mn, r) }
```

Lastly, convert everything to NKFC form for maximum compatibility and space saving. All three strings are now equal.

Note that this type of comparison is done with one single assumption that belies it all: there is one language that we're doing our comparisons in—English. **Café** in French means **coffee** as well as **coffee shop**. This kind of normalization, where we remove diacritical marks, works so long as removing a diacritic mark does not change the meaning of the word. We'd have to be more careful around normalization when dealing with multiple languages. But for this project, this is a good enough assumption.

With this new knowledge, we will need to update our `processor` type:

```
type processor struct {
tfidf *tfidf.TFIDF
corpus *corpus.Corpus
transformer transformer.Transformer
locations map[string]int
locCount int
}
func newProcessor() *processor {
c, err := corpus.Construct(corpus.WithWords([]string{mention, hashtag,
retweet, url}))
dieIfErr(err)
t := transform.Chain(norm.NFD, transform.RemoveFunc(isMn), norm.NFKC)
return &processor{
tfidf: tfidf.New(),
corpus: c,
transformer: t,
locations: make(map[string]int),
}
}
```

The first line of our `p.single` function would have to change too, from this:

```
func (p *processor) single(a string) (wordID int, ok bool) {
word := strings.ToLower(a)
```

It will change to this:

```
func (p *processor) single(a string) (wordID int, ok bool) {
word, _, err := transform.String(p.transformer, a)
dieIfErr(err)
word = strings.ToLower(word)
```

If you're feeling extra hard-working, try making `strings.ToLower` a `transform.Transformer`. It is harder than you might expect, but not as hard as it appears.

Preprocessing stopwords

Enough about normalization. We now turn our focus to `stopwords`.

Recall from `Chapter 2`, *Linear Regression–House Price Prediction*, that `stopwords` are words such as **the**, **there**, **from**, and so on. They're connective words, useful in understanding the specific context of sentences, but for a naive statistical analysis, they often add nothing more than noise. So, we have to remove them.

A check for `stopwords` is simple. If a word matches a `stopwords`, we'll return `false` for whether to add the word ID into the sentence:

```
if _, ok = stopwords[word]; ok {
 return -1, false
 }
```

Where does the list of `stopwords` come from? It's simple enough that I just wrote this in `stopwords.go`:

```
const sw = `a about above across after afterwards again against all almost
alone along already also although always am among amongst amoungst amount
an and another any anyhow anyone anything anyway anywhere are around as at
back be became because become becomes becoming been before beforehand
behind being below beside besides between beyond bill both bottom but by
call can cannot can't cant co co. computer con could couldnt couldn't cry
de describe detail did didn didn't didnt do does doesn doesn't doesnt doing
don done down due during each eg e.g eight either eleven else elsewhere
empty enough etc even ever every everyone everything everywhere except few
fifteen fify fill find fire first five for former formerly forty found four
from front full further get give go had has hasnt hasn't hasn have he hence
her here hereafter hereby herein hereupon hers herself him himself his how
however hundred i ie i.e. if in inc indeed interest into is it its itself
just keep kg km last latter latterly least less ltd made make many may me
meanwhile might mill mine more moreover most mostly move much must my
```

myself name namely neither never nevertheless next nine no nobody none
noone nor not nothing now nowhere of off often on once one only onto or
other others otherwise our ours ourselves out over own part per perhaps
please put quite rather re really regarding same say see seem seemed
seeming seems serious several she should show side since sincere six sixty
so some somehow someone something sometime sometimes somewhere still such
system take ten than that the their them themselves then thence there
thereafter thereby therefore therein thereupon these they thick thin third
this those though three through throughout thru thus to together too top
toward towards twelve twenty two un under unless until up upon us used
using various very via was we well were what whatever when whence whenever
where whereafter whereas whereby wherein whereupon wherever whether which
while whither who whoever whole whom whose why will with within without
would yet you your yours yourself yourselves`

```
var stopwords = make(map[string]struct{})
func init() {
  for _, s := range strings.Split(sw, " ") {
  stopwords[s] = struct{}{}
  }
  }
```

And that's it! A tweet with content that looks like this—*an apple a day keeps the doctor away* would have the IDs for *apple, day, doctor,* and *away.*

The list of stopwords is adapted from the list that is used in the `lingo` package. The list of stopwords in the `lingo` package is meant to be used on lemmatized words. Because we're not lemmatizing, some words were manually added. It's not perfect but works well enough for our purpose.

Preprocessing Twitter entities

After we've removed the stopwords, it's time to process the special Twitter entities:

```
if strings.HasPrefix(word, "#") {
return p.corpus.Add(hashtag), true
}
if strings.HasPrefix(word, "@") {
return p.corpus.Add(mention), true
}
if strings.HasPrefix(word, "http://") {
return p.corpus.Add(url), true
}
```

These are straightforwards enough.

If a word begins with "#", then it's a hashtag. We might want to come back to this later, so it's good to keep this in mind.

Any word that begins with a "@" is a mention. This is a little tricky. Sometimes, people tweet things such as I am @PlaceName, indicating a location, as opposed to mentioning a user (indeed, one may find @PlaceName does not exist). Or, alternatively, people may tweet something such as I am @ PlaceName. In this case, the solo "@" would still be treated as a mention. I found that for the former (@PlaceName), it doesn't really matter if the word is treated as a mention. Twitter's API does indeed return a list of mentions that you may check against. But for my personal timeline, this was extra work that isn't necessary. So, think of this as an extra credit project—check against the list of mentions from the API.

Of course, we shan't be as lazy as to leave everything to extra credit; simple checks can be made—if @ is solo, then we shouldn't treat it as a mention. It should be treated as at.

Now, we check for URLs. The line if strings.HasPrefix(word, "http://") checks for a http:// prefix. This isn't good. This doesn't account for URLs with a https scheme.

Now we know how to modify this section of the code. It looks like this:

```
switch {
case strings.HasPrefix(word, "#"):
return p.corpus.Add(hashtag), true
case strings.HasPrefix(word, "@"):
if len(word) == 0 {
return p.corpus.Add("at"), true
}
return p.corpus.Add(mention), true
case strings.HasPrefix(word, "http"):
return p.corpus.Add(url), true
}
```

Lastly, a final line of code is added to handle historical tweets before retweets were supported by Twitter:

```
if word == "rt" {
return p.corpus.Add(retweet), false
}
```

Processing a single tweet

Consider the following snippet of code:

```
for _, tt := range a {
for _, word := range strings.Fields(tt.FullText) {
wordID, ok := p.single(word)
if ok {
tt.ids = append(tt.ids, wordID)
}
if word == "rt" {
tt.isRT = true
}
}
p.tfidf.Add(tt)
}
```

What it says is after we've preprocessed every single word, we simply add that word to the TFIDF.

Clustering

The purpose of this project is to clean up the amount of tweets that I have to read. If there is a reading budget of 100 tweets, I don't want to be reading 50 tweets on the same topic; they may well represent different viewpoints, but in general for skimming purposes, are not relevant to my interests. Clustering provides a good solution to this problem.

First, if the tweets are clustered, the 50 tweets on the same topic will be grouped in the same cluster. This allows me to dig in deeper if I wish. Otherwise, I can just skip those tweets and move on.

In this project, we wish to use K-means. To do so, we'll use Marcin Praski's `clusters` library. To install it, simply run `go get -u github.com/mpraski/clusters`. It's a good library, and it comes built in with multiple clustering algorithms. I introduced K-means before, but we're also going to be using DBSCAN.

Last, we're going to be using the DMMClust algorithm to compare against. The DMMClust algorithm is in a different library. To install it, simply run `go get -u github.com/go-nlp/dmmclust`. The purpose of DMMClust is to cluster small texts using an innovative process.

Clustering with K-means

As a recap, here's what we did so far—we processed each tweet in a list of tweets from the home timeline to be a slice of `float64`. These represent the coordinates in the higher-dimensional space. Now, all we need to do is the following:

1. Create a clusterer.
2. Create a `[][]float64` representing all the tweets from the timeline.
3. Train the clusterer.
4. Predict which tweet belongs in which cluster.

It can be done as follows:

```
func main() {
tweets := mock()
p := newProcessor()
p.process(tweets)
// create a clusterer
  c, err := clusters.KMeans(10000, 25, clusters.EuclideanDistance)
  dieIfErr(err)
data := asMatrix(tweets)
  dieIfErr(c.Learn(data))clusters := c.Guesses()
  for i, clust := range clusters{
fmt.Printf("%d: %q\n", clust, tweets[i].FullText)
  }
  }
```

Surprised? Let's break it down.

The first few lines are for processing `tweets`:

```
tweets := mock()
p := newProcessor()
p.process(tweets)
```

We then create a clusterer:

```
// create a clusterer
c, err := clusters.KMeans(10000, 25, clusters.EuclideanDistance)
dieIfErr(err)
```

Here, we say we want a K-means clusterer. We'll train on the data 10,000 times, and we want it to find 25 clusters, using the `EuclideanDistance` method to calculate distances. The Euclidean distance is your bog standard distance calculation, the same one you'd use to calculate the distance between two points in the exercises in the K-means section before. There are other methods of calculating distances, which are more suited for textual data. Later in this chapter, I'll show you how to create a distance function, the Jacard distance, which is much better than Euclidean distance when used on text.

After we've created a clusterer, we need to convert our list of `tweets` into a matrix. We then train the clusterer:

```
data := asMatrix(tweets)
dieIfErr(c.Learn(data))
```

And, finally, we display the `clusters`:

```
clusters := c.Guesses()
for i, clust := range clusters{
fmt.Printf("%d: %q\n", clust, tweets[i].FullText)
}
```

Clustering with DBSCAN

Clustering with DBSCAN using Marcin's package is equally simple. In fact, you would just need to change one single line of code from this:

```
c, err := clusters.KMeans(10000, 25, clusters.EuclideanDistance)
```

You would change it to this:

```
c, err := clusters.DBSCAN(eps, minPts, clusters.EuclideanDistance)
```

Now, of course, the question is what values should `eps` and `minPts` be?

`eps` represents the minimum distance required for two points to be considered a neighbor. `minPts` is the minimum number of points to form a dense cluster. Let's address `eps` first.

How do we know what the best distance is? A good way to figure this out is usually to visualize the data. In fact, this is what the original inventors of the DBSCAN algorithm suggests. But what exactly are we to visualize?

We want to visualize the distance between the tweets. Given a dataset, we can compute a distance matrix that looks something like this:

```
|  | A | B | C | ... |
|--|--|--|--|--|--|
| A |  |  |  |  |
| B |  |  |  |  |
| C |  |  |  |  |
| ... |  |  |  |  |
```

To do so, we write the following function:

```go
func knn(a [][]float64, k int, distance func(a, b []float64) float64)
([][]float64, []float64) {
var distances [][]float64
for _, row := range a {
var dists []float64
for _, row2 := range a {
dist := distance(row, row2)
dists = append(dists, dist)
}
sort.Sort(sort.Float64Slice(dists))
topK := dists[:k]
distances = append(distances, topK)
}
var lastCol []float64
for _, d := range distances {
l := d[len(d)-1]
lastCol = append(lastCol, l)
}
sort.Sort(sort.Float64Slice(lastCol))
return distances, lastCol
}
```

This function takes a matrix of floats; each row represents a tweet, and finds the top k-nearest neighbors. Let's walk through the algorithm. As we walk though the algorithm, bear in mind that each row is a tweet; you can think of each row therefore as a very complicated coordinate.

The first thing we want to do is to find the distance between a tweet and another tweet, hence the following block:

```
var distances [][]float64
for _, row := range a {
var dists []float64
for _, row2 := range a {
dist := distance(row, row2)
dists = append(dists, dist)
}
```

Of particular note are the two expressions `for _, row := range a` and `for _, row2 := range a`. In a normal KNN function, you'd have two matrices, `a` and `b`, and you'd find the distance between a tweet in `a` and a tweet in `b`. But for the purposes of drawing this chart, we are going to compare tweets within the same dataset.

Once we acquired all the distances, we want to find the closest neighbors, so we sort the list and then put them in the distance matrix:

```
sort.Sort(sort.Float64Slice(dists))
topK := dists[:k]
distances = append(distances, topK)
```

This, in a very quick way, is how to do K-nearest neighbors. Of course, it's not the most efficient. The algorithm I've shown here is $O(n^2)$. There are better ways of doing things, but for the purpose of this project, this suffices.

After that, we grab the last column of the matrix and sort the last column. This is what we wish to plot. The plotting code is not unlike that seen in previous chapters. I shall provide it here with no further elaboration on how to use it:

```
func plotKNNDist(a []float64) plotter.XYs {
points := make(plotter.XYs, len(a))
for i, val := range a {
points[i].X = float64(i)
points[i].Y = val
}
return points
}
```

When I plot the real Twitter data to figure out the ideal `eps`, I get the following output:

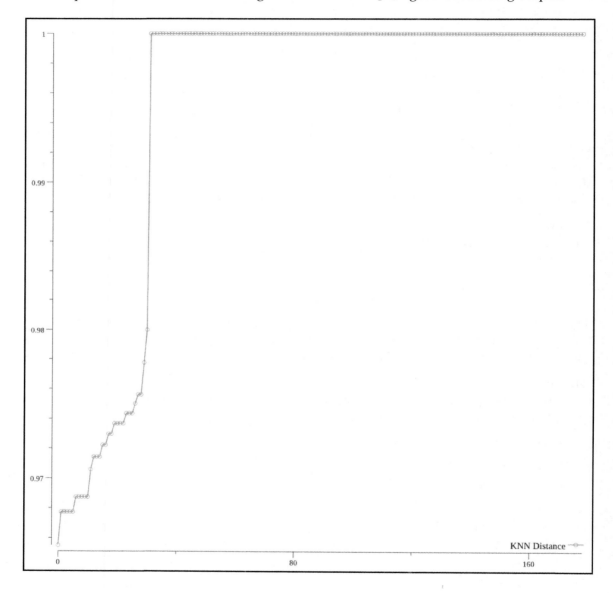

What you want to find is an `elbow` or `knee` in the picture. Unfortunately, as you can tell, there are many of them. This is going to make clustering with the DBSCAN algorithm difficult. What this means is that the data is rather noisy.

One of the things that is of particular importance is the distance function used. I will go into this a little further in following sections on tweaking the program.

Clustering with DMMClust

Having been somewhat discouraged by the distance plot of my Twitter home feed, I looked into another way of clustering tweets. To that end, I used the `dmmclust` library (of which I am the primary author). The purpose of the DMMClust algorithm is that it is able to handle small texts quite well. Indeed, it was written to handle the problem of having small text.

What exactly is a small text? Most text clustering research out there is done on texts with large amounts of words. Twitter, up to very recently, only supported 140 characters. As you may imagine, the amount of information that 140 characters to be transmitted as human language is not very much.

The DMMClust algorithm works very much like students joining high school social clubs. Imagine the tweets as a bunch of students. Each student randomly joins a social club. Within each social club, they may like their fellow members of the club, or they may not. If they do not like the people in the group, they are allowed to change social clubs. This happens until all the clubs have people who like each other the most, or until the amount of iterations runs out.

This, in a nutshell, is how the DMMClust algorithm works.

Real data

Up to this point, we've been working on an example JSON that the Twitter documentation provides. I assume by now you have your Twitter API access. So, let's get real Twitter data!

To get your API keys from the developer portal, click on the **Get Started** link. You will come to a page such as this:

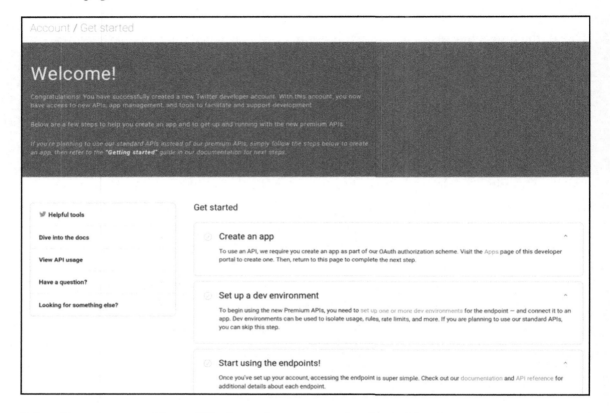

Select **Create an app**. You will be brought to a page that looks like this:

I had previously created a Twitter app a long time ago (it had very similar features to the one we're creating in this project); hence, I have an app there already. Click on the blue **Create an app** button at the top right. You will be brought to the following form:

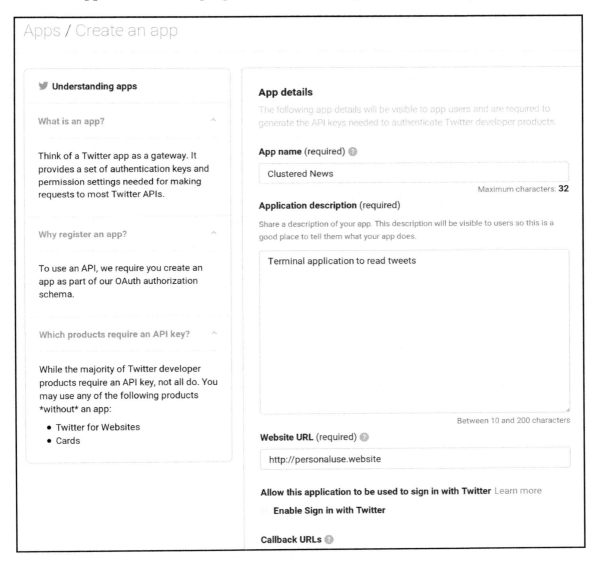

Fill in the form then click **submit**. It might take a few days before you receive an email saying the app has been approved for development. Be sure to be truthful in the description. Lastly, you should then be able to click into your app, and get the following page, which shows your API key and secret:

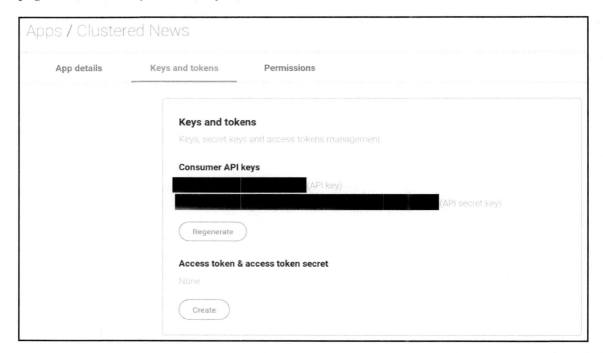

Click **Create** to create your access token and access token secret. You'll be needing them.

Now that we have our API access key, this is how you'd access Twitter using the Anaconda package:

```
const (
ACCESSTOKEN = "_____"
ACCESSTOKENSECRET = "_____"
CONSUMERKEY = "_____"
CONSUMERSECRET = "_____"
)
func main() {
twitter := anaconda.NewTwitterApiWithCredentials(ACCESSTOKEN,
ACCESSTOKENSECRET, CONSUMERKEY, CONSUMERSECRET)
raw, err := twitter.GetHomeTimeline(nil)
f, err := os.OpenFile("dev.json", os.O_TRUNC|os.O_WRONLY|os.O_CREATE, 0644)
dieIfErr(err)
```

```
enc := json.NewEncoder(f)
enc.Encode(raw)
f.Close()
}
```

At first glance, this snippet of code is a little weird. Let's go through the code line by line. The first six lines deal with the access tokens and keys. Obviously, they should not be hardcoded in. A good way to handle secrets like these is to put them in environment variables. I'll leave that as an exercise to the reader. We'll move on to the rest of the code:

```
twitter := anaconda.NewTwitterApiWithCredentials(ACCESSTOKEN,
ACCESSTOKENSECRET, CONSUMERKEY, CONSUMERSECRET)
raw, err := twitter.GetHomeTimeline(nil)
```

These two lines uses the Anaconda library to get the tweets found in the Home timeline. The `nil` being passed in may be of interest. Why would one do this? The `GetHomeTimeline` method takes a map of `url.Values`. The package can be found in the standard library as `net/url`. Values is defined thus:

```
type Values map[string][]string
```

But what do the values represent? It turns out that you may pass some parameters to the Twitter API. The parameters and what they do are enumerated here: `https://developer.twitter.com/en/docs/tweets/timelines/api-reference/get-statuses-home_timeline`. I don't wish to limit anything, so passing in `nil` is acceptable.

The result is `[]anaconda.Tweet`, all neatly packaged up for us to use. The following few lines are therefore quite odd:

```
f, err := os.OpenFile("dev.json", os.O_TRUNC|os.O_WRONLY|os.O_CREATE,
0644)
dieIfErr(err)
enc := json.NewEncoder(f)
enc.Encode(raw)
f.Close()
```

Why would I want to save this as a JSON file? The answer is simple—when using machine learning algorithms, you may need to tune the algorithm. Saving the request as a JSON file serves two purposes:

- It allows for consistency. Under active development, you would expect to tweak the algorithm a lot. If the JSON file keeps changing, how do you know if it's the tweaks that are making the improvements, and not because the JSON has changed?

- Being a good citizen. Twitter's API is rate limited. This means you cannot request the same thing over and over again too many times. While testing and tuning machine learning algorithms, you are likely to have to repeatedly process your data over and over again. Instead of hammering the Twitter servers, you should be a good citizen and use a locally cached copy.

We defined `load` earlier. Again, we shall see its usefulness in the context of tweaking the algorithms.

The program

Once we've done that, we may move the previous `main()` into a different function, leaving ourselves with a blank canvas for `main()` again. We're now ready for the meat of the program. This is a skeleton program. You're encouraged to actually actively change the program while writing this:

```
func main() {
  f, err := os.Open("dev.json")
  dieIfErr(err)
  tweets := load(f)
  p := newProcessor()
  tweets = p.process(tweets)
expC := 20
  distances, last := knn(asMatrix(tweets), expC, clusters.EuclideanDistance)
  log.Printf("distances %v | %v", distances, last)
// plot for DBSCAN elbows
  plt, err := plot.New()
  dieIfErr(err)
  plotutil.AddLinePoints(plt, "KNN Distance", plotKNNDist(last))
  plt.Save(25*vg.Centimeter, 25*vg.Centimeter, "KNNDist.png")
// actually do the clustering
  dmmClust := dmm(tweets, expC, p.corpus.Size())
  kmeansClust := kmeans(tweets, expC)
  dbscanClust, clustCount := dbscan(tweets)
// print output
  log.Printf("len(tweets)%d", len(tweets))
  var buf bytes.Buffer
bc := byClusters2(dmmClust, expC)
  lc, tweetCount := largestCluster2(dmmClust)
  fmt.Fprintf(&buf, "Largest Cluster %d - %d tweets\n", lc, tweetCount)
  for i, t := range bc {
  fmt.Fprintf(&buf, "CLUSTER %d: %d\n", i, len(t))
  for _, c := range t {
  fmt.Fprintf(&buf, "\t%v\n", tweets[c].clean2)
```

```
  }
  }
  fmt.Fprintf(&buf, "==============\n")
  bc2 := byClusters(kmeansClust, expC)
  for i, t := range bc2 {
  fmt.Fprintf(&buf, "CLUSTER %d: %d\n", i, len(t))
  for _, c := range t {
  fmt.Fprintf(&buf, "\t%v\n", tweets[c].clean2)
  }
  }
  fmt.Fprintf(&buf, "==============\n")
  bc3 := byClusters(dbscanClust, clustCount)
  for i, t := range bc3 {
  fmt.Fprintf(&buf, "CLUSTER %d: %d\n", i, len(t))
  for _, c := range t {
  fmt.Fprintf(&buf, "\t%v\n", tweets[c].clean2)
  }
  }
  log.Println(buf.String())
  }
```

There are some utility functions that I have yet to show you. Now it's time to define them:

```
  func dmm(a []*processedTweet, expC int, corpusSize int) []dmmclust.Cluster
  {
  conf := dmmclust.Config{
  K: expC,
  Vocabulary: corpusSize,
  Iter: 1000,
  Alpha: 0.0,
  Beta: 0.01,
  Score: dmmclust.Algorithm4,
  Sampler: dmmclust.NewGibbs(rand.New(rand.NewSource(1337))),
  }
  dmmClust, err := dmmclust.FindClusters(toDocs(a), conf)
  dieIfErr(err)
  return dmmClust
  }
  func kmeans(a []*processedTweet, expC int) []int {
  // create a clusterer
  kmeans, err := clusters.KMeans(100000, expC, clusters.EuclideanDistance)
  dieIfErr(err)
  data := asMatrix(a)
  dieIfErr(kmeans.Learn(data))
  return kmeans.Guesses()
  }
  func dbscan(a []*processedTweet) ([]int, int) {
  dbscan, err := clusters.DBSCAN(5, 0.965, 8, clusters.EuclideanDistance)
```

```go
    dieIfErr(err)
    data := asMatrix(a)
    dieIfErr(dbscan.Learn(data))
    clust := dbscan.Guesses()
counter := make(map[int]struct{})
    for _, c := range clust {
    counter[c] = struct{}{}
    }
    return clust, len(counter)
    }
func largestCluster(clusters []int) (int, int) {
    cc := make(map[int]int)
    for _, c := range clusters {
    cc[c]++
    }
var retVal, maxVal int
for k, v := range cc {
    if v > maxVal {
    retVal = k
    maxVal = v
    }
    }
    return retVal, cc[retVal]
    }
func largestCluster2(clusters []dmmclust.Cluster) (int, int) {
    cc := make(map[int]int)
    for _, c := range clusters {
    cc[c.ID()]++
    }
var retVal, maxVal int
for k, v := range cc {
    if v > maxVal {
    retVal = k
    maxVal = v
    }
    }
    return retVal, cc[retVal]
    }
func byClusters(a []int, expectedClusters int) (retVal [][]int) {
    if expectedClusters == 0 {
    return nil
    }
    retVal = make([][]int, expectedClusters)
    var i, v int
    defer func() {
    if r := recover(); r != nil {
    log.Printf("exp %v | %v", expectedClusters, v)
    panic(r)
```

```
    }
  } ()
  for i, v = range a {
  if v == -1 {
  // retVal[0] = append(retVal[0], i)
  continue
  }
  retVal[v-1] = append(retVal[v-1], i)
  }
  return retVal
}
func byClusters2(a []dmmclust.Cluster, expectedClusters int) (retVal
[][]int) {
  retVal = make([][]int, expectedClusters)
  for i, v := range a {
  retVal[v.ID()] = append(retVal[v.ID()], i)
  }
  return retVal
}
```

These are some of the utility functions that may be found in `utils.go`. They mainly help with tweaking the program. Now run the program by typing `go run *.go`.

Tweaking the program

If you have been following up to this point, you may get very poor results from all the clustering algorithms. I'd like to remind you that the stated objective of this book in general is to impart an understanding of what it's like to do data science in Go. For the most part, I have advocated a method that can be described as think hard about the problem, then write the answers down. But the reality is that often trial and error are required.

The solution that works for me on my Twitter home timeline may not work for you. For example, this code works well on a friend's Twitter feed. Why is this? He follows a lot of similar people who talk about similar things at the same time. It's a little harder to cluster tweets in my Twitter home feed. I follow a diverse array of people. The people I follow don't have set schedules of tweeting and do not generally interact with other Twitter users. Therefore, the tweets are generally quite diverse already.

It is with this in mind that I encourage you to experiment and tweak your program. In the subsections that follow, I shall outline what worked for me. It may not work for you.

Tweaking distances

Up to this point, we had been using Euclidean distance as provided by the `Marcin` library. The Euclidean distance is computed as follows:

$$EuclideanDistance(\mathbf{q},\mathbf{p}) = \sqrt{\sum_{i=1}^n (q_i - p_i)^2}.$$

The `EuclideanDistance` is a good metric to use when it comes to coordinates in a Cartesian space. Indeed, earlier I had drawn up an analogy of thinking of a tweet as a bunch of coordinates in space, to explain K-means and DBSCAN. The reality is that text documents aren't really in Cartesian space. You may think of them as being in Cartesian space, but they are not strictly so.

So, allow me to introduce another type of distance, one that is more suited to dealing with textual elements in a bag-of-words-style setting that we're currently doing, the Jaccard distance.

The Jaccard distance is defined as follows:

$$d_J(A,B) = 1 - J(A,B) = { { |A \cup B| - |A \cap B| } \over |A \cup B| }$$

Here, A and B are sets of words in each tweet. The implementation of the Jaccard distance in Go is rudimentary, but it works:

```go
func jaccard(a, b []float64) float64 {
setA, setB := make(map[int]struct{}), make(map[int]struct{})
union := make(map[int]struct{})
for i := range a {
if a[i] != 0 {
union[i] = struct{}{}
setA[i] = struct{}{}
}
}
for i := range b {
if b[i] != 0 {
union[i] = struct{}{}
setB[i] = struct{}{}
}
}
intersection := 0.0
 for k := range setA {
if _, ok := setB[k]; ok {
intersection++
}
}
```

```
return 1 - (intersection / float64(len(union)))
 }
```

Tweaking the preprocessing step

One thing you may note is that the preprocessing of tweets is very minimal, and some of the rules are odd. For example, all hashtags are treated as one, as are all links and mentions. When this project started, it seemed like a good reason. There is no other justification than it seemed like a good reason; one always needs a springboard from which to jump off in any project. A flimsy excuse at that point is as good as any other.

Nonetheless, I have tweaked my preprocessing steps. These are the functions that I finally settled on. Do observe the difference between this and the original, listed in previous sections:

```
var nl = regexp.MustCompile("\n+")
var ht = regexp.MustCompile("&.+?;")
func (p *processor) single(word string) (wordID int, ok bool) {
if _, ok = stopwords[word]; ok {
return -1, false
}
switch {
case strings.HasPrefix(word, "#"):
word = strings.TrimPrefix(word, "#")
case word == "@":
return -1, false // at is a stop word!
case strings.HasPrefix(word, "http"):
return -1, false
}
if word == "rt" {
return -1, false
}
return p.corpus.Add(word), true
}
func (p *processor) process(a []*processedTweet) []*processedTweet {
// remove things from consideration
i := 0
for _, tt := range a {
if tt.Lang == "en" {
a[i] = tt
i++
}
}
a = a[:i]
var err error
```

```
    for _, tt := range a {
    if tt.RetweetedStatus != nil {
    tt.Tweet = *tt.RetweetedStatus
    }
  tt.clean, _, err = transform.String(p.transformer, tt.FullText)
    dieIfErr(err)
    tt.clean = strings.ToLower(tt.clean)
    tt.clean = nl.ReplaceAllString(tt.clean, "\n")
    tt.clean = ht.ReplaceAllString(tt.clean, "")
    tt.clean = stripPunct(tt.clean)
    log.Printf("%v", tt.clean)
    for _, word := range strings.Fields(tt.clean) {
    // word = corpus.Singularize(word)
    wordID, ok := p.single(word)
    if ok {
    tt.ids = append(tt.ids, wordID)
    tt.clean2 += " "
    tt.clean2 += word
    }
  if word == "rt" {
  tt.isRT = true
  }
  }
    p.tfidf.Add(tt)
    log.Printf("%v", tt.clean2)
    }
  p.tfidf.CalculateIDF()
   // calculate scores
   for _, tt := range a {
   tt.textVec = p.tfidf.Score(tt)
   }
 // normalize text vector
   size := p.corpus.Size()
   for _, tt := range a {
   tt.normTextVec = make([]float64, size)
   for i := range tt.ids {
   tt.normTextVec[tt.ids[i]] = tt.textVec[i]
   }
   }
   return a
   }
func stripPunct(a string) string {
  const punct = ",.?;:'\"!'*-""
  return strings.Map(func(r rune) rune {
  if strings.IndexRune(punct, r) < 0 {
  return r
  }
  return -1
```

```
}, a)
}
```

The most notable thing that I have changed is that I now consider a hashtag a word. Mentions are removed. As for URLs, in one of the attempts at clustering, I realized that the clustering algorithms were clustering all the tweets with a URL into the same cluster. That realization made me remove hashtags, mentions, and URLs. Hashtags have the # removed and are treated as if they were normal words.

Furthermore, you may note that I added some quick and dirty ways to `clean` certain things:

```
tt.clean = strings.ToLower(tt.clean)
tt.clean = nl.ReplaceAllString(tt.clean, "\n")
tt.clean = ht.ReplaceAllString(tt.clean, "")
tt.clean = stripPunct(tt.clean)
```

Here, I used regular expressions to replace multiple newlines with just one, and to replace all HTML-encoded text with nothing. Lastly, I removed all punctuation.

In a more formal setting, I would use a proper lexer to handle my text. The lexer I'd use would come from Lingo (`github.com/chewxy/lingo`). But given that Twitter is a low value environment, there wasn't much point in doing so. A proper lexer like the one in lingo flags text as multiple things, allowing for easy removal.

Another thing you might notice is that I changed the definition of what a tweet is mid-flight:

```
if tt.RetweetedStatus != nil {
tt.Tweet = *tt.RetweetedStatus
}
```

This block of code says if a tweet is indeed a retweeted status, replace the tweet with the retweeted tweet. This works for me. But it may not work for you. I personally consider any retweet to be the same as repeating a tweet. So, I do not see why they should be separate. Additionally, Twitter allows for users to comment on a retweet. If you want to include that, you'd have to change the logic a little bit more. Either way, the way I got to this was by manually inspecting the JSON file I had saved.

It's asking these questions and then making a judgment call what is important in doing data science, either in Go or any other language. It's not about blindly applying algorithms. Rather, it's always driven by what the data tells you.

One last thing that you may note is this curious block of code:

```
// remove things from consideration
i := 0
for _, tt := range a {
if tt.Lang == "en" {
a[i] = tt
i++
}
}
a = a[:i]
```

Here, I only consider English tweets. I follow many people who tweet in a variety of languages. At any given time, my home timeline would have about 15% of tweets in French, Chinese, Japanese, or German. Clustering tweets in a different language is a whole different ballgame, so I chose to omit them.

Summary

In this chapter, we have learned how to cluster tweets using a variety of clustering methods. Though frequently touted as one of the most robust algorithms, we've shown that DBSCAN has problems with clustering tweets due to the nature of tweets being noisy. Instead, we see that older, more traditional methods, as well as a new method of clustering, would yield better results.

This points to a lesson—there is no one machine-learning algorithm to rule them all; there is no ultimate algorithm. Instead, we need to try more than one thing. In the chapters that follow, this theme will be more apparent, and we shall approach these with more rigor. In the next chapter, we will learn about basics of neural networks and apply them on handwriting to recognize digits.

6
Neural Networks - MNIST Handwriting Recognition

Imagine, you were a postal worker. Your would be job to deliver letters. Most of the time, the recipient's name and address would be printed and quite legible, and your job becomes quite easy. But come Thanksgiving and Christmas, the number of envelopes with handwritten addresses increases as people give their personal touches and flourishes. And, to be frank, some people (me included) just have terrible handwriting.

Blame it on schools for no longer emphasizing cursive handwriting if you must, but the problem remains: handwriting is hard to read and interpret. God forbid you have to deliver a letter penned by a doctor (good luck doing that!).

Imagine, instead, if you had built a machine learning system that allows you to read handwriting. That's what we will be doing this chapter and the next; we will be building a type of machine-learning algorithm known as an artificial neural network, and in the next chapter, we will be expanding on the concept with deep learning.

In this chapter, we will learn the basics of neural networks, see how it's inspired by biological neurons, find a better way of representing them, and finally apply neural networks on handwriting to recognize digits.

A neural network

The term **neural network** can mean one of two things in modern parlance. The first refers to a network of neurons found in your brain. These neurons form specific networks and pathways and are vital to you understanding this very sentence. The second meaning of the term refers to an artificial neural network; that is, things we build in software to emulate a neural network in the brain.

This, of course, has led to very many unfortunate comparisons between a biological neural network and an artificial neural network. To understand why, we must start at the beginning.

 From here on, I shall spell **neuron** with a British spelling denoting a real neuron cell, while the American spelling, **neuron,** will be reserved for the artificial variant.

This following diagram is of a neuron:

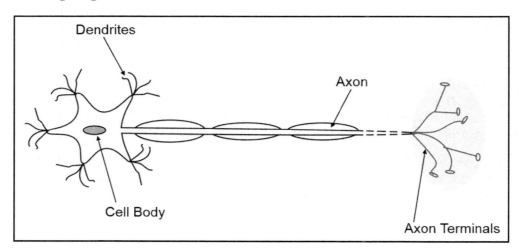

In general, a neuron typically consists of the soma (the general body of the cell that contains its nucleus), an optional axon covered in a kind of fatty tissue known as **myelin**, and dendrites. The latter two components (the axon and dendrites) are particularly interesting because together they form a structure known as a synapse. Specifically, it's the end of an axon the terminal) that forms such synapses.

The vast majority of synapses in mammalian brains are between axon terminals and dendrites. The typical flow of signals (chemical or electrical impulses) goes from one neuron, travels along the axon, and deposits its signal onto the next.

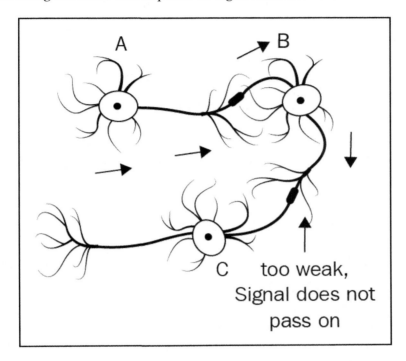

In the image above, we have three neurons, labelled A, B, and C. Imagine A receives a signal from an external source (like your eyes). It receives a signal that is strong enough that it passes the signal down the axon, which touches the dendrites of B via a synapse. B receives the signal and decides it doesn't warrant passing along the signal to C, so nothing goes down the axon of B.

And so we will now explore how you might emulate this.

Emulating a neural network

Let's simplify the preceding diagram of the neural network:

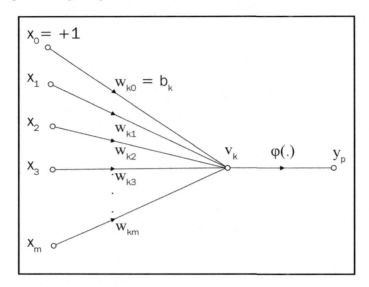

We'll have a circle represent the body of the neuron, and we'll call it the **neuron**. The "dendrites" of the neuron receive inputs from other neurons (unshown) and add up all the inputs. Each input represents an input from another neuron; so, if you see three inputs, it means that this neuron is connected to three other neurons.

If the sum of the inputs exceeds a threshold value, then we can say the neuron "fires" or is activated. This simulates the activation potential of an actual neuron. For simplicity, let's say if it fires, then the output will be 1; otherwise, it will be 0. Here is a good emulation of it in Go code:

```go
func neuron(threshold int, inputs ...int) int {
  var total int
  for _, in := range inputs {
    total += in
  }
  if total > threshold {
    return 1
  }
  return 0
}
```

This is generally known as a **perceptron**, and it's a faithful emulation of how neurons work, if your knowledge of how neurons work is stuck in the 1940s and 1950s.

Here is a rather interesting anecdote: As I was writing this section, King Princess' 1950 started playing in the background and I thought it would be rather apt to imagine ourselves in the 1950s, developing the perceptron. There remains a problem: the artificial network we emulated so far cannot learn! It is programmed to do whatever the inputs tell it to do.

What does it mean for an artificial neural network "to learn" exactly? There's an idea that arose in neuroscience in the 1950s, called the **Hebbian Rule**, which can be briefly summed up as: *Neurons that fire together grow together*. This gives rise to an idea that some synapses are thicker; hence, they have stronger connections, and other synapses are thinner; hence, they have weaker connections.

To emulate this, we would need to introduce the concept of a weighted value, the weight of which corresponds to the strength of the input from another neuron. Here's a good approximation of this idea:

```
func neuron(threshold, weights, inputs []int) int {
  if len(weights) != len(inputs) {
    panic("Expected length of weights to be the same as the length of
inputs")
  }
  var total int
  for i, in := range inputs {
    total += weights[i]*in
  }
  if total > threshold {
    return 1
  }
  return 0
}
```

At this point, if you are familiar with linear algebra, you might think to yourself that total is essentially a vector product. You would be absolutely correct. Additionally, if the threshold is 0, then you have simply applied a heaviside step function:

```
func heaviside(a float64) float64 {
  if a >= 0 {
    return 1
  }
  return 0
}
```

In other words, we can summarize a single neuron in the following way:

```
func neuron(weights, inputs []float64) float64 {
  return heaviside(vectorDot(weights, inputs))
}
```

Note in the last two examples, I switched over from `int` to a more canonical `float64`. The point remains the same: a single neuron is simply a function applied to a vector product.

A single neuron does not do much. But stack a bunch of them together and arrange them by layers like so, and then suddenly they start to do more:

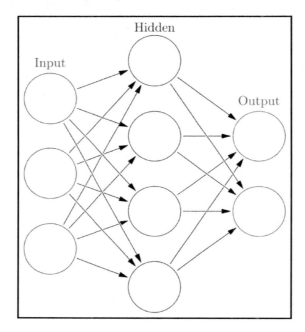

Now we come to the part that requires a conceptual leap: if a neuron is essentially just a vector product, *stacking* the neurons simply makes it a matrix!

Given an image can be represented as a flat slice of `float64`, the `vectorDot` function is replaced with `matVecMul`, which is a function that multiplies a matrix and vector to return a vector. We can write a function representing the neural layer like so:

```
func affine(weights [][]float64, inputs []float64) []float64 {
  return activation(matVecMul(weights, inputs))
}
```

Linear algebra 101

I want to take a detour to talk about linear algebra. It's featured quite a bit so far in this book, although it was scarcely mentioned by name. In fact linear algebra underlies every chapter we've done so far.

Imagine you have two equations:

$$y_1 = x_1 + 2x_2$$
$$y_2 = 3x_1 + 5x_2$$

Let's say y_1 and y_2 is 4 and 1, respectively. We can now write the following equations as such:

$$4 = x_1 + 2x_2$$
$$1 = 3x_1 + 5x_2$$

And we can solve it using basic algebra (please do work it out on your own): $x_1 = 2$ and $x_2 = 1$.

What if you have three, four, or five simultaneous equations? It starts to get cumbersome to calculate these values. Instead, we invented a new notation: the matrix notation, which will allow us to solve simultaneous equations faster.

It had been used for about 100 years without a name (it was first termed "matrix" by James Sylvester) and formal rules were being used until Arthur Cayley formalized the rules in 1858. Nonetheless, the idea of grouping together parts of an equation into a bunch had been long used.

We start by "factoring" out the equations into their parts:

$$\frac{y_1 = \begin{bmatrix} 1 & 2 \end{bmatrix} \begin{bmatrix} x_1 & x_2 \end{bmatrix}}{y_2 = \begin{bmatrix} 3 & 5 \end{bmatrix} \begin{bmatrix} x_1 & x_2 \end{bmatrix}}$$

The horizontal line indicates that it's two different equations, not that they are ratios. Of course, we realize that we've been making too many repetitions so we simplify the matrix of x_1 and x_2

$$\begin{bmatrix} y_1 \\ y_2 \end{bmatrix} = \begin{bmatrix} 1 & 2 \\ 3 & 5 \end{bmatrix} \begin{bmatrix} x_1 & x_2 \end{bmatrix}$$

Here, you can see that x_1 and x_2 is only ever written once. It's rather unneat to write it the way we just wrote it, so instead we write it like so to be neater:

$$\begin{bmatrix} y_1 \\ y_2 \end{bmatrix} = \begin{bmatrix} 1 & 2 \\ 3 & 5 \end{bmatrix} \begin{bmatrix} x_1 \\ x_2 \end{bmatrix}$$

Not only do we write it like so, we give specific rule on how to read this notation:

$$y_1 = \begin{bmatrix} 1 & 2 \end{bmatrix} \begin{bmatrix} x_1 \\ x_2 \end{bmatrix}$$
$$= 1 \times x_1 + 2 \times x_2$$

$$y_2 = \begin{bmatrix} 3 & 5 \end{bmatrix} \begin{bmatrix} x_1 \\ x_2 \end{bmatrix}$$
$$= 3 \times x_1 + 5 \times x_2$$

We should give the matrices names so we can refer to them later on:

$$\mathbf{y} = \begin{bmatrix} y_1 \\ y_2 \end{bmatrix}$$

$$\mathbf{W} = \begin{bmatrix} 1 & 2 \\ 3 & 5 \end{bmatrix}$$

$$\mathbf{x} = \begin{bmatrix} x_1 \\ x_2 \end{bmatrix}$$

 The bold indicates that the variable holds multiple values. An uppercase indicates a matrix ($\mathbf{W}$), and lowercase indicates a vector ($\mathbf{x}$ and $\mathbf{y}$. This is to distinguish it from scalar variables (variables that only hold one value), which are typically written without boldface (for example, x and y).

To solve the equations, the solution is simply this:

$$\mathbf{x} = \mathbf{W}^{-1}\mathbf{y}$$

The $^{-1}$ superscript indicates an inverse is to be taken. This is rather consistent with normal algebra.

Consider a problem $y = wx$ where you are asked to solve for x. The solution is simply $x = \dfrac{y}{w}$. Or we can rewrite it as a series of multiplications as $x = \dfrac{1}{w} \times y$. And what do we know about fractions where one is the numerator? They can simply be written as a power to the -1. Hence, we arrive at this solution equation: $x = w^{-1}y$

Now if you squint very carefully, the scalar version of the equation looks very much like the matrix notation version of the equation.

How to calculate the inverse of a matrix is not what this book aims to do. Instead, I encourage you to pick up a linear algebra text book. I highly recommend Sheldon Axler's *Linear Algebra Done Right* (Springer Books).

To recap, here are the main points:

- Matrix multiplication and notation were invented to solve simultaneous equations.
- To solve the simultaneous equation, we treat the equation as though the variables were scalar variables and use inverses.

Now comes the interesting part. Using the same two equations, we will turn the question around. What if we knew what x_1 and x_2 is instead? The equations would now look something like this:

$$4 = w_1 \times 2 + w_2 \times 1$$
$$1 = w_3 \times 2 + w_3 \times 1$$

Writing it in matrix form, we get the following:

$$\begin{bmatrix} 4 \\ 1 \end{bmatrix} = \begin{bmatrix} w_1 & w_2 \\ w_3 & w_4 \end{bmatrix} \begin{bmatrix} 2 \\ 1 \end{bmatrix}$$

Careful readers would have caught an error by now: there are *four* variables (w_1, w_2, w_3, and w_4), but only *two* equations. From high-school math, we learn that you can't solve a system of equations where there are fewer equations than there are variables!

The thing is, your high school math teacher kind of lied to you. It is sort of possible to solve this, and you've already done so yourself in `Chapter 2`, *Linear Regression - House Price Prediction*.

In fact, most machine learning problems can be re-expressed in linear algebra, specifically of this form:

$$given \ \mathbf{y} = \mathbf{Wx}, \ solve \ for \ \mathbf{W}$$

And this in my opinion, is the right way to think about artificial neural networks: a series of mathematical functions, not an analogue of biological neurons. We will explore this a bit more in the next chapter. In fact, this understanding is vital to the understanding of deep learning and why it works.

For now, it suffices to follow on with the more common notion that an artificial neural network is similar in actions to a biologically inspired neural network.

Exploring activation functions

The thing about linear algebra is, it's linear. It is useful when the change of the output is proportional to the change in input. The real world is full of non-linear functions and equations. Solving non-linear equation is hard with a capital H. But we've got a trick. We can take a linear equation, and then add a non-linearity to it. This way, the function becomes non-linear!

Following from this view, you can view an artificial neural network as a generic version of all the previous chapters we've gone through so far.

Throughout the history of artificial neural networks, the community has favored particular activation functions in a fashionable way. In the early days, the Heaviside function was favored. Gradually, the community moved toward favoring differentiable, continuous functions, such as sigmoid and tanh. But lately, the pendulum of fashion has swung back toward the harder, seemingly discontinuous functions. The key is that we've learned new tricks on how to differentiate functions, such as the **rectified linear unit (ReLu)**.

Here are some of the more popular activation functions over time:

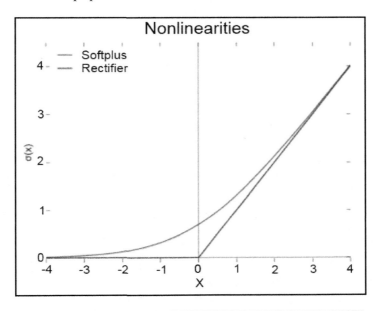

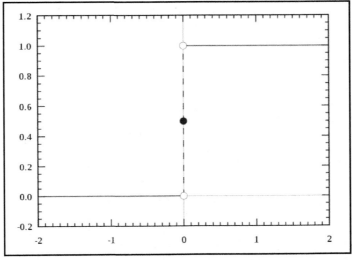

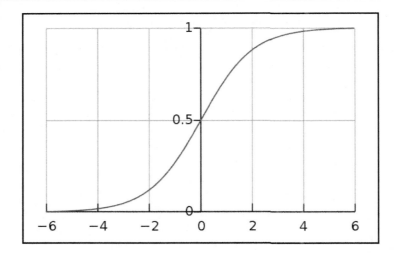

One thing to note about these is that these functions are all nonlinear and they all have a hard limit on the y axis.

The vertical ranges of the activation functions are limited, but the horizontal ranges are not. We can use biases to adjust how our activation functions look.

It should be noted that biases can be zero. It also means that we can omit biases. Most of the time, for more complex projects, this is fine, though adding biases will add to the accuracy of the neural network.

Learning

I want you to think about how you learn. Not the learning styles, mind; no, I want you to give your learning process a long hard deep thought. Think of the various ways you learn. Maybe you've touched a stove while it's hot once. Or if you ever learned a new language, maybe you started out by memorizing phrases before becoming fluent. Think about all the chapters that had preceded this. What do they have in common?

In broad strokes, learning is done by means of corrections. If you touched a stove while it's hot, you made a mistake. The correction is to never touch a stove when it's hot ever again. You've learned how not to touch the stove while it's hot.

Similarly, the way a neural network learns is by means of correction. If we want to train a machine to learn to classify handwriting, we would need to provide some sample images, and tell the machine which are the correct labels. If the machine predicted the labels wrongly, we need to tell it to change something in the neural network and try again.

What can be changed? The weights of course. The inputs can't be changed; they're inputs. But we can always try different weights. Hence, the process of learning can be broken down into two steps:

- Telling the neural network that it is wrong when it made a mistake.
- Updating the weights so that the next try will yield a better result.

When broken down like this, we have a good idea of how to proceed next. One way would be a binary determination mechanism: if the neural network predicted the correct answer, don't update the weights. If it's wrong, update the weights.

How to update the weights, then? Well, one way would be to completely replace the weight matrix with new values and try again. Since the weight matrix is filled from values pulled from a random distribution, the new weight matrix would be a new random matrix.

It should be quite obvious that these two methods, when combined, would take a very very long time before the neural network learns anything; it's as if we're simply guessing our way into the correct weight matrices.

Instead, modern neural networks use the concept of **backpropagation** to tell the neural network that it's made a mistake, and some form of **gradient descent** to update the weights.

The specifics of backpropagation and gradient descent are outside the scope of this chapter (and book). I'll, however, briefly run through the big ideas by sharing a story. I was having lunch with a couple of friends who also work in machine learning and that lunch ended with us arguing. This was because I had casually mentioned that backpropagation was "discovered", as opposed to "invented". My friends were adamant that backpropagation was invented, not discovered. My reasoning was simple: Mathematics is "discovered" if multiple people stumble upon it with the same formulation. Mathematics is "invented" if there were no parallel discovery of it.

Backpropagation, in various forms, has been constantly rediscovered over time. The first time backpropagation was discovered was in the invention of linear regression. I should note that it was a very specific form of backpropagation specific to linear regression: the sum of squared errors can be propagated back to its inputs by differentiating the result of the sum of squared errors with regard to the inputs.

We start with a cost. Remember how we have to tell the neural network that it's made a mistake. We do so by telling the neural network the cost of making a prediction. This is called a cost function. We can define a cost so that when the neural network makes a correct prediction, the cost is low, and when the neural network makes a wrong prediction, the cost is high.

Imagine for now, that the cost function is $cost = x^2$. How do you know at what values of x the cost will be lowest? From high-school math, we know that the solution is to differentiate $cost$ with regard to x and solve for the solution when it's 0:

$$\frac{dcost}{dx} = 0$$

Backpropagation takes the same cue. In short, backpropagtion is just a bunch of partial differentiations with regard to the weights. The main difference between our toy example and real backpropagation is that the derivation of our expression is easy to solve. For more complex mathematical expressions, it can be computationally too expensive to compute the solution. Instead, we rely on gradient descent to find the answer.

Gradient descent assumes we start our x somewhere and we update the x iteratively toward the lowest cost. In each iteration, we update the weights. The simplest form of gradient descent is to add the gradient of the weights to the weights themselves.

The key takeaway is the powerful notion that you can tell the inputs that an error has occurred by performing differentiation of the function and finding a point at which the derivatives are at its minimum.

The project

The project we're embarking on is the one as mentioned in the opening paragraphs. The dataset which we are going to classify is a collection of handwritten numbers originally collected by the National Institute of Standards and Technology and later modified by Yann LeCun's team. Our goal is to classify the handwritten numbers as either one of 0, 1, 2... 9.

We're going to build a basic neural network with the understanding that neural networks are applied linear algebra, and we'll be using Gorgonia for this and the next chapter.

To install Gorgonia, simply run `go get -u gorgonia.org/gorgonia` and `go get -u gorgonia.org/tensor`.

Gorgonia

Gorgonia is a library that facilitates efficient mathematical operations for the purposes of building deep neural networks. It operates on the fundamental understanding that neural networks are mathematical expressions. As such it is quite easy to build neural networks using Gorgonia.

A note on the chapters: Because Gorgonia is a relatively huge library, parts of this chapter will elide over some things about Gorgonia but will be expanded upon in the next chapter, as well as another Packt book, *Hands On Deep Learning in Go*.

Getting the data

The data for the MNIST data can be found in the repository for this chapter. In its original form, it's not in a standard image format. So, we will need to parse the data into an acceptable format.

The dataset comes in two parts: labels and images. So here are a couple of functions, designed to read and parse the MNIST file:

```go
// Image holds the pixel intensities of an image.
// 255 is foreground (black), 0 is background (white).
type RawImage []byte

// Label is a digit label in 0 to 9
type Label uint8


const numLabels = 10
const pixelRange = 255

const (
    imageMagic = 0x00000803
    labelMagic = 0x00000801
    Width = 28
    Height = 28
)

func readLabelFile(r io.Reader, e error) (labels []Label, err error) {
    if e != nil {
        return nil, e
    }

    var magic, n int32
    if err = binary.Read(r, binary.BigEndian, &magic); err != nil {
```

```
      return nil, err
    }
    if magic != labelMagic {
      return nil, os.ErrInvalid
    }
    if err = binary.Read(r, binary.BigEndian, &n); err != nil {
      return nil, err
    }
    labels = make([]Label, n)
    for i := 0; i < int(n); i++ {
      var l Label
      if err := binary.Read(r, binary.BigEndian, &l); err != nil {
        return nil, err
      }
      labels[i] = l
    }
    return labels, nil
  }

  func readImageFile(r io.Reader, e error) (imgs []RawImage, err error) {
    if e != nil {
      return nil, e
    }

    var magic, n, nrow, ncol int32
    if err = binary.Read(r, binary.BigEndian, &magic); err != nil {
      return nil, err
    }
    if magic != imageMagic {
      return nil, err /*os.ErrInvalid*/
    }
    if err = binary.Read(r, binary.BigEndian, &n); err != nil {
      return nil, err
    }
    if err = binary.Read(r, binary.BigEndian, &nrow); err != nil {
      return nil, err
    }
    if err = binary.Read(r, binary.BigEndian, &ncol); err != nil {
      return nil, err
    }
    imgs = make([]RawImage, n)
    m := int(nrow * ncol)
    for i := 0; i < int(n); i++ {
      imgs[i] = make(RawImage, m)
      m_, err := io.ReadFull(r, imgs[i])
      if err != nil {
        return nil, err
      }
```

```
    if m_ != int(m) {
      return nil, os.ErrInvalid
    }
  }
  return imgs, nil
}
```

First, the functions read the file from a `io.Reader` and reading a set of `int32`s. These are the metadata of the file. The first `int32` is a magic number that is used to indicate if a file is a labels file or a file of images. `n` indicates the number of images or labels the file contains. `nrow` and `ncol` are metadata that exists in the file, and indicates how many rows/columns there are in each image.

Zooming into the `readImageFile` function, we can see that after all the metadata has been read, we know to create a `[]RawImage` of size `n`. The image format used in the MNIST dataset is essentially a slice of 784 bytes (28 columns and 28 rows). Each byte therefore represents a pixel in the image. The value of each byte represents how bright the pixel is, ranging from 0 to 255:

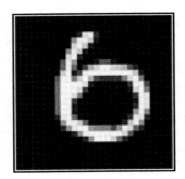

The preceding image is an example of an MNIST image blown up. At the top-left corner, the index of the pixel in a flat slice is 0. At the top right corner, the index of the pixel in a flat slice is 27. At the bottom-left corner, the index of the pixel in a flat slice is 755. And, finally, at the bottom-right corner, the index is 727. This is an important concept to keep in mind: A 2D image can be represented as a 1D slice.

Acceptable format

What is an acceptable format to represent the image? A slice of bytes is useful for reading and displaying the image, but it's not particularly useful for doing any machine learning. Rather, we should want to represent the image as a slice of floating points. So, here's a function to convert a byte into a `float64`:

```
func pixelWeight(px byte) float64 {
  retVal := float64(px)/pixelRange*0.9 + 0.1
  if retVal == 1.0 {
    return 0.999
  }
  return retVal
}
```

This is essentially a scaling function that scales from 0-255 to between 0.0 and 1.0. There is an additional check; if the value is 1.0, we return 0.999 instead of 1. This is mainly due to the fact that when values are 1.0, numerical instability tends to happen, as mathematical functions tend to act weirdly. So instead, replace 1.0 with values that are very close to 1.

So now, we can make a `RawImage` into a `[]float64`. And because we have `N` images in the form of `[]RawImage`, we can make it into a `[][]float64`, or a matrix.

From images to a matrix

So far we've established that we can convert a list of images in a special format in to a slice of slices of `float64`. Recall from earlier, that when you stack neurons together they form a matrix, and the activation of a neural layer is simply a matrix-vector multiplication. And when the inputs are stacked together, it's simply matrix-matrix multiplication.

We technically can build a neural network with just `[][]float64`. But the end result will be quite slow. Collectively as a species, we have had approximately 40 years of developing algorithms for efficient linear algebra operations, such as matrix multiplication and matrix-vector multiplication. This collection of algorithms are generally known as BLAS (Basic Linear Algebra Subprograms).

We have been, up to this point in the book, using libraries built on top of a library that provide BLAS functions, namely Gonum's BLAS library. If you had been following the book up to this point, you would have it installed already. Otherwise, run `go get -u gonum.org/v1/gonum/...`, which would install the entire suite of Gonum libraries.

Because of the way BLAS works in general, we need a better way of representing matrices than `[][]float64`. Here we have two options:

- Gonum's `mat` library
- Gorgonia's `tensor` library

Why Gorgonia's `tensor`? The reason for `tensor` is quite simple. It plays well with Gorgonia itself, which requires multidimensional arrays. Gonum's `mat` only takes up to two dimensions, while in the next chapter we'll see a use of four-dimensional arrays.

What is a tensor?

Fundamentally tensors are very much like vectors. The idea is stolen from physics. Imagine pushing a box on a two-dimensional plane. If you push the box with a force of 1 Newton along the x axis, there is no force applied to the y axis. You would write the vector as such: `[1, 0]`. If the box were moving along the x axis with at a speed of 10 km/h and along the y axis with a speed of 2 km/h, you would write the vector as such: `[10, 2]`. Note that they are unitless: the first example was a vector of Newtons, the second example was a vector with km/h as its units.

In short, it is a representation of something (a force, a speed, or anything with magnitude and direction) applied to a direction. From this idea, computer science co-opted the name vector. But in Go, they're called a **slice**.

So what is a tensor? Eliding a lot of the details but without a loss of generality, a tensor is like a vector. Except multidimensional. Imagine if you were to describe two speeds along the plane (imagine a silly putty being stretched in two directions at different speeds): `[1, 0]` and `[10, 2]`. You would write it as such:
```
[ 1 0]
[10 2]
```

This is also called a matrix (when it's two-dimensional). It's called a 3-Tensor when it's three-dimensional, 4-Tensor when its four-dimensional, and so on and so forth. Note that if you have a third speed (that is, the silly putty being stretched in a third direction), you wouldn't have a 3-Tensor. Instead you'd still have a matrix, with three rows.

To visualize a 3-Tensor while building on the previous example, imagine if you will, that the two directions that the silly putty was being pulled at was a slice in time. Then imagine another slice in time where the same silly putty is pulled in two directions again. So now you'd have two matrices. A 3-Tensor is what happens when you imagine stacking these matrices together.

To convert a `[]RawImage` to a `tensor.Tensor`, the code is as follows:

```
func prepareX(M []RawImage) (retVal tensor.Tensor) {
  rows := len(M)
  cols := len(M[0])

  b := make([]float64, 0, rows*cols)
  for i := 0; i < rows; i++ {
    for j := 0; j < len(M[i]); j++ {
      b = append(b, pixelWeight(M[i][j]))
    }
  }
  return tensor.New(tensor.WithShape(rows, cols), tensor.WithBacking(b))
}
```

Gorgonia may be a bit confusing to beginners. So let me explain the code line by line. But first, you must be aware that like Gonum matrices, Gorgonia tensors, no matter how many dimensions, are also internally represented as a flat slice. Gorgonia tensors are a little more flexible in the sense that they can take more than a flat slice of `float64` (it takes slices of other types too). This is called the backing slice or array. This is one of the fundamental reasons why performing linear algebra operations is more efficient in Gonum and Gorgonia than using plain `[][]float64`.

`rows := len(M)` and `cols := len(M[0])` are pretty self explanatory. We want to know the rows (that is, number of images) and columns (the number of pixels in the image).

`b := make([]float64, 0, rows*cols)` creates the backing array with a capacity of `rows * cols`. This backing array is called a backing *array* because throughout the lifetime of `b`, the size will not change. Here we start with a length of `0` because we want to use the `append` function later on.

`a := make([]T, 0, capacity)` is a good pattern to use to pre-allocate a slice. Consider a snippet that looks like this:

```
a := make([]int, 0)
    for i := 0; i < 10; i++ {
        a = append(a, i)
    }
```

During the first call to append, the Go runtime will look at the capacity of `a`, and find it's `0`. So it will allocate some memory to create a slice of size 1. Then on the second call to append, the Go runtime will look at the capacity of `a` and find that it's `1`, which is insufficient. So it will allocate twice the current capacity of the slice. On the fourth iteration, it will find the capacity of `a` is insufficient for appending and once again allocates twice the current capacity of the slice.

The thing about allocation is that it is an expensive operation. Occasionally the Go runtime may not only have to allocate memory, but copy the memory to a new location. This adds to the cost of appending to a slice.

So instead, if we know the capacity of the slice upfront, it's best to allocate all of it in one shot. We can specify the length, but it's often a cause of indexing errors. So my recommendation is to allocate with the capacity and a length of `0`. That way, you can safely use append without having to worry about indexing errors.

After creating a backing slice, we simply populate the backing slice with the values of the pixel, converted to a `float64` using the `pixelWeight` function that we described earlier.

Finally, we call `tensor.New(tensor.WithShape(rows, cols)`, `tensor.WithBacking(b))`, which returns a `*tensor.Dense`. The `tensor.WithShape(rows, cols)` construction option creates a `*tensor.Dense` with the specified shape while `tensor.WithBacking(b)` simply uses the already pre-allocated and pre-filled `b` as a backing slice.

The `tensor` library will simply reuse the entire backing array so that fewer allocations are made. What this means is you have to be careful when handling `b`. Modifying the contents of `b` afterward will change the content in the `tensor.Dense` as well. Given that `b` was created in the `prepareX` function, once the function has returned, there's no way to modify the contents of `b`. This is a good way to prevent accidental modification.

From labels to one-hot vectors

Recall that neural networks built in Gorgonia only take tensor.Tensors as inputs.
Therefore, the labels will also have to be converted into tensor.Tensor. The function is
quite similar to prepareX:

```
func prepareY(N []Label) (retVal tensor.Tensor) {
  rows := len(N)
  cols := 10

  b := make([]float64, 0, rows*cols)
  for i := 0; i < rows; i++ {
    for j := 0; j < 10; j++ {
      if j == int(N[i]) {
        b = append(b, 1)
      } else {
        b = append(b, 0)
      }
    }
  }
  return tensor.New(tensor.WithShape(rows, cols), tensor.WithBacking(b))
}
```

What we're building here is a matrix with *N* rows and ten columns. The specifics of why we
build a matrix of (N, 10) will be explored in the next chapter, but for now let's zoom into
an imaginary row. Imagine the first label, (int(N[i])), is 7. The row will look like this:

```
[0, 0, 0, 0, 0, 0, 0, 1, 0, 0]
```

This is called a one-hot vector encoding. It will be useful to us later, and will expanded
upon in the next chapter.

Visualization

It's also useful to have visualization when we are dealing with image data. Earlier we had
converted our image pixels from a byte to a float64 using pixelWeight. It'd be
instructive to also have the reverse function:

```
func reversePixelWeight(px float64) byte {
  return byte(((px - 0.001) / 0.999) * pixelRange)
}
```

Here's how to visualize 100 of the images:

```go
// visualize visualizes the first N images given a data tensor that is made
up of float64s.
// It's arranged into (rows, 10) image.
// Row counts are calculated by dividing N by 10 - we only ever want 10
columns.
// For simplicity's sake, we will truncate any remainders.
func visualize(data tensor.Tensor, rows, cols int, filename string) (err
error) {
  N := rows * cols

  sliced := data
  if N > 1 {
    sliced, err = data.Slice(makeRS(0, N), nil) // data[0:N, :] in python
    if err != nil {
      return err
    }
  }

  if err = sliced.Reshape(rows, cols, 28, 28); err != nil {
    return err
  }

  imCols := 28 * cols
  imRows := 28 * rows
  rect := image.Rect(0, 0, imCols, imRows)
  canvas := image.NewGray(rect)

  for i := 0; i < cols; i++ {
    for j := 0; j < rows; j++ {
      var patch tensor.Tensor
      if patch, err = sliced.Slice(makeRS(i, i+1), makeRS(j, j+1)); err !=
nil {
        return err
      }

      patchData := patch.Data().([]float64)
      for k, px := range patchData {
        x := j*28 + k%28
        y := i*28 + k/28
        c := color.Gray{reversePixelWeight(px)}
        canvas.Set(x, y, c)
      }
    }
  }

  var f io.WriteCloser
```

```
if f, err = os.Create(filename); err != nil {
  return err
}

if err = png.Encode(f, canvas); err != nil {
  f.Close()
  return err
}

if err = f.Close(); err != nil {
  return err
}
return nil
}
```

The dataset is a huge slice of images. We need to figure out how many we want first; hence, `N := rows * cols`. Having the number we want, we then slice using `data.Slice(makeRS(0, N), nil)`, which slices the tensor along the first axis. The sliced tensor is then reshaped into a four-dimensional array with `sliced.Reshape(rows, cols, 28,28)`. The way you can think about it is to have a stacked rows and columns of 28x28 images.

A primer on slicing

A `*tensor.Dense` acts very much like a standard Go slice; just as you can slice `a[0:2]`, you can do the same with Gorgonia's tensors. The `.Slice()` method for all tensors accepts a `tensor.Slice` descriptor, defined as:

```
type Slice interface {
    Start() int
    End() int
    Step() int
}
```

As such, we would have to make our own data type that fulfills the `Slice` interface. It's defined in the `utils.go` file of this project. `makeRS(0, N)` simply reads as if we were doing `data[0:N]`. Details and reasoning for this API can be found on the Gorgonia tensor Godoc page.

Then a grayscale image is created using the built-in image package: `canvas :=`
`image.NewGray(rect)`. A `image.Gray` is essentially a slice of bytes and each byte is a
pixel. What we need to do next is to fill up the pixels. Quite simply, we simply loop
through the columns and rows in each patch, and we fill it up with the correct value
extracted from the tensor. The `reversePixelWeight` function is used to convert the float
into a byte, which is then converted into a `color.Gray`. The pixel in the canvas is then set
using `canvas.Set(x, y, c)`.

Following that, the canvas is encoded as a PNG. *Et voilà*, our visualization is done!

Now Calling the visualize in the main function as such:

```
func main() {
  imgs, err := readImageFile(os.Open("train-images-idx3-ubyte"))
  if err != nil {
    log.Fatal(err)
  }
  log.Printf("len imgs %d", len(imgs))

  data := prepareX(imgs)
  visualize(data, 100, "image.png")
}
```

This yields the following image:

Preprocessing

What we are going to do next is to "whiten" our data using a **Zero Phase Component Analysis (ZCA)**. The definitions of ZCA is beyond the scope of this chapter, but briefly, ZCA is very much like **Principal Component Analysis (PCA)**. In our 784-pixel slice, there is a high probability that the pixels are correlated with one another. What PCA does is it finds the set of pixels that are uncorrelated with one another. It does this by looking at all the images at once and figuring out how each column correlates with one another:

```go
func zca(data tensor.Tensor) (retVal tensor.Tensor, err error) {
  var dataᵀ, data2, sigma tensor.Tensor
  data2 = data.Clone().(tensor.Tensor)

  if err := minusMean(data2); err != nil {
    return nil, err
  }
  if dataᵀ, err = tensor.T(data2); err != nil {
    return nil, err
  }

  if sigma, err = tensor.MatMul(dataᵀ, data2); err != nil {
    return nil, err
  }

  cols := sigma.Shape()[1]
  if _, err = tensor.Div(sigma, float64(cols-1), tensor.UseUnsafe()); err
!= nil {
    return nil, err
  }

  s, u, _, err := sigma.(*tensor.Dense).SVD(true, true)
  if err != nil {
    return nil, err
  }

  var diag, uᵀ, tmp tensor.Tensor
  if diag, err = s.Apply(invSqrt(0.1), tensor.UseUnsafe()); err != nil {
    return nil, err
  }
  diag = tensor.New(tensor.AsDenseDiag(diag))

  if uᵀ, err = tensor.T(u); err != nil {
    return nil, err
  }

  if tmp, err = tensor.MatMul(u, diag); err != nil {
    return nil, err
```

```
    }

    if tmp, err = tensor.MatMul(tmp, uᵀ); err != nil {
        return nil, err
    }

    if err = tmp.T(); err != nil {
        return nil, err
    }

    return tensor.MatMul(data, tmp)
}

func invSqrt(epsilon float64) func(float64) float64 {
    return func(a float64) float64 {
        return 1 / math.Sqrt(a+epsilon)
    }
}
```

This is a pretty large chunk of code. Let's go through the code. But first, let's understand the key ideas behind ZCA before going through the code that implements it..

First, recall what PCA does: it finds the set of inputs (columns and pixels, to be used interchangeably) that are least correlated with one another. What ZCA does is then to take the principal components found and multiply them by the inputs to transform the inputs so that they become less correlated with one another.

First, we want to subtract the row mean. To do that, we first make a clone of the data (we'll see why later), then subtract the mean with this function:

```
func minusMean(a tensor.Tensor) error {
    nat, err := native.MatrixF64(a.(*tensor.Dense))
    if err != nil {
        return err
    }
    for _, row := range nat {
        mean := avg(row)
        vecf64.Trans(row, -mean)
    }

    rows, cols := a.Shape()[0], a.Shape()[1]

    mean := make([]float64, cols)
    for j := 0; j < cols; j++ {
        var colMean float64
        for i := 0; i < rows; i++ {
            colMean += nat[i][j]
```

```
    }
    colMean /= float64(rows)
    mean[j] = colMean
  }

  for _, row := range nat {
    vecf64.Sub(row, mean)
  }

  return nil
}
```

After all the preceding spiel about efficiency of a flat slice versus a `[][]float64`, what I am going to suggest next is going to sound counter-intuitive. But please bear with me. `native.MatrixF64` takes a `*tensor.Dense` and returns a `[][]float64`, which we call `nat`. `nat` shares the same allocation as the tensor `a`. No extra allocations are made, and any modification made to `nat` will show up in `a`. In this scenario, we should treat `[][]float64` as an easy way to iterate through the values in the tensor. This can be seen here:

```
for j := 0; j < cols; j++ {
  var colMean float64
  for i := 0; i < rows; i++ {
    colMean += nat[i][j]
  }
  colMean /= float64(rows)
  mean[j] = colMean
}
```

Like in the `visualize` function, we first iterate through the columns, albeit for a different purpose. We want to find the mean of each column. We then store the mean of each column in the mean variable. This allows us to subtract the column mean:

```
for _, row := range nat {
  vecf64.Sub(row, mean)
}
```

This block of code uses the `vecf64` package that comes with Gorgonia to subtract a slice from another slice, element-wise. It's rather the same as the following:

```
for _, row := range nat {
  for j := range row {
    row[j] -= mean[j]
  }
}
```

The only real reason to use `vecf64` is that it's optimized to perform the operation with SIMD instructions: instead of doing `row[j] -= mean[j]` one at a time, it performs `row[j] -= mean[j], row[j+1] -= mean[j+1], row[j+2] -= mean[j+2]`, and `row[j+3] -= mean[j+3]` simultaneously.

After we've subtracted the mean, we find its transpose and make a copy of it:

```
if data^T, err = tensor.T(data2); err != nil {
  return nil, err
}
```

Typically, you would find the transpose of a `tensor.Tensor` by using something like `data2.T()`. But this does not return a copy of it. Instead, the `tensor.T` function clones the data structure, then performs a transposition on it. The reason for that? We're about to use both the tranpose and `data2` to find `Sigma` (more on matrix multiplication will be expounded in the next chapter):

```
var sigma tensor.Tensor
if sigma, err = tensor.MatMul(data^T, data2); err != nil {
  return nil, err
}
```

After we have found `sigma`, we divide it by the number of columns-1. This provides an unbiased estimator. The `tensor.UseUnsafe` option is used to indicate that the result should be stored back into the `sigma` tensor:

```
cols := sigma.Shape()[1]
if _, err = tensor.Div(sigma, float64(cols-1), tensor.UseUnsafe()); err
!= nil {
   return nil, err
}
```

All this is done so that we can perform an SVD on `sigma`:

```
s, u, _, err := sigma.(*tensor.Dense).SVD(true, true)
if err != nil {
  return nil, err
}
```

Singular Value Decomposition, if you are not familiar with it, is a method among many that breaks down a matrix into its constituents. Why would you want to do so? For one, it makes parts of calculations of some things easier. What it does is to factorize $\mathbf{A}$, a (M, N) matrix into a (M, N) matrix called $\mathbf{S}$, a (M,M) matrix called $\mathbf{U}$, and a (N, N) matrix called $\mathbf{V}$. To reconstruct A, the formula is simply:

$$\mathbf{A} = \mathbf{U}\mathbf{S}\mathbf{V}^{T}$$

The decomposed parts will then be used. In our case, we're not particularly interested about the right singular values V, so we'll ignore it for now. The decomposed parts are simply used to transform the images, which can be found in the tailend of the function body.

After preprocessing, we can once more visualize the first 100 or so images:

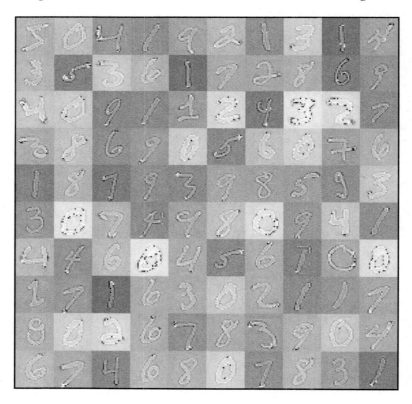

Building a neural network

Finally, let's build a neural network! We'll be building a simple three-layer neural network with one hidden layer. A three-layer neural network has two weight matrices, so we can define the neural network as such:

```
type NN struct {
  hidden, final *tensor.Dense
  b0, b1 float64
}
```

`hidden` represents the weight matrix between the input layer and hidden layer, while `final` represents the weight matrix between the hidden layer and the final layer.

This is a graphical representation of our *NN data structure:

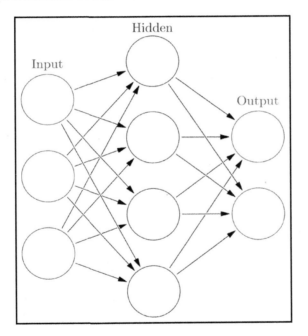

The input layer is the slice of 784 `float64` which is then fed forward (that is, a matrix multiplication followed by an activation function) to form the hidden layer. The hidden layer is then fed forward to form the final layer. The final layer is a vector of ten `float64`, which is exactly the one-hot encoding that we discussed earlier. You can think of them as pseud-probabilities, because the values don't exactly sum up to 1.

A key thing to note: b0 and b1 are bias values for the hidden layer and the final layer, respectively. They are not actually used mainly due to the mess; it's quite difficult to get the correct differentiation. A challenge for the reader is to later incorporate the use of b0 and b1.

And to create a new neural network, we have the New function:

```
func New(input, hidden, output int) (retVal *NN) {
  r := make([]float64, hidden*input)
  r2 := make([]float64, hidden*output)
  fillRandom(r, float64(len(r)))
  fillRandom(r2, float64(len(r2)))
  hiddenT := tensor.New(tensor.WithShape(hidden, input),
tensor.WithBacking(r))
  finalT := tensor.New(tensor.WithShape(output, hidden),
tensor.WithBacking(r2))
  return &NN{
    hidden: hiddenT,
    final: finalT,
  }
}
```

The fillRandom function fills a []float64 with random values. In our case, we fill it up from random values drawn from a uniform distribution. Here, we use the distuv package from Gonum:

```
func fillRandom(a []float64, v float64) {
  dist := distuv.Uniform{
    Min: -1 / math.Sqrt(v),
    Max: 1 / math.Sqrt(v),
  }
  for i := range a {
    a[i] = dist.Rand()
  }
}
```

After the slices r and r2 have been filled, the tensors hiddenT and finalT are created, and the *NN is returned.

Feed forward

Now that we have a conceptual idea of how the neural network works, let's write the forward propagation function. We'll call it `Predict` because, well, to predict, you merely need to run the function forward:

```
func (nn *NN) Predict(a tensor.Tensor) (int, error) {
  if a.Dims() != 1 {
    return -1, errors.New("Expected a vector")
  }

  var m maybe
  hidden := m.do(func() (tensor.Tensor, error) { return
nn.hidden.MatVecMul(a) })
  act0 := m.do(func() (tensor.Tensor, error) { return hidden.Apply(sigmoid,
tensor.UseUnsafe()) })

  final := m.do(func() (tensor.Tensor, error) { return
tensor.MatVecMul(nn.final, act0) })
  pred := m.do(func() (tensor.Tensor, error) { return final.Apply(sigmoid,
tensor.UseUnsafe()) })

  if m.err != nil {
    return -1, m.err
  }
  return argmax(pred.Data().([]float64)), nil
}
```

This is fairly straightforward, except for a few control structures. I should first explain that the API of the tensor package is quite expressive in the sense in that it allows the user multiple ways of doing the same thing, albeit with different type signatures. Briefly, the patterns are the following:

- `tensor.BINARYOPERATION(a, b tensor.Tensor, opts ...tensor.FuncOpt) (tensor.Tensor, error)`
- `tensor.UNARYOPERATION(a tensor.Tensor, opts ...tensor.FuncOpt)(tensor.Tensor, error)`
- `(a *tensor.Dense) BINARYOPERATION (b *tensor.Dense, opts ...tensor.FuncOpt) (*tensor.Dense, error)`
- `(a *tensor.Dense) UNARYOPERATION(opts ...tensor.FuncOpt) (*tensor.Dense, error)`

Key things to note are package level operations (`tensor.Add`, `tensor.Sub`, and so on) take one or more `tensor.Tensor`s and return a `tensor.Tensor` and an `error`. There are multiple things that fulfill a `tensor.Tensor` interface, and the tensor package provides two structural types that fulfill the interface:

- `*tensor.Dense`: A representation of of a densely packed tensor
- `*tensor.CS`: A memory-efficient representation of a sparsely packed tensor with the data arranged in compressed sparse columns/row format

For the most part, the most commonly used type of `tensor.Tensor` is the `*tensor.Dense` type. The `*tensor.CS` data structure is only used for very specific memory-constrained optimizations for specific algorithms. We shan't talk more about the `*tensor.CS` type in this chapter.

In addition to the package level operations, each specific type also has methods that they implement. `*tensor.Dense`'s methods (`.Add(...)`, `.Sub(...)`, and so on) take one or more `*tensor.Dense` and return `*tensor.Dense` and an error.

Handling errors with maybe

With that quick introduction out of the way, we can now talk about the `maybe` type.

One of the things you may have already noticed is that almost all the operations return an error. Indeed, there are very few functions and methods that do not return an error. The logic behind this is simple: most of the errors are actually recoverable and have suitable recovery strategies.

However, for this project, we have one error recovery strategy: bubble up the error to the `main` function, where a `log.Fatal` will be called and the error will be inspected for debugging.

So, I defined `maybe` as follows:

```
type maybe struct {
  err error
}

func (m *maybe) do(fn func() (tensor.Tensor, error)) tensor.Tensor {
  if m.err != nil {
    return nil
  }

  var retVal tensor.Tensor
```

```
if retVal, m.err = fn(); m.err == nil {
    return retVal
}
m.err = errors.WithStack(m.err)
return nil
}
```

This way, it is able to handle any function as long as it's wrapped within a closure.

Why do this? I personally do not enjoy this structure. I taught it to a few students of mine as a cool trick, and since then they claimed that the resulting code was more understandable than having blocks of:

```
if foo, err := bar(); err != nil {
    return err
}
```

I can definitely empathize with this view. It is most useful in my opinion in the prototyping phase, especially when it is not clear yet when and where to handle the error (in our case, return early). Leaving the returning of an error until the end of the function can be useful. In production code though, I would prefer to be as explicit as possible about error-handling strategies.

This can be further augmented by abstracting common function calls into methods. For example, we see this line, `m.do(func() (tensor.Tensor, error) { return hidden.Apply(sigmoid, tensor.UseUnsafe()) })` , twice in the preceding snippet. If we want to prioritize understandability while leaving the structure mostly intact, we could abstract it away by creating a new method:

```
func (m *maybe) sigmoid(a tensor.Tensor) (retVal tensor.Tensor){
    if m.err != nil {
        return nil
    }
    if retVal, m.err = a.Apply(sigmoid); m.err == nil {
        return retVal
    }
    m.err = errors.WithStack(m.err)
    return nil
}
```

And we would just call `m.sigmoid(hidden)` instead. This is one of the many error-handling strategies that programmers can employ to help them. Remember, you're a programmer; you are allowed and even expected to program your way out!

Explaining the feed forward function

With all that done, let's walk through the the feed forward function, line by line.

First, recall from the section, *Emulating a neural network*, that we can define a neural network as follows:

```
func affine(weights [][]float64, inputs []float64) []float64 {
   return activation(matVecMul(weights, inputs))
}
```

We do the first matrix multiplication as part of calculating the first hidden layer: `hidden := m.do(func() (tensor.Tensor, error) { return nn.hidden.MatVecMul(a)) })`. `MatVecMul` is used because we're multiplying a matrix by a vector.

Then we perform the second part of calculating a layer: `act0 := m.do(func() (tensor.Tensor, error) { return hidden.Apply(sigmoid, tensor.UseUnsafe()) })`. Once again, the `tensor.UseUnsafe()` function option is used to tell the function to not allocate a new tensor. *Voila*! We've successfully calculated the first layer.

The same two steps are repeated for the final layer, and we get a one-hot-ish vector. Do note that for the first step, I used `tensor.MatVecMul(nn.final, act0)` instead of `nn.final.MatVecMul(act0)`. This was done to show that both functions are indeed the same, and they just take different types (the method takes a concrete type while the package function takes an abstract data type). They are otherwise identical in function.

 Notice how the `affine` function is quite easy to read, whereas the other functions are quite difficult to read? Read through the section about `maybe` and see if you can come up with a way to write it in such a way that it reads more like affine.
Is there a way to abstract the function into a function like `affine` so that you could just call a single function and not repeat yourself?

Before we return the result, we need to perform a check to see if anything in the prece-ing steps have errored. Think about what are the errors that could happen. They would, in my experience, predominantly be shape related errors. In this specific project, a shape error should be considered a failure, so we return a nil result and the error.

The reason why we would have to check for errors at this point is because we are about to use `pred`. If `pred` is nil (which it would be if an error had occurred earlier), trying to access the `.Data()` function would cause a panic.

Anyway, after the check, we call the `.Data()` method, which returns the raw data as a flat slice. It's an `interface{}` type though, so we would have to convert it back to a `[]float64` before inspecting the data further. Because the result is a vector, it is no different in data layout from a `[]float64`, so we can directly call `argmax` on it.

`argmax` simply returns the index of the greatest value in the slice. It's defined thus:

```
func affine(weights [][]float64, inputs []float64) []float64 {
    return activation(matVecMul(weights, inputs))
}
```

And thus, we have managed to write a feed forward function for our neural network.

Costs

Having written a fairly straightforward feed forward function, let's now look at how to make the neural network learn.

Recall that we said earlier that a neural network learns when you tell it that it's made a mistake? More technically, we ask the question: what kind of cost function can we use so that it is able to convey to the neural network accurately about what the true value is.

The cost function we want to use for this project is the sum of squared errors. What is an error? Well, an error is simply the difference between the real value and the predicted value. Does this mean that if the real value is 7, and the neural network predicted 2, the cost would just be 7-2 ? No. This is because we should not treat the labels as numbers. They are labels.

So what do we subtract? Recall the one-hot vector that we created earlier? If we peek inside the `Predict` function, we can see that `pred`, the result of the final activation is a slice of ten `float64`s. That's what we're going to subtract. Because both are slices of ten `float64`s, we would have to subtract them element-wise.

Merely subtracting the slices would not be useful; the results may be negative. Imagine if you were tasked to find the lowest possible costs for a product. If someone came up to you and told you that their product costs negative amounts and that they would pay you to use it, would you not use it? So to prevent that, we take the square of the errors.

To calculate the sum of squared errors, we simply square the result. Because we're training the neural network one image at a time, the sum is simply the squared errors of that one image.

Backpropagation

The section on costs is a little sparse for good reason. Furthermore, there is a twist: we're not going to entirely calculate the full cost function, mainly because we don't need to for this specific case. Costs are heavily tied to the notion of backpropagation. Now we're going to do some mathematical trickery.

Recall that our cost was the sum of squared errors. We can write it like so:

$$cost = (y - pred)^2$$

Now what I am about to describe can sound very much like cheating, but it's a valid strategy. The derivative with regard to prediction is this:

$$\frac{\delta cost}{\delta pred} = 2(y - pred)$$

To make things a bit easier on ourselves, let's redefine the cost as this:

$$cost = \frac{1}{2}(y - pred)^2$$

It doesn't make a difference to the process of finding the lowest cost. Think about it; imagine a highest cost and a lowest cost. The difference between them if there is a $\frac{1}{2}$ multiplier in front of them does not change the fact that the lowest cost is still lower than the highest cost. Take some time to work this out on your own to convince yourself that having a constant multiplier doesn't change the process.

The derivative of a `sigmoid` function is:

$$\frac{d\sigma(x)}{dx} = \sigma(x)(1 - \sigma(x))$$

From there, we can work out the derivation of the cost function with regard to the weights matrix. How to work out the full backpropagation will be explained in the next chapter. For now, here is the code:

```
// backpropagation
outputErrors := m.do(func() (tensor.Tensor, error) { return tensor.Sub(y,
pred) })
cost = sum(outputErrors.Data().([]float64))
hidErrs := m.do(func() (tensor.Tensor, error) {
  if err := nn.final.T(); err != nil {
    return nil, err
  }
  defer nn.final.UT()
  return tensor.MatMul(nn.final, outputErrors)
})

if m.err != nil {
  return 0, m.err
}

dpred := m.do(func() (tensor.Tensor, error) { return pred.Apply(dsigmoid,
tensor.UseUnsafe()) })
m.do(func() (tensor.Tensor, error) { return tensor.Mul(pred,
outputErrors, tensor.UseUnsafe()) })
// m.do(func() (tensor.Tensor, error) { err := act0.T(); return act0, err
})
dpred_dfinal := m.do(func() (tensor.Tensor, error) {
  if err := act0.T(); err != nil {
    return nil, err
  }
  defer act0.UT()
  return tensor.MatMul(outputErrors, act0)
})

dact0 := m.do(func() (tensor.Tensor, error) { return act0.Apply(dsigmoid)
})
m.do(func() (tensor.Tensor, error) { return tensor.Mul(hidErrs, dact0,
tensor.UseUnsafe()) })
m.do(func() (tensor.Tensor, error) { err :=
hidErrs.Reshape(hidErrs.Shape()[0], 1); return hidErrs, err })
// m.do(func() (tensor.Tensor, error) { err := x.T(); return x, err })
dcost_dhidden := m.do(func() (tensor.Tensor, error) {
  if err := x.T(); err != nil {
    return nil, err
  }
  defer x.UT()
  return tensor.MatMul(hidErrs, x)
})
```

And there we have it, the derivatives of the cost with regard to the inputs matrices.

The thing to do with the derivatives is to use them as gradients to update the input matrices. To do that, use a simple gradient descent algorithm; we simply add the gradient to the values itself. But we don't want to add the full value of the gradient. If we do that and our starting value is very close to the minima, we'd overshoot it. So we need to multiply the gradients by some small value, known as the learn rate:

```
    // gradient update
    m.do(func() (tensor.Tensor, error) { return tensor.Mul(dcost_dfinal,
learnRate, tensor.UseUnsafe()) })
    m.do(func() (tensor.Tensor, error) { return tensor.Mul(dcost_dhidden,
learnRate, tensor.UseUnsafe()) })
    m.do(func() (tensor.Tensor, error) { return tensor.Add(nn.final,
dcost_dfinal, tensor.UseUnsafe()) })
    m.do(func() (tensor.Tensor, error) { return tensor.Add(nn.hidden,
dcost_dhidden, tensor.UseUnsafe()) })
```

And this is the training function in full:

```
    // X is the image, Y is a one hot vector
    func (nn *NN) Train(x, y tensor.Tensor, learnRate float64) (cost float64,
err error) {
      // predict
      var m maybe
      m.do(func() (tensor.Tensor, error) { err := x.Reshape(x.Shape()[0], 1);
return x, err })
      m.do(func() (tensor.Tensor, error) { err := y.Reshape(10, 1); return y,
err })

      hidden := m.do(func() (tensor.Tensor, error) { return
tensor.MatMul(nn.hidden, x) })
      act0 := m.do(func() (tensor.Tensor, error) { return hidden.Apply(sigmoid,
tensor.UseUnsafe()) })

      final := m.do(func() (tensor.Tensor, error) { return
tensor.MatMul(nn.final, act0) })
      pred := m.do(func() (tensor.Tensor, error) { return final.Apply(sigmoid,
tensor.UseUnsafe()) })
      // log.Printf("pred %v, correct %v", argmax(pred.Data().([]float64)),
argmax(y.Data().([]float64)))

      // backpropagation.
      outputErrors := m.do(func() (tensor.Tensor, error) { return tensor.Sub(y,
pred) })
      cost = sum(outputErrors.Data().([]float64))

      hidErrs := m.do(func() (tensor.Tensor, error) {
```

```
      if err := nn.final.T(); err != nil {
        return nil, err
      }
      defer nn.final.UT()
      return tensor.MatMul(nn.final, outputErrors)
  })

  if m.err != nil {
    return 0, m.err
  }

  dpred := m.do(func() (tensor.Tensor, error) { return pred.Apply(dsigmoid,
tensor.UseUnsafe()) })
  m.do(func() (tensor.Tensor, error) { return tensor.Mul(pred,
outputErrors, tensor.UseUnsafe()) })
  // m.do(func() (tensor.Tensor, error) { err := act0.T(); return act0, err
})
  dpred_dfinal := m.do(func() (tensor.Tensor, error) {
    if err := act0.T(); err != nil {
      return nil, err
    }
    defer act0.UT()
    return tensor.MatMul(outputErrors, act0)
  })

  dact0 := m.do(func() (tensor.Tensor, error) { return act0.Apply(dsigmoid)
})
  m.do(func() (tensor.Tensor, error) { return tensor.Mul(hidErrs, dact0,
tensor.UseUnsafe()) })
  m.do(func() (tensor.Tensor, error) { err :=
hidErrs.Reshape(hidErrs.Shape()[0], 1); return hidErrs, err })
  // m.do(func() (tensor.Tensor, error) { err := x.T(); return x, err })
  dcost_dhidden := m.do(func() (tensor.Tensor, error) {
    if err := x.T(); err != nil {
      return nil, err
    }
    defer x.UT()
    return tensor.MatMul(hidErrs, x)
  })

  // gradient update
  m.do(func() (tensor.Tensor, error) { return tensor.Mul(dcost_dfinal,
learnRate, tensor.UseUnsafe()) })
  m.do(func() (tensor.Tensor, error) { return tensor.Mul(dcost_dhidden,
learnRate, tensor.UseUnsafe()) })
  m.do(func() (tensor.Tensor, error) { return tensor.Add(nn.final,
dcost_dfinal, tensor.UseUnsafe()) })
  m.do(func() (tensor.Tensor, error) { return tensor.Add(nn.hidden,
```

```
dcost_dhidden, tensor.UseUnsafe()) })
  return cost, m.err
```

There are several observations to be made:

- You may note that parts of the body of the `Predict` method are repeated at the top of the `Train` method
- The `tensor.UseUnsafe()` function option is used a lot

This is going to be a pain point when we start scaling up into deeper networks. As such, in the next chapter, we will explore the possible solutions to these problems.

Training the neural network

Our main looks like this so far:

```
func main() {
  imgs, err := readImageFile(os.Open("train-images-idx3-ubyte"))
  if err != nil {
    log.Fatal(err)
  }
  labels, err := readLabelFile(os.Open("train-labels-idx1-ubyte"))
  if err != nil {
    log.Fatal(err)
  }

  log.Printf("len imgs %d", len(imgs))
  data := prepareX(imgs)
  lbl := prepareY(labels)
  visualize(data, 10, 10, "image.png")

  data2, err := zca(data)
  if err != nil {
    log.Fatal(err)
  }
  visualize(data2, 10, 10, "image2.png")

  nat, err := native.MatrixF64(data2.(*tensor.Dense))
  if err != nil {
    log.Fatal(err)
  }

  log.Printf("Start Training")
  nn := New(784, 100, 10)
  costs := make([]float64, 0, data2.Shape()[0])
```

```
for e := 0; e < 5; e++ {
  data2Shape := data2.Shape()
  var oneimg, onelabel tensor.Tensor
  for i := 0; i < data2Shape[0]; i++ {
    if oneimg, err = data2.Slice(makeRS(i, i+1)); err != nil {
      log.Fatalf("Unable to slice one image %d", i)
    }
    if onelabel, err = lbl.Slice(makeRS(i, i+1)); err != nil {
      log.Fatalf("Unable to slice one label %d", i)
    }
    var cost float64
    if cost, err = nn.Train(oneimg, onelabel, 0.1); err != nil {
      log.Fatalf("Training error: %+v", err)
    }
    costs = append(costs, cost)
  }
  log.Printf("%d\t%v", e, avg(costs))
  shuffleX(nat)
  costs = costs[:0]
}
log.Printf("End training")
}
```

Here are the steps in brief:

1. Load image files.
2. Load label files.
3. Convert image files into `*tensor.Dense`.
4. Convert label files into `*tensor.Dense`.
5. Visualize 100 of the images.
6. Perform ZCA whitening on the images.
7. Visualize the whitened images.
8. Create a native iterator for the dataset.
9. Create the neural network with a 100 unit hidden layer.
10. Create a slice of the costs. This is so we can keep track of the average cost over time.
11. Within each epoch, slice the input into single image slices.
12. Within each epoch, slice the output labels into single slices.
13. Within each epoch, call `nn.Train()` with a learn rate of `0.1` and use the sliced single image and single labels as a training example.
14. Train for five epochs.

How would we know that the neural network has learned well? One way is to monitor the costs. If the neural network is learning, the average costs over time will drop. There may be bumps, of course, but the overall big picture should be that the cost does not end up higher than when the program first runs.

Cross-validation

Another way we could test how well the neural network is learning is to cross-validate. The neural network could learn very well on the training data, in essence, memorizing which collections of pixels will result in a particular label. However, to check that the machine learning algorithm generalizes well, we need to show the neural network some data it's never seen before.

Here's the code to do so:

```
log.Printf("Start testing")
testImgs, err := readImageFile(os.Open("t10k-images.idx3-ubyte"))
if err != nil {
  log.Fatal(err)
}

testlabels, err := readLabelFile(os.Open("t10k-labels.idx1-ubyte"))
if err != nil {
  log.Fatal(err)
}

testData := prepareX(testImgs)
testLbl := prepareY(testlabels)
shape := testData.Shape()
testData2, err := zca(testData)
if err != nil {
  log.Fatal(err)
}

visualize(testData, 10, 10, "testData.png")
visualize(testData2, 10, 10, "testData2.png")

var correct, total float64
var oneimg, onelabel tensor.Tensor
var predicted, errcount int
for i := 0; i < shape[0]; i++ {
  if oneimg, err = testData.Slice(makeRS(i, i+1)); err != nil {
    log.Fatalf("Unable to slice one image %d", i)
  }
  if onelabel, err = testLbl.Slice(makeRS(i, i+1)); err != nil {
```

```
      log.Fatalf("Unable to slice one label %d", i)
    }
    if predicted, err = nn.Predict(oneimg); err != nil {
      log.Fatalf("Failed to predict %d", i)
    }

    label := argmax(onelabel.Data().([]float64))
    if predicted == label {
      correct++
    } else if errcount < 5 {
      visualize(oneimg, 1, 1, fmt.Sprintf("%d_%d_%d.png", i, label,
predicted))
      errcount++
    }
    total++
  }
  fmt.Printf("Correct/Totals: %v/%v = %1.3f\n", correct, total,
correct/total)
```

Note that the code is largely the same as the code before in the `main` function. The exception is that instead of calling `nn.Train`, we call `nn.Predict`. Then we check to see whether the label is the same as what we predicted.

Here are the tweakable parameters:

After running (it takes 6.5 minutes), and tweaking various parameters, I ran the code and got the following results:

```
$ go build . -o chapter7
 $ ./chapter7
 Corerct/Totals: 9719/10000 = 0.972
```

A simple three-layer neural network leads to a 97% accuracy! This is, of course, not close to state of the art. We'll build one that goes up to 99.xx% in the next chapter, but requires a big shift of mindset.

 Training a neural network takes time. It's often wise to want to save the result of the neural network. The `*tensor.Dense type` implements `gob.GobEncoder` and `gob.GobDecoder` and to save the neural network to disk, simply save the weights (`nn.hidden` and `nn.final`). For an additional challenge, write a gob encoder for those weight matrices and save/load the functionality.

Furthermore, let's have a look at a few of the things that was wrongly classified. In the preceding code, this snippet writes out five wrong predictions:

```
if predicted == label {
  correct++
} else if errcount < 5 {
  visualize(oneimg, 1, 1, fmt.Sprintf("%d_%d_%d.png", i, label,
predicted))
  errcount++
}
```

And here they are:

In the first image, the neural network classified it as a 0, while the true value is 6. As you can see, it is an easy mistake to make. The second image shows a 2, and the neural network classified it as a 4. You may be inclined to think that looks a bit like a 4. And, lastly, if you are an American reader, the chances are you have been exposed to the Palmer handwriting method. If so, I'll bet that you might classify the last picture as a 7, instead of a 2, which is exactly what the neural network predicts. Unfortunately, the real label is that it's a 2. Some people just have terrible handwriting.

Summary

In this chapter, we've learned how to write a simple neural network with one hidden layer that performs remarkably well. Along the way, we've learned how to perform ZCA whitening so that the data can be cleaned. There are some difficulties with this model, of course; you'd have to pre-calculate the derivatives by hand before you coded it.

The key takeaway point is that a simple neural network can do a lot! While this version of the code is very Gorgonia's tensor-centric, the principles are exactly the same, even if using Gonum's mat. In fact, Gorgonia's tensor uses Gonum's awesome matrix multiplication library underneath.

In the next chapter, we will revisit the notion of a neural network on the same dataset to get a 99% accuracy, but our mindsets of how to approach a neural network will have to change. I would advise re-reading the section on linear algebra to get a stronger grasp on things.

7
Convolutional Neural Networks - MNIST Handwriting Recognition

In the previous chapter, I posited a scenario where you are a postal worker trying to recognize handwriting. In that, we ended up with a neural network built on top of Gorgonia. In this chapter, we'll look at the same scenario, but we'll augment our ideas of what a neural network is and write a more advanced neural network, one that was, until very recently, state of the art.

Specifically, in this chapter, we are going to build a **Convolutional Neural Network (CNN)**. A CNN is a type of deep learning network that has been popular in recent years.

Everything you know about neurons is wrong

In the previous chapter, I mentioned that everything you know about neural networks is wrong. Here, I repeat that claim. Most literature out there on a neural network starts with a comparison with biological neurones and ends there. This leads readers to often assume that it is. I'd like to make a point that artificial neural networks are *nothing* like their biological namesake.

Instead, in the last chapter, I spent a significant amount of the chapter describing linear algebra, and explained that the twist is that you can express almost any **machine learning (ML)** problem as linear algebra. I shall continue to do so in this chapter.

Rather than think of artificial neural networks as analogies of real-life neural networks, I personally encourage you to think of artificial neural networks as mathematical equations. The non-linearities introduced by the activation functions, combined with linear combinations allows for artificial neural networks to be able to approximate any function.

Neural networks – a redux

The fundamental understanding that neural networks are mathematical expressions leads to really simple and easy implementations of neural networks. Recall from the previous chapter that a neural network can be written like this:

```
func affine(weights [][]float64, inputs []float64) []float64 {
    return activation(matVecMul(weights, inputs))
}
```

If we rewrite the code as a mathematical equation, we can write a neural network like this:

$$act = \sigma(w'x + b)$$

A side note: $w'x$ is the same as xw.

We can simply write it out using Gorgonia, like this:

```
import (
    G "gorgonia.org/gorgonia"
)

var Float tensor.Float = tensor.Float64
func main() {
    g := G.NewGraph()
    x := G.NewMatrix(g, Float, G.WithName("x"), G.WithShape(N, 728))
    w := G.NewMatrix(g, Float, G.WithName("w"), G.WithShape(728, 800),
        G.WithInit(G.Uniform(1.0)))
    b := G.NewMatrix(g, Float, G.WithName("b"), G.WithShape(N, 800),
        G.WithInit(G.Zeroes()))
    xw, _ := G.Mul(x, w)
    xwb, _ := G.Add(xw, b)
    act, _ := G.Sigmoid(xwb)

    w2 := G.NewMatrix(g, Float, G.WithName("w2"), G.WithShape(800, 10),
```

```
        G.WithInit(G.Uniform(1.0)))
    b2 := G.NewMatrix(g, Float, G.WithName("b2"), G.WithShape(N, 10),
        G.WithInit(G.Zeroes()))
    xw2, _ := G.Mul(act, w2)
    xwb2, _ := G.Add(xw2, b2)
    sm, _ := G.SoftMax(xwb2)
}
```

The preceding code is a representation of the following neural network in images:

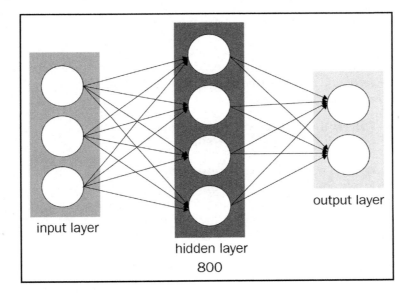

The middle layer consists of 800 hidden units.

Of course, the preceding code hides a lot of things. You can't really expect a neural network from scratch in fewer than 20 lines, can you? To understand what is happening, we need to take a brief detour into understanding what Gorgonia is.

Gorgonia

Gorgonia is a library that provides primitives for working with mathematical expressions specific to deep learning. When working with a ML related project, you will start to find yourself more introspective about the world, and questioning assumptions all the time. This is a good thing.

Consider what happens in your mind when you read the following mathematical expression:

$$1 + 1 = 5$$

You should instantly think *hang on, that's false*. Why does your brain think this?

That's mainly because your brain evaluated the mathematical expression. In general, there are three parts to the expression: the left-hand side, the equal symbol, and the right-hand side. Your brain evaluated each part separately and then evaluated the expression as false.

When we read mathematical expressions, we automatically evaluate the expressions in our mind that we take evaluation for granted. In Gorgonia, what we take for granted is made explicit. There are two general *parts* to using Gorgonia: defining an expression and evaluating an expression.

Since you are most probably a programmer, you can think of the first part as writing a program, and the second part can be thought of as running a program.

When describing a neural network in Gorgonia, it's often instructive to imagine yourself writing in another programming language, one that is specific to building neural networks. This is because the patterns used in Gorgonia are not unlike a new programming language. Indeed, Gorgonia was built from ground-up with the idea that it's a programming language without a syntactical frontend. As such, in this section, I will often ask you to imagine writing in another Go-like language.

Why?

A good question to ask is *why?* Why bother with this separation of processes? After all, the preceding code could be rewritten as the previous chapter's `Predict` function:

```
func (nn *NN) Predict(a tensor.Tensor) (int, error) {
  if a.Dims() != 1 {
    return nil, errors.New("Expected a vector")
  }

  var m maybe
  act0 := m.sigmoid(m.matVecMul(nn.hidden, a))
  pred := m.sigmoid(m.matVecMul(nn.final, act0))
  if m.err != nil {
    return -1, m.err
  }
  return argmax(pred.Data().([]float64)), nil
}
```

Here, we define the network in Go, and when we run the Go code, the neural network is run as it is being defined. What's the problem we face that we need to introduce the idea of separating the definition of the neural network and running it? We've already seen the problem when we wrote the `Train` method.

If you recall, in the last chapter, I said that writing the `Train` method requires us to actually copy and paste code from the `Predict` method. To refresh your memory, here's the `Train` method:

```go
// X is the image, Y is a one hot vector
func (nn *NN) Train(x, y tensor.Tensor, learnRate float64) (cost float64,
err error) {
  // predict
  var m maybe
  m.reshape(x, s.Shape()[0], 1)
  m.reshape(y, 10, 1)
  act0 := m.sigmoid(m.matmul(nn.hidden, x))
  pred := m.sigmoid(m.matmul(nn.final, act0))

  // backpropagation.
  outputErrors := m.sub(y, pred))
  cost = sum(outputErrors.Data().([]float64))

  hidErrs := m.do(func() (tensor.Tensor, error) {
    if err := nn.final.T(); err != nil {
      return nil, err
    }
    defer nn.final.UT()
    return tensor.MatMul(nn.final, outputErrors)
  })
  dpred := m.mul(m.dsigmoid(pred), outputErrors, tensor.UseUnsafe())
  dpred_dfinal := m.dmatmul(outputErrors, act0)
    if err := act0.T(); err != nil {
      return nil, err
    }
    defer act0.UT()
    return tensor.MatMul(outputErrors, act0)
  })

  m.reshape(m.mul(hidErrs, m.dsigmoid(act0), tensor.UseUnsafe()),
            hidErrs.Shape()[0], 1)
  dcost_dhidden := m.do(func() (tensor.Tensor, error) {
    if err := x.T(); err != nil {
      return nil, err
    }
    defer x.UT()
    return tensor.MatMul(hidErrs, x)
```

```
    })

    // gradient update
    m.mul(dpred_dfinal, learnRate, tensor.UseUnsafe())
    m.mul(dcost_dhidden, learnRate, tensor.UseUnsafe())
    m.add(nn.final, dpred_dfinal, tensor.UseUnsafe())
    m.add(nn.hidden, dcost_dhidden, tensor.UseUnsafe())
    return cost, m.err
}
```

Let's go through an exercise of refactoring to highlight the problem. Taking off our ML hat for a bit, and putting on our software engineer hat, let's see how we can refactor `Train` and `Predict`, even if conceptually. We see in the `Train` method that we need access to `act0` and `pred` in order to backpropagate the errors. Where in `Predict` `act0` and `pred` are terminal values (that is, we don't use them after the function has returned), in `Train`, they are not.

So, here, we can create a new method; let's call it `fwd`:

```
func (nn *NN) fwd(x tensor.Tensor) (act0, pred tensor.Tensor, err error) {
    var m maybe
    m.reshape(x, s.Shape()[0], 1)
    act0 := m.sigmoid(m.matmul(nn.hidden, x))
    pred := m.sigmoid(m.matmul(nn.final, act0))
    return act0, pred, m.err
}
```

And we can refactor `Predict` to look like this:

```
func (nn *NN) Predict(a tensor.Tensor) (int, error) {
    if a.Dims() != 1 {
        return nil, errors.New("Expected a vector")
    }

    var err error
    var pred tensor.Tensor
    if _, pred, err = nn.fwd(a); err!= nil {
        return -1, err
    }
    return argmax(pred.Data().([]float64)), nil
}
```

And the `Train` method would look like this:

```
// X is the image, Y is a one hot vector
func (nn *NN) Train(x, y tensor.Tensor, learnRate float64) (cost float64,
err error) {
```

```
// predict
var act0, pred tensor.Tensor
if act0, pred, err = nn.fwd(); err != nil {
  return math.Inf(1), err
}

var m maybe
m.reshape(y, 10, 1)
// backpropagation.
outputErrors := m.sub(y, pred))
cost = sum(outputErrors.Data().([]float64))

hidErrs := m.do(func() (tensor.Tensor, error) {
  if err := nn.final.T(); err != nil {
    return nil, err
  }
  defer nn.final.UT()
  return tensor.MatMul(nn.final, outputErrors)
})
dpred := m.mul(m.dsigmoid(pred), outputErrors, tensor.UseUnsafe())
dpred_dfinal := m.dmatmul(outputErrors, act0)
  if err := act0.T(); err != nil {
    return nil, err
  }
  defer act0.UT()
  return tensor.MatMul(outputErrors, act0)
})

m.reshape(m.mul(hidErrs, m.dsigmoid(act0), tensor.UseUnsafe()),
          hidErrs.Shape()[0], 1)
dcost_dhidden := m.do(func() (tensor.Tensor, error) {
  if err := x.T(); err != nil {
    return nil, err
  }
  defer x.UT()
  return tensor.MatMul(hidErrs, x)
})

// gradient update
m.mul(dpred_dfinal, learnRate, tensor.UseUnsafe())
m.mul(dcost_dhidden, learnRate, tensor.UseUnsafe())
m.add(nn.final, dpred_dfinal, tensor.UseUnsafe())
m.add(nn.hidden, dcost_dhidden, tensor.UseUnsafe())
return cost, m.err
}
```

This looks better. What exactly are we doing here? We are programming. We are rearranging one form of syntax into another form of syntax but we are not changing the semantics, the meaning of the program. The refactored program has exactly the same meaning as the pre-refactored program.

Programming

Wait a minute, you might say to yourself. What do I mean by *the meaning of the program?* This is a surprisingly deep topic that involves a whole branch of mathematics known as **homotopy**. But for all practical intents and purposes of this chapter, let's define the *meaning* of a program to be the extensional definition of the program. If two programs compile and run, take the exact same inputs, and return the same exact output every time, we say two programs are equal.

These two programs would be equal:

Program A	Program B
fmt.Println("Hello World")	fmt.Printf("Hello " + "World\n")

Intentionally, if we visualize the programs as an **Abstract Syntax Tree (AST)**, they look slightly different:

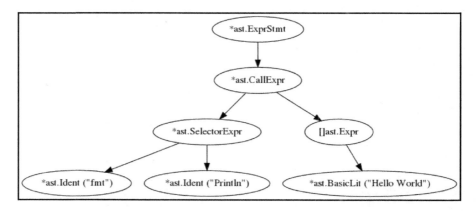

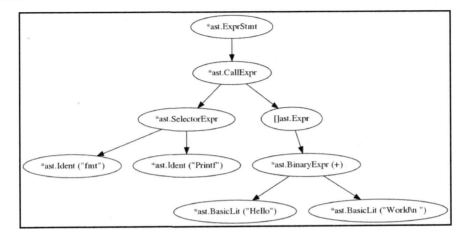

The syntax for both programs are different, but they are semantically the same. We can refactor program B into program A, by eliminating the +.

But note what we did here: we took a program and represented it as an AST. Through syntax, we manipulated the AST. This is the essence of programming.

What is a tensor? – part 2

In the previous chapter, there was an info box that introduced the concept of a tensor. That info box was a little simplified. If you google what a tensor is, you will get very conflicting results, which only serve to confuse. I don't want to add to the confusion. Instead, I shall only briefly touch on tensors in a way that will be relevant to our project, and in a way very much like how a typical textbook on Euclidean geometry introduces the concept of a point: by holding it to be self-evident from use cases.

Likewise, we will hold tensors to be self-evident from use. First, we will look at the concept of multiplication:

- First, let's define a vector: $x = \begin{bmatrix} 2 & 3 \end{bmatrix}$. You can think of it as this diagram:

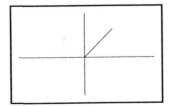

- Next, let's multiply the vector by a scalar value: 2. The result is something like this:

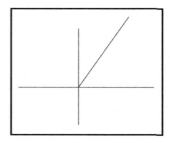

There are two observations:

- The general direction of the arrow doesn't change.
- Only the length changes. In physics terms, this is called the magnitude. If the vector represents the distance travelled, you would have traveled twice the distance along the same direction.

So, how would you change directions by using multiplications alone? What do you have to multiply to change directions? Let's try the following matrix, which we will call T, for transformation:

$$\mathbf{T} = \begin{bmatrix} -1 & 2 \\ 3 & -4 \end{bmatrix}$$

Now if we multiply the transformation matrix with the vector, we get the following:

$$\begin{aligned} \mathbf{Tx} &= \mathbf{T} \cdot \mathbf{x} \\ &= \begin{bmatrix} -1 & 2 \\ 3 & -4 \end{bmatrix} \begin{bmatrix} 2 \\ 3 \end{bmatrix} \\ &= \begin{bmatrix} 4 \\ -6 \end{bmatrix} \end{aligned}$$

And if we plot out the starting vector and the ending vector, we get the resultant output:

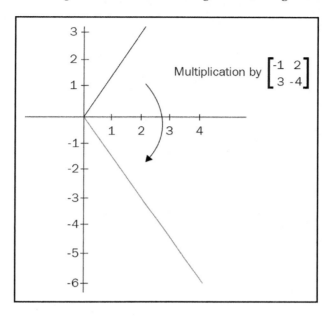

As we can see, the direction has changed. The magnitude too has changed.

Now, you might be saying, *hang on, isn't this just Linear Algebra 101?*. Yes, it is. But to really understand a tensor, we must learn how to construct one. The matrix that we just used is also a tensor of rank-2. The proper name for a tensor of rank-2 is a **dyad**.

Why the mixing of naming conventions? Here's a bit of fun trivia. When I was writing the earliest versions of Gorgonia, I was musing about the terrible naming conventions computer science has had, a fact that Bjarne Stroustrup himself lamented. The canonical name for a rank-2 tensor is called a **dyad**, but can be represented as a matrix. I was struggling to properly call it; after all, there are power in names and to name it is to tame it.

At around the same time as I was developing the earliest versions of Gorgonia, I was following a most excellent BBC TV series called **Orphan Black**, in which the Dyad Institute is the primary foe of the protagonists. They were quite villainous and that clearly left an impact in my mind. I decided against naming it thus. In retrospect, this seemed like a rather silly decision.

Now let's consider the transformation dyad. You can think of the dyad as a vector u times a vector v. To write it out in equation form:

$$\mathbf{T} = \mathbf{uv}$$
$$\mathbf{u} = ???$$
$$\mathbf{v} = ???$$

At this point, you may be familiar with the previous chapter's notion of linear algebra. You might think to yourself: if two vectors multiply, that'd end up with a scalar value, no? If so, how would you multiply two vectors and get a matrix out of it?

Here, we'd need to introduce a new type of multiplication: the outer product (and by contrast, the multiplication introduced in the previous chapter is an inner product). We write outer products with this symbol: $\otimes$.

Specifically speaking, the outer product, also known as a dyad product, is defined as such:

$$\mathbf{u} \otimes \mathbf{v} = \mathbf{u} \cdot \mathbf{v}^T$$
$$= \begin{bmatrix} u_1 \\ u_2 \end{bmatrix} \cdot \begin{bmatrix} v_1 & v_2 \end{bmatrix}$$
$$= \begin{bmatrix} u_1 v_1 & u_1 v_2 \\ u_2 v_1 & u_2 v_2 \end{bmatrix}$$

We won't be particularly interested in the specifics of u and v in this chapter. However, being able to construct a dyad from its constituent vectors is an integral part of what a tensor is all about.

Specifically, we can replace T with uv:

$$\mathbf{Tx} = \mathbf{T} \cdot \mathbf{x}$$
$$= \mathbf{uv} \cdot \mathbf{x}$$
$$= \mathbf{u}(\mathbf{v} \cdot \mathbf{x})$$
$$= \mathbf{u}\lambda$$
$$= \lambda\mathbf{u}$$

Now we get λ as the scalar magnitude change and u as the directional change.

So what is the big fuss with tensors? I can give two reasons.

Firstly, the idea that dyads can be formed from vectors generalizes upward. A three-tensor, or triad can be formed by a dyad product *uvw*, a four-tensor or a tetrad can be formed by a dyad product *uvwx*, and so on and so forth. This affords us a mental shortcut that will be very useful to us when we see shapes that are associated with tensors.

The useful mental model of what a tensor can be thought as is the following: a vector is like a list of things, a dyad is like a list of vectors, a triad is like a list of dyads, and so on and so forth. This is absolutely helpful when thinking of images, like those that we've seen in the previous chapter:

An image can be seen as a (28, 28) matrix. A list of ten images would have the shape (10, 28, 28). If we wanted to arrange the images in such a way that it's a list of lists of ten images, it'd have a shape of (10, 10, 28, 28).

All this comes with a caveat of course: a tensor can only be defined in the presence of transformation. As a physics professor once told me: *that which transforms like a tensor is a tensor*. A tensor devoid of any transformation is just an *n*-dimensional array of data. The data must transform, or flow from tensor to tensor in an equation. In this regards, I think that TensorFlow is a ridiculously well-named product.

For more information on tensors, I would recommend the relatively dense text book, *Linear Algebra and Geometry* by Kostrikin (I failed to finish this book, but it was this book that gave me what I believe to be a strong-ish understanding of tensors). More on the flow of tensors can be found in Spivak's *Manifold Calculus*.

All expressions are graphs

Now we can finally return to the preceding example.

Our problem, if you recall, is that we had to specify the neural network twice: once for prediction and once for learning purposes. We then refactored the program so that we don't have to specify the network twice. Additionally, we had to manually write out the expression for the backpropagation. This is error prone, especially when dealing with larger neural networks like the one we're about to build in this chapter. Is there a better way? The answer is yes.

Once we understand and fully internalize that neural networks are essentially mathematical expressions, we can take the learning's from tensors, and model a neural network where the entire neural network is a flow of tensors.

Recall that tensors can only be defined in the presence of transformation; then, any operation that transforms tensor(s), used in concert with data structures that hold data are tensors. Also, recall that computer programs can be represented as abstract syntax trees. Mathematical expressions can be represented as a program. Therefore, mathematical expressions can also be represented as an abstract syntax tree.

More accurate, however, is that mathematical expressions can be expressed as a graph; a directed acyclic graph, to be specific. We call this the **expression graph**.

This distinction matters. Trees cannot share nodes. Graphs can. Let's consider, for example, the following mathematical expression:

$$y = abc + abd$$

Here are the representations as a graph and as a tree:

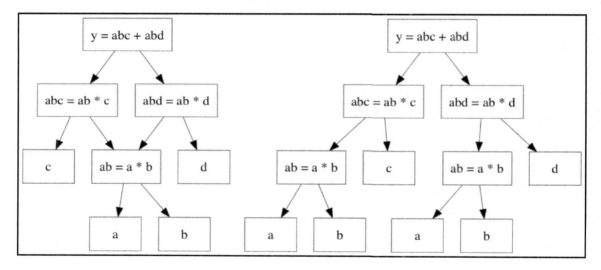

On the left, we have a directed acyclic graph, and on the right, we have a tree. Note that in the tree variant of the mathematical equation, there are repeat nodes. Both are rooted at $y = abc + abd$. The arrow should be read as *depends on*. $y = abc + abd$ depends on two other nodes, $abc = ab * c$ and $abd = ab * d$, and so on and so forth.

Both the graph and tree are valid representations of the same mathematical equation, of course.

Why bother representing a mathematical expression as a graph or a tree? Recall that an abstract syntax tree represents a computation. If a mathematical expression, represented as a graph or a tree, has a shared notion of computation, then it also represents an abstract syntax tree.

Indeed, we can take each node in the graph or tree, and perform a computation on it. If each node is a representation of a computation, then logic holds that fewer nodes means faster computations (and less memory usage). Therefore, we should prefer to use the directed acyclic graph representation.

And now we come to the major benefit of representing a mathematical expression as a graph: we get differentiation for free.

If you recall from the previous chapter, backpropagation is essentially differentiating the cost with regards to the inputs. The gradients, once calculated, can then be used to update the values of the weights themselves. Having a graph structure, we wouldn't have to write the backpropagation parts. Instead, if we have a virtual machine that executes the graph, starting at the leaves and moving toward the root, the virtual machine can automatically perform differentiation on the values as it traverses the graph from leaf to root.

Alternatively, if we don't want to do automatic differentiation, we can also perform symbolic differentiation by manipulating the graph in the same way that we manipulated the AST in the *What is programming* section, by adding and coalescing nodes.

In this way, we can now shift our view of a neural network to this:

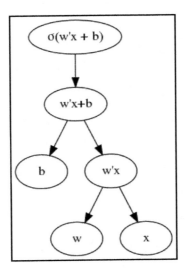

Describing a neural network

Now let's get back to the task of writing a neural network and thinking of it in terms of a mathematical expression expressed as a graph. Recall that the code looks something like this:

```
import (
  G "gorgonia.org/gorgonia"
)

var Float tensor.Float = tensor.Float64
func main() {
  g := G.NewGraph()
  x := G.NewMatrix(g, Float, G.WithName("x"), G.WithShape(N, 728))
  w := G.NewMatrix(g, Float, G.WithName("w"), G.WithShape(728, 800),
                   G.WithInit(G.Uniform(1.0)))
  b := G.NewMatrix(g, Float, G.WithName("b"), G.WithShape(N, 800),
                   G.WithInit(G.Zeroes()))
  xw, _ := G.Mul(x, w)
  xwb, _ := G.Add(xw, b)
  act, _ := G.Sigmoid(xwb)

  w2 := G.NewMatrix(g, Float, G.WithName("w2"), G.WithShape(800, 10),
                    G.WithInit(G.Uniform(1.0)))
  b2 := G.NewMatrix(g, Float, G.WithName("b2"), G.WithShape(N, 10),
                    G.WithInit(G.Zeroes()))
  xw2, _ := G.Mul(act, w2)
  xwb2, _ := G.Add(xw2, b2)
  sm, _ := G.SoftMax(xwb2)
}
```

Now let's go through this code.

First, we create a new expression graph with `g := G.NewGraph()`. An expression graph is a holder object to hold the mathematical expression. Why would we want an expression graph? The mathematical expression that represents a neural network is contained in the `*gorgonia.ExpressionGraph` object.

Mathematical expressions are only interesting if we use variables. $1 + 1 = 2$ is quite an uninteresting expression because you can't do much with this expression. The only thing you can do with it is to evaluate the expression and see if it returns true or false. $a + 1 = 2$ is slightly more interesting. But, then again, a can only be 1.

Consider, however, the expression $a + b = 2$. With two variables, it suddenly becomes a lot more interesting. The values that a and b can take are dependent on one another, and there is a whole range of possible pairs of numbers that can fit into a and b.

Recall that each layer of neural network is just a mathematical expression that reads like this: $act = \sigma(w'x + b)$. In this case, w, x, and b are variables. So, we create them. Note that in this case, Gorgonia treats variables as a programming language does: you have to tell the system what the variable represents.

In Go, you would do that by typing `var x Foo`, which tells the Go compiler that `x` should be a type `Foo`. In Gorgonia, the mathematical variables are declared by using `NewMatrix`, `NewVector`, `NewScalar`, and `NewTensor`. `x := G.NewMatrix(g, Float, G.WithName, G.WithShape(N, 728))` simply says `x` is a matrix in expression graph `g` with a name `x`, and has a shape of `(N, 728)`.

Here, readers may observe that `728` is a familiar number. In fact, what this tells us is that `x` represents the input, which is N images. `x`, therefore, is a matrix of N rows, where each row represents a single image (728 floating points).

The eagle-eyed reader would note that `w` and `b` have extra options, where the declaration of `x` does not. You see, `NewMatrix` simply declares the variable in the expression graph. There is no value associated with it. This allows for flexibility when the value is attached to a variable. However, with regards to the weight matrix, we want to start the equation with some initial values. `G.WithInit(G.Uniform(1.0))` is a construction option that populates the weight matrix with values pulled from a uniform distribution with a gain of `1.0`. If you imagine yourself coding in another language specific to building neural networks, it'd look something like this: `var w Matrix(728, 800) = Uniform(1.0)`.

Following that, we simply write out the mathematical equation: xw is simply a matrix multiplication between x and w; hence, `xw, _ := G.Mul(x, w)`. At this point, it should be clarified that we are merely describing the computation that is supposed to happen. It is yet to happen. In this way, it is not dissimilar to writing a program; writing code does not equal running the program.

`G.Mul` and most operations in Gorgonia actually returns an error. For the purposes of this demonstration, we're ignoring any errors that may arise from symbolically multiplying `x` and `w`. What could possibly go wrong with simple multiplication? Well, we're dealing with matrix multiplication, so the shapes must have matching inner dimensions. A (N, 728) matrix can only be multiplied by a (728, M) matrix, which leads to an (N, M) matrix. If the second matrix does not have 728 rows, then an error will happen. So, in real production code, error handling is a **must**.

Speaking of *must*, Gorgonia comes with a utility function, called, **G.Must**. Taking a cue from the `text/template` and `html/template` libraries found in the standard library, the `G.Must` function panics when an error occur. To use, simply write this: `xw :=` `G.Must(G.Mul(x,w))`.

After the inputs are multiplied with the weights, we add to the biases using `G.Add(xw, b)`. Again, errors may occur, but in this example, we're eliding the checks of errors.

Lastly, we take the result and perform a non-linearity: a sigmoid function, with `G.Sigmoid(xwb)`. This layer is now complete. Its shape, if you follow, would be (N, 800).

The completed layer is then used as an input for the following layer. The next layer has a similar layout as the first layer, except instead of a sigmoid non-linearity, a `G.SoftMax` is used. This ensures that each row in the resulting matrix sums 1.

One-hot vector

Perhaps, not so coincidentally, the last layer has the shape of (N, 10). N is the number of input images (which we've gotten from `x`) ; that's fairly self-explanatory. It also means that there is a clean mapping from input to output. What's not self-explanatory is the 10. Why 10? Simply put, there are 10 possible numbers we want to predict - 0, 1, 2, 3, 4, 5, 6, 7, 8, 9:

	0	1	2	3...10
0	0.1	0.1	0.2	...*
1				
2				
⋮				
N				

The preceding diagram is an example result matrix. Recall that we used `G.SoftMax` to ensure that each row sums up to 1. Therefore, we can interpret the numbers in each column of each row to be the probability that it is the specific digit that we're predicting. To find the digit we're predicting, simply find the highest probability in each column.

In the previous chapter, I introduced the concept of one-hot vector encoding. To recap, it takes a slice of labels and returns a matrix.

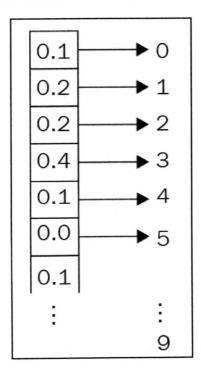

Now, this is clearly a matter of encoding. Who's to say that column 0 would have to represent 0? We could of course come up with a completely crazy encoding like such and the neural network would still work:

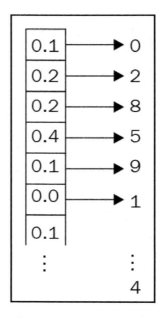

Of course, we would not be using such a scheme for encoding; it would be a massive source of programmer error. Instead, we would go for the standard encoding of a one-hot vector.

I hope this has given you a taste of how powerful the notion of an expression graph can be. One thing we haven't touched upon yet is the execution of the graph. How do you run a graph? We'll look further into that in the next section.

The project

With all that done, it's time to get on to the project! Once again, we are going to recognize handwritten digits. But this time around, we're going to build a CNN for that. Instead of just using the `tensor` package of Gorgonia, this time we're going to use all of Gorgonia.

Once again, to install Gorgonia, simply run `go get -u gorgonia.org/gorgonia` and `go get -u gorgonia.org/tensor`.

Getting the data

The data is the same data as in the previous chapter: the MNIST dataset. It can be found in the repository for this chapter, and we'll be using a function we wrote in the previous chapter to acquire the data:

```go
// Image holds the pixel intensities of an image.
// 255 is foreground (black), 0 is background (white).
type RawImage []byte

// Label is a digit label in 0 to 9
type Label uint8


const numLabels = 10
const pixelRange = 255

const (
  imageMagic = 0x00000803
  labelMagic = 0x00000801
  Width = 28
  Height = 28
)

func readLabelFile(r io.Reader, e error) (labels []Label, err error) {
  if e != nil {
    return nil, e
  }

  var magic, n int32
  if err = binary.Read(r, binary.BigEndian, &magic); err != nil {
    return nil, err
  }
  if magic != labelMagic {
    return nil, os.ErrInvalid
  }
  if err = binary.Read(r, binary.BigEndian, &n); err != nil {
    return nil, err
  }
  labels = make([]Label, n)
  for i := 0; i < int(n); i++ {
    var l Label
    if err := binary.Read(r, binary.BigEndian, &l); err != nil {
      return nil, err
    }
    labels[i] = l
  }
}
```

```
    return labels, nil
}

func readImageFile(r io.Reader, e error) (imgs []RawImage, err error) {
  if e != nil {
    return nil, e
  }

  var magic, n, nrow, ncol int32
  if err = binary.Read(r, binary.BigEndian, &magic); err != nil {
    return nil, err
  }
  if magic != imageMagic {
    return nil, err /*os.ErrInvalid*/
  }
  if err = binary.Read(r, binary.BigEndian, &n); err != nil {
    return nil, err
  }
  if err = binary.Read(r, binary.BigEndian, &nrow); err != nil {
    return nil, err
  }
  if err = binary.Read(r, binary.BigEndian, &ncol); err != nil {
    return nil, err
  }
  imgs = make([]RawImage, n)
  m := int(nrow * ncol)
  for i := 0; i < int(n); i++ {
    imgs[i] = make(RawImage, m)
    m_, err := io.ReadFull(r, imgs[i])
    if err != nil {
      return nil, err
    }
    if m_ != int(m) {
      return nil, os.ErrInvalid
    }
  }
  return imgs, nil
```

Other things from the previous chapter

Obviously, there is a lot from the previous chapter that we can reuse:

- The range normalization function (pixelWeight) and its isometric counterpart (reversePixelWeight)
- prepareX and prepareY
- The visualize function

For convenience sake, here they are again:

```
func pixelWeight(px byte) float64 {
    retVal := (float64(px) / 255 * 0.999) + 0.001
    if retVal == 1.0 {
        return 0.999
    }
    return retVal
}
func reversePixelWeight(px float64) byte {
    return byte(((px - 0.001) / 0.999) * 255)
}
func prepareX(M []RawImage) (retVal tensor.Tensor) {
    rows := len(M)
    cols := len(M[0])

    b := make([]float64, 0, rows*cols)
    for i := 0; i < rows; i++ {
        for j := 0; j < len(M[i]); j++ {
            b = append(b, pixelWeight(M[i][j]))
        }
    }
    return tensor.New(tensor.WithShape(rows, cols), tensor.WithBacking(b))
}
func prepareY(N []Label) (retVal tensor.Tensor) {
    rows := len(N)
    cols := 10

    b := make([]float64, 0, rows*cols)
    for i := 0; i < rows; i++ {
        for j := 0; j < 10; j++ {
            if j == int(N[i]) {
                b = append(b, 0.999)
            } else {
                b = append(b, 0.001)
            }
        }
    }
}
```

```
        return tensor.New(tensor.WithShape(rows, cols), tensor.WithBacking(b))
}
func visualize(data tensor.Tensor, rows, cols int, filename string) (err
error) {
    N := rows * cols

    sliced := data
    if N > 1 {
        sliced, err = data.Slice(makeRS(0, N), nil) // data[0:N, :] in
python
        if err != nil {
            return err
        }
    }

    if err = sliced.Reshape(rows, cols, 28, 28); err != nil {
        return err
    }

    imCols := 28 * cols
    imRows := 28 * rows
    rect := image.Rect(0, 0, imCols, imRows)
    canvas := image.NewGray(rect)

    for i := 0; i < cols; i++ {
        for j := 0; j < rows; j++ {
            var patch tensor.Tensor
            if patch, err = sliced.Slice(makeRS(i, i+1), makeRS(j,
                                        j+1)); err != nil {
                return err
            }

            patchData := patch.Data().([]float64)
            for k, px := range patchData {
                x := j*28 + k%28
                y := i*28 + k/28
                c := color.Gray{reversePixelWeight(px)}
                canvas.Set(x, y, c)
            }
        }
    }

    var f io.WriteCloser
    if f, err = os.Create(filename); err != nil {
        return err
    }

    if err = png.Encode(f, canvas); err != nil {
```

```
        f.Close()
        return err
    }

    if err = f.Close(); err != nil {
        return err
    }
    return nil
}
```

CNNs

What we will be building is a CNN. So, what is a Convolutional Neural Network? As its name suggests, it's a neural network, not unlike the one we have built in the previous chapter. So, clearly, there are elements that are similar. There are also elements that are not similar, for if they were similar, we wouldn't have this chapter.

What are convolutions?

The main difference between the neural network we built in the previous chapter and a CNN is the convolutional layer. Recall that the neural network was able to learn features related to digits. In order to be more accurate, the neural network layers need to learn more specific features. One way to do this is to add more layers; more layers would lead to more features being learned, giving rise to deep learning.

On a spring evening of 1877, people dressed in what modern-day people would consider as *black-tie* gathered at the Royal Institute, in London. The speaker for the evening was Francis Galton, the same Galton we met in `Chapter 1`, *How to Solve All Machine Learning Problems*. In his talk, Galton brought out a curious device, which he called a **quincunx**. It was a vertical wooden board with wooden pegs sticking out of it, arranged in a uniform, but interleaved manner. The front of it was covered with glass and there was an opening at the top. Tiny balls are then dropped from the top and as they hit the pegs, bounce left or right, and fall to the corresponding chutes. This continues until the balls collect at the bottom:

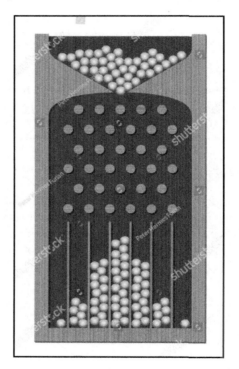

A curious shape begins to form. It's the shape modern statisticians have come to recognize as the binomial distribution. Most statistical textbooks end the story about here. The quincunx, now known as the Galton Board, illustrates, very clearly and firmly, the idea of the central limit theorem.

Our story, of course, doesn't end there. Recall in `Chapter 1`, *How to Solve All Machine Learning Problems*, that I mentioned that Galton was very much interested in hereditary issues. A few years earlier, Galton had published a book called *Hereditary Genius*. He had collected data on *eminent* persons in Great Britain across the preceding centuries, and much to his dismay, he found that *eminent* parentage tended to lead to un-eminent children. He called this a **reversion to the mediocre**:

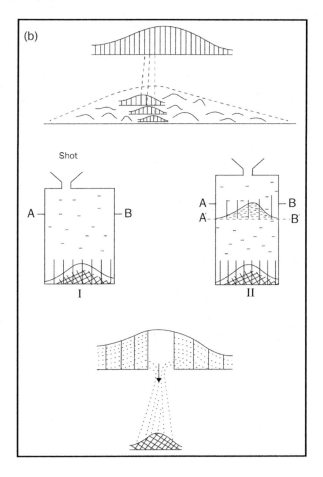

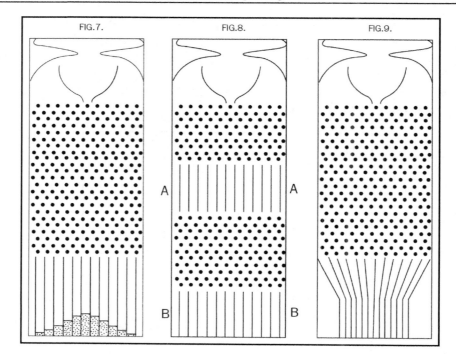

And, yet, he reasoned, the mathematics doesn't show such things! He explained this by showing off a quincunx with two layers. A two-layered quincunx was a stand-in for the generational effect. The top layer would essentially be the distribution of a feature (say, height). Upon dropping to the second layer, the beads would cause the distribution to *flatten out*, which is not what he had observed. Instead, he surmised that there has to be another factor which causes the regression to the mean. To illustrate his idea, he installed chutes as the controlling factor, which causes a regression to the mean. A mere 40 years later, the rediscovery of Mendel's pea experiments would reveal genetics to be the factor. That is a story for another day.

What we're interested in is why the distribution would *flatten out*. While the standard *it's physics!* would suffice as an answer, there remains interesting questions that we could ask. Let's look at a simplified depiction:

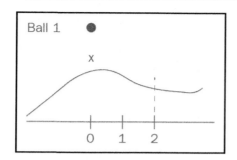

Here, we evaluate the probability that the ball will drop and hit a position. The curve indicates the probability of the ball landing at position B. Now, we add a second layer:

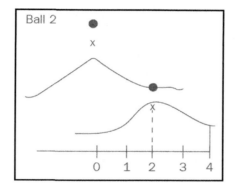

Say, from the previous layer, the ball landed at position 2. Now, what is the probability that the ball's final resting place is at position D?

To calculate this, we need to know all the possible ways that the ball can end up at position D. Limiting our option to A to D only, here they are:

Level 1 Position	L1 Horizontal Distance	Level 2 position	L2 Horizontal Distance
A	0	D	3
B	1	D	2
C	2	D	1
D	3	D	0

Now we can ask the question in terms of probability. The horizontal distances in the table are an encoding that allows us to ask the question probabilistically and generically. The probability of the ball travelling horizontally by one unit can be represented as *P(1)*, the probability of the ball travelling horizontally by two units can be represented as *P(2)*, and so on.

And to calculate the probability that the ball ends up in D after two levels is essentially summing up all the probabilities:

$$P(\text{lands on } D) = P(0) \cdot P(3) + P(1) \cdot P(2) + P(2) \cdot P(1) + P(3) \cdot P(0)$$

We can write it as such:

$$P(c = a + b) = \sum P_1(a) \cdot P_2(b)$$

We can read it as the probability of the final distance being $c = a+b$ is the sum of $P\_1(a)$, with the probability of level 1, where the ball traveled horizontally by a and $P\_2(b)$, with the probability of level 2, where the ball traveled horizontally by b.

And this is the typical definition of convolution:

$$(f * g)(t) = \int f(\tau) \cdot g(t - \tau) d\tau$$

If the integral scares you, we can equivalently rewrite this as a summation operation (this is only valid because we are considering discrete values; for continuous real values, integrations have to be used):

$$(f * g)(t) = \sum f(\tau) \cdot g(t - \tau)$$

Now, if you squint very carefully, this equation looks a lot like the preceding probability equation. Instead of b, we can rewrite it as $c - a$:

$$P(c) = \sum P_1(a) \cdot P_2(c - a)$$

And what are probabilities, but functions? There is, after all, a reason we write probabilities in the format $P(a)$. We can indeed genericize the probability equation to the convolution definition.

However, for now, let's strengthen our intuitions about what convolutions are. For that, we'll keep the notion that the function we're talking about has probabilities. First, we should note that the probability of the ball ending up in a particular location is dependent on where it starts. But imagine if the platform for the second platform moves horizontally:

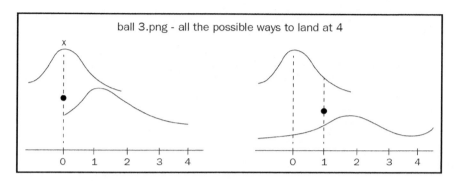

Now the probability of the final resting place of the ball is highly dependent on where the initial starting position is, as well as where the second layer's starting position is. The ball may not even land on the bottom!

So, here's a good mental shortcut of thinking about convolutions: t's as if one function in one layer is *sliding* across a second function.

So, convolutions are what cause the *flattening* of Galton's quincunx. In essence, it is a function that slides on top of the probability function, flattening it out as it moves along the horizontal dimension. This is a one-dimensional convolution; the ball only travels along one dimension.

A two-dimensional convolution is similar to a one-dimensional convolution. Instead, there are two *distances* or metrics that we're considering for each layer:

$$P(c = (b_1, b_2)) = \sum P_1(a_1, a_2) \cdot P_2(b_1, b_2)$$

But this equation is nigh impenetrable. Instead, here's a convenient series of pictures of how it works, step by step:

Convolution (Step 1):

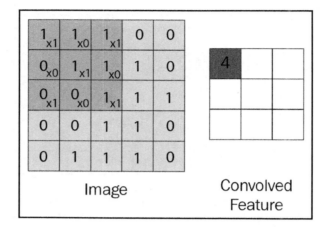

Convolution (Step 2):

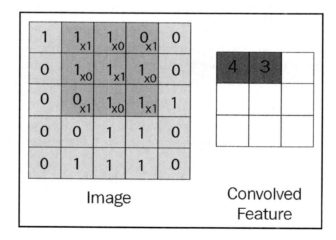

Convolution (Step 3):

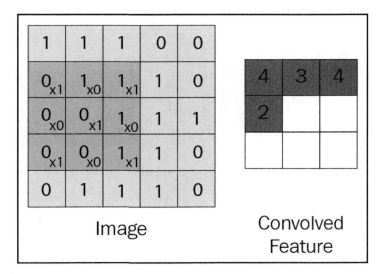

Convolution (Step 4):

Convolution (Step 5):

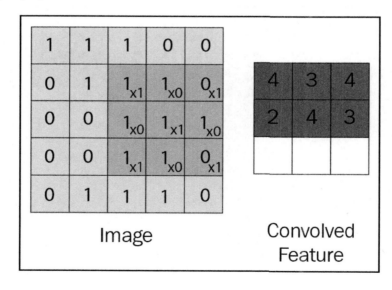

Convolution (Step 6):

Convolution (Step 7):

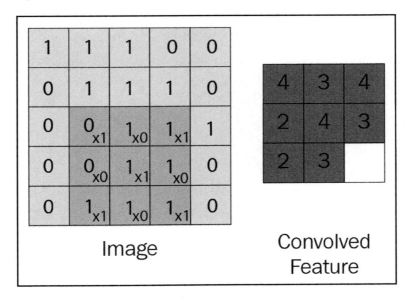

Convolution (Step 8):

Convolution (Step 9):

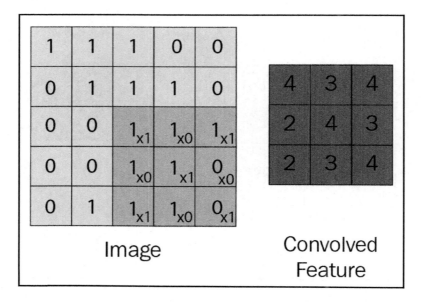

Again, you can think of this as sliding a function that slides over another function (the input) in two dimensions. The function that slides, performs the standard linear algebra transformation of multiplication followed by addition.

You can see this in action in an image-processing example that is undoubtedly very common: Instagram.

How Instagram filters work

I am going to assume that you are familiar with Instagram. If not, I both envy and pity you; but here's the gist of Instagram: it's a photo sharing service that has a selling point of allowing users to apply filters to their images. The filters would change the color of the images, often to enhance the subject.

How do those filters work? Convolutions!

For example, let's define a filter:

$$k = \begin{bmatrix} \frac{1}{16} & \frac{1}{8} & \frac{1}{16} \\ \frac{1}{8} & \frac{1}{4} & \frac{1}{8} \\ \frac{1}{16} & \frac{1}{8} & \frac{1}{16} \end{bmatrix}$$

To convolve, we simply slide the filter across the following diagram (it's a *very* famous artwork by an artist called Piet Chew):

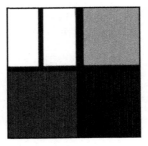

Applying the preceding filter would yield something such as the following:

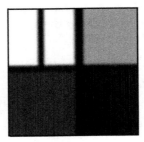

Yes, the filter blurs images!

Here's an example written in Go to emphasize the idea:

```go
func main() {
  kb := []float64{
    1 / 16.0, 1 / 8.0, 1 / 16.0,
    1 / 8.0, 1 / 4.0, 1 / 8.0,
    1 / 16.0, 1 / 8.0, 1 / 16.0,
  }
  k := tensor.New(tensor.WithShape(3,3), tensor.WithBacking(kb))

  for _, row := range imgIt {
    for j, px := range row {
      var acc float64

      for _, krow := range kIt {
        for _, kpx := range krow {
          acc += px * kpx
        }
      }
      row[j] = acc
    }
  }
}
```

The function is quite slow and inefficient, of course. Gorgonia itself comes with a much more sophisticated algorithm

Back to neural networks

OK, so we now know that convolutions are important in the use of filters. But how does this relate to neural networks?

Recall that a neural network is defined as a linear transform ($w'x + b$) with a non-linearity applied on it (written as $\sigma(w'x + b)$). Note that x, the input image, is acted upon as a whole. This would be like having a single filter across the entire image. But what if we could process the image one small section at a time?

To add to that, in the preceding section, I showed how a simple filter could be used to blur an image. Filters could also be used to sharpen an image, picking out features that matter and blurring out features that don't. So, what if a machine could learn what filter to create?

That's the reason why we would want to use a convolution in a neural network:

- Convolutions act on small parts of the image at a time, leaving only features that matter
- We can learn the specific filters

This gives a lot of fine-tuned control to the machine. Now, instead of a rough feature detector that works on the whole image at once, we can build many filters, each specializing to a specific feature, thus allowing us to extract the features necessary for the classification of numbers.

Max-pooling

Now we have in our minds a conceptual machine that will learn the filters that it needs to apply to extract features from an image. But, at the same time, we don't want the machine to overfit on the learning. A filter that is overly specific to the training data is not useful in real life. If a filter learns, for example, that all human faces have two eyes, a nose, and a mouth, and that's all, it wouldn't be able to classify a picture of a person with half their face obscured.

So, in an attempt to teach a ML algorithm to be able to generalize better, we simply give it less information. Max-pooling is one such process, as is *dropout* (see the next section).

How max pooling works is it partitions the input data into non-overlapping regions, and simply finds the maximum value of that region:

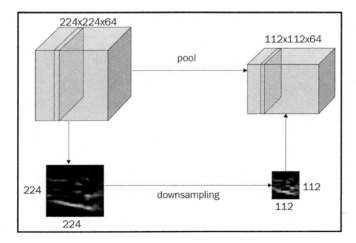

There is, of course, an implicit understanding that this definitely changes the shape of the output. In fact, you will observe that it shrinks the image.

Dropout

The result after max-pooling is minimum information within the output. But this may still be too much information; the machine may still overfit. Therefore, a very interesting quandary arises: what if some of the activations were randomly zeroed?

This is the basis of dropout. It's a remarkably simple idea that improves upon the machine learning algorithm's ability to generalize, simply by having deleterious effects on information. With every iteration, random activations are zeroed. This forces the algorithm to only learn what is really important. How it does so involves structural algebra and is a story for another day.

For the purposes of this project, Gorgonia actually handles dropout by means of element-wise multiplication by a randomly generated matrix of 1s and 0s.

Describing a CNN

Having said all that, the neural network is very easy to build. First, we define a neural network as such:

```
type convnet struct {
    g                   *gorgonia.ExprGraph
    w0, w1, w2, w3, w4 *gorgonia.Node // weights. the number at the back
indicates which layer it's used for
    d0, d1, d2, d3      float64        // dropout probabilities

    out    *gorgonia.Node
    outVal gorgonia.Value
}
```

Here, we defined a neural network with four layers. A convnet layer is similar to a linear layer in many ways. It can, for example, be written as an equation:

$$DropOut(MaxPool(\sigma(w * x)))$$

Note that in this specific example, I consider dropout and max-pool to be part of the same layer. In many literatures, they are considered to be separate layers.

I personally do not see the necessity to consider them as separate layers. After all, everything is just a mathematical equation; composing functions comes naturally.

A mathematical equation on its own without structure is quite meaningless. Unfortunately, we do not have technology usable enough to simply define the structure of a data type (the hotness is in dependently-typed languages, such as Idris, but they are not yet at the level of usability or performance that is necessary for deep learning). Instead, we have to constrain our data structure by providing a function to define a `convnet`:

```
func newConvNet(g *gorgonia.ExprGraph) *convnet {
  w0 := gorgonia.NewTensor(g, dt, 4, gorgonia.WithShape(32, 1, 3, 3),
            gorgonia.WithName("w0"),
            gorgonia.WithInit(gorgonia.GlorotN(1.0)))
  w1 := gorgonia.NewTensor(g, dt, 4, gorgonia.WithShape(64, 32, 3, 3),
            gorgonia.WithName("w1"),
            gorgonia.WithInit(gorgonia.GlorotN(1.0)))
  w2 := gorgonia.NewTensor(g, dt, 4, gorgonia.WithShape(128, 64, 3, 3),
            gorgonia.WithName("w2"),
            gorgonia.WithInit(gorgonia.GlorotN(1.0)))
  w3 := gorgonia.NewMatrix(g, dt, gorgonia.WithShape(128*3*3, 625),
            gorgonia.WithName("w3"),
            gorgonia.WithInit(gorgonia.GlorotN(1.0)))
  w4 := gorgonia.NewMatrix(g, dt, gorgonia.WithShape(625, 10),
            gorgonia.WithName("w4"),
            gorgonia.WithInit(gorgonia.GlorotN(1.0)))
  return &convnet{
    g: g,
    w0: w0,
    w1: w1,
    w2: w2,
    w3: w3,
    w4: w4,

    d0: 0.2,
    d1: 0.2,
    d2: 0.2,
    d3: 0.55,
  }
}
```

We'll start with `dt`. This is essentially a global variable denoting what data type we would like to work in. For the purposes of this project, we can use `var dt = tensor.Float64`, to indicate that we would like to work with `float64` throughout the entire project. This allows us to immediately reuse the functions from the previous chapter without having to handle different data types. Note that if we do plan to use `float32`, the computation speed immediately doubles. In the repository to this chapter, you might note that the code uses `float32`.

We'll start with `d0` all the way to `d3`. This is fairly simple. For the first three layers, we want 20% of the activations to be randomly zeroed. But for the last layer, we want 55% of the activations to be randomly zeroed. In really broad strokes, this causes an information bottleneck, which will cause the machine to learn only the really important features.

Take a look at how `w0` is defined. Here, we're saying `w0` is a variable called `w0`. It is a tensor with the shape of (32, 1, 3, 3). This is typically called the **Number of Batches, Channels, Height, Width (NCHW/BCHW)** format. In short, what we're saying is that there are 32 filters we wish to learn, each filter has a height and width of (3, 3), and it has one color channel. MNIST is, after all, black and white.

 BCHW is not the only format! Some deep learning frameworks prefer to use BHWC formats. The reason for preferring one format over another is purely operational. Some convolution algorithms work better with NCHW; some work better with BHWC. The ones in Gorgonia works only in BCHW.

The choice of a 3 x 3 filter is purely unprincipled but not without precedence. You could choose a 5 x 5 filter, or a 2 x 1 filter, or really, a filter of any shape. However, it has to be said that a 3 x 3 filter is probably the most universal filter that can work on all sorts of images. Square filters of these sorts are common in image-processing algorithms, so it is in accordance to such traditions that we chose a 3 x 3.

The weights for the higher layers start to look a bit more interesting. For example, `w1` has a shape of (64, 32, 3, 3). Why? In order to understand why, we need to explore the interplay between the activation functions and the shapes. Here's the entire forward function of the `convnet`:

```
// This function is particularly verbose for educational reasons. In
reality, you'd wrap up the layers within a layer struct type and perform
per-layer activations
func (m *convnet) fwd(x *gorgonia.Node) (err error) {
    var c0, c1, c2, fc *gorgonia.Node
    var a0, a1, a2, a3 *gorgonia.Node
    var p0, p1, p2 *gorgonia.Node
```

```go
    var l0, l1, l2, l3 *gorgonia.Node

    // LAYER 0
    // here we convolve with stride = (1, 1) and padding = (1, 1),
    // which is your bog standard convolution for convnet
    if c0, err = gorgonia.Conv2d(x, m.w0, tensor.Shape{3, 3}, []int{1, 1},
[]int{1, 1}, []int{1, 1}); err != nil {
        return errors.Wrap(err, "Layer 0 Convolution failed")
    }
    if a0, err = gorgonia.Rectify(c0); err != nil {
        return errors.Wrap(err, "Layer 0 activation failed")
    }
    if p0, err = gorgonia.MaxPool2D(a0, tensor.Shape{2, 2}, []int{0, 0},
[]int{2, 2}); err != nil {
        return errors.Wrap(err, "Layer 0 Maxpooling failed")
    }
    if l0, err = gorgonia.Dropout(p0, m.d0); err != nil {
        return errors.Wrap(err, "Unable to apply a dropout")
    }

    // Layer 1
    if c1, err = gorgonia.Conv2d(l0, m.w1, tensor.Shape{3, 3}, []int{1, 1},
[]int{1, 1}, []int{1, 1}); err != nil {
        return errors.Wrap(err, "Layer 1 Convolution failed")
    }
    if a1, err = gorgonia.Rectify(c1); err != nil {
        return errors.Wrap(err, "Layer 1 activation failed")
    }
    if p1, err = gorgonia.MaxPool2D(a1, tensor.Shape{2, 2}, []int{0, 0},
[]int{2, 2}); err != nil {
        return errors.Wrap(err, "Layer 1 Maxpooling failed")
    }
    if l1, err = gorgonia.Dropout(p1, m.d1); err != nil {
        return errors.Wrap(err, "Unable to apply a dropout to layer 1")
    }

    // Layer 2
    if c2, err = gorgonia.Conv2d(l1, m.w2, tensor.Shape{3, 3}, []int{1, 1},
[]int{1, 1}, []int{1, 1}); err != nil {
        return errors.Wrap(err, "Layer 2 Convolution failed")
    }
    if a2, err = gorgonia.Rectify(c2); err != nil {
        return errors.Wrap(err, "Layer 2 activation failed")
    }
    if p2, err = gorgonia.MaxPool2D(a2, tensor.Shape{2, 2}, []int{0, 0},
[]int{2, 2}); err != nil {
        return errors.Wrap(err, "Layer 2 Maxpooling failed")
    }
```

```
    log.Printf("p2 shape %v", p2.Shape())

    var r2 *gorgonia.Node
    b, c, h, w := p2.Shape()[0], p2.Shape()[1], p2.Shape()[2],
p2.Shape()[3]
    if r2, err = gorgonia.Reshape(p2, tensor.Shape{b, c * h * w}); err !=
nil {
        return errors.Wrap(err, "Unable to reshape layer 2")
    }
    log.Printf("r2 shape %v", r2.Shape())
    if l2, err = gorgonia.Dropout(r2, m.d2); err != nil {
        return errors.Wrap(err, "Unable to apply a dropout on layer 2")
    }

    // Layer 3
    if fc, err = gorgonia.Mul(l2, m.w3); err != nil {
        return errors.Wrapf(err, "Unable to multiply l2 and w3")
    }
    if a3, err = gorgonia.Rectify(fc); err != nil {
        return errors.Wrapf(err, "Unable to activate fc")
    }
    if l3, err = gorgonia.Dropout(a3, m.d3); err != nil {
        return errors.Wrapf(err, "Unable to apply a dropout on layer 3")
    }

    // output decode
    var out *gorgonia.Node
    if out, err = gorgonia.Mul(l3, m.w4); err != nil {
        return errors.Wrapf(err, "Unable to multiply l3 and w4")
    }
    m.out, err = gorgonia.SoftMax(out)
    gorgonia.Read(m.out, &m.outVal)
    return
}
```

It should be noted that convolution layers do change the shape of the inputs. Given an (N, 1, 28, 28) input, the `Conv2d` function will return a (N, 32, 28, 28) output, precisely because there are now 32 filters. The `MaxPool2d` will return an output with the shape of (N, 32, 14, 14); recall that the purpose of max-pooling is to reduce the amount of information in the neural network. It just happens that max-pooling with a shape of (2, 2) will nicely halve the length and width of the image (and reduce the amount of information by four times).

The output of layer 0 would have a shape of (N, 32, 14, 14). If we stick to our explanations of our shapes from earlier, where it was in the format of (N, C, H, W), we would be quite stumped. What does it mean to have 32 channels? To answer that, let's look at how we encode a color image in terms of BCHW:

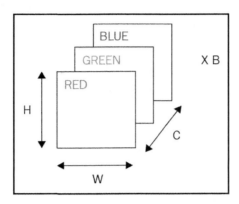

Note that we encode it as three separate layers, stacked onto one another. This is a clue as to how to think about having 32 channels. Of course, each of the 32 channels as the result of applying each of the 32 filters; the extracted features, so to speak. The result can, of course, be stacked in the same way color channels be stacked.

For the most part, however, the mere act of symbol pushing is all that is required to build a deep learning system; no real intelligence is required. This, of course mirrors, the Chinese Room Puzzle thought experiment, and I have quite a bit to say on that, though it's not really the time nor the place.

The more interesting parts is in the construction of Layer 3. Layers 1 and 2 are constructed very similarly to Layer 0, but Layer 3 has a slightly different construction. The reason is because the output of Layer 2 is a rank-4 tensor, but in order to perform matrix multiplication, it needs to be reshaped into a rank-2 tensor.

Lastly, the final layer, which decodes the output, uses a softmax activation function to ensure that the result we get is probability.

And really, there you have it. A CNN, written in a very neat way that does not obfuscate the mathematical definitions.

Backpropagation

For the convnet to learn, what is required is backpropagation, which propagates the errors, and a gradient descent function to update the weight matrices. To do this is relatively simple with Gorgonia, so simple that we can actually put it into our main function without impacting understandability:

```go
func main() {
    flag.Parse()
    parseDtype()
    imgs, err := readImageFile(os.Open("train-images-idx3-ubyte"))
    if err != nil {
        log.Fatal(err)
    }
    labels, err := readLabelFile(os.Open("train-labels-idx1-ubyte"))
    if err != nil {
        log.Fatal(err)
    }

    inputs := prepareX(imgs)
    targets := prepareY(labels)

    // the data is in (numExamples, 784).
    // In order to use a convnet, we need to massage the data
    // into this format (batchsize, numberOfChannels, height, width).
    //
    // This translates into (numExamples, 1, 28, 28).
    //
    // This is because the convolution operators actually understand height
and width.
    //
    // The 1 indicates that there is only one channel (MNIST data is black
and white).
    numExamples := inputs.Shape()[0]
    bs := *batchsize

    if err := inputs.Reshape(numExamples, 1, 28, 28); err != nil {
        log.Fatal(err)
    }
    g := gorgonia.NewGraph()
    x := gorgonia.NewTensor(g, dt, 4, gorgonia.WithShape(bs, 1, 28, 28),
gorgonia.WithName("x"))
    y := gorgonia.NewMatrix(g, dt, gorgonia.WithShape(bs, 10),
gorgonia.WithName("y"))
    m := newConvNet(g)
    if err = m.fwd(x); err != nil {
        log.Fatalf("%+v", err)
```

```
    }
    losses := gorgonia.Must(gorgonia.HadamardProd(m.out, y))
    cost := gorgonia.Must(gorgonia.Mean(losses))
    cost = gorgonia.Must(gorgonia.Neg(cost))

    // we wanna track costs
    var costVal gorgonia.Value
    gorgonia.Read(cost, &costVal)

    if _, err = gorgonia.Grad(cost, m.learnables()...); err != nil {
        log.Fatal(err)
    }
```

For the errors, we use a simple cross-entropy by multiplying the expected output element-wise and then averaging it, as shown in this snippet:

```
    losses := gorgonia.Must(gorgonia.HadamardProd(m.out, y))
    cost := gorgonia.Must(gorgonia.Mean(losses))
    cost = gorgonia.Must(gorgonia.Neg(cost))
```

Following that, we simply call `gorgonia.Grad(cost, m.learnables()...)`, which performs symbolic backpropagation. What is `m.learnables()`?, you may ask. It's simply the variables that we wish the machine to learn. The definition is as such:

```
func (m *convnet) learnables() gorgonia.Nodes {
    return gorgonia.Nodes{m.w0, m.w1, m.w2, m.w3, m.w4}
}
```

Again, it's fairly simple.

One additional comment I want the reader to note is `gorgonia.Read(cost, &costVal)`. `Read` is one of the more confusing parts of Gorgonia. But when framed correctly, it is quite simple to understand.

Earlier, in the section *Describing a neural network*, I likened Gorgonia to writing in another programming language. If so, then `Read` is the equivalent of `io.WriteFile`. What `gorgonia.Read(cost, &costVal)` says is that when the mathematical expression gets evaluated, make a copy of the result of `cost` and store it in `costVal`. This is necessary because of the way mathematical expressions are evaluated within the Gorgonia system.

 Why is it called `Read` instead of `Write`? I initially modeled Gorgonia to be quite monadic (in the Haskell sense of monad), and as a result, one would *read out* a value. After a span of three years, the name sort of stuck.

Running the neural network

Observe that up to this point, we've merely described the computations we need to perform. The neural network doesn't actually run; this is simply a description on the neural network to run.

We need to be able to evaluate the mathematical expression. In order to do so, we need to compile the expression into a program that can be executed. Here's the code to do it:

```
vm := gorgonia.NewTapeMachine(g,
    gorgonia.WithPrecompiled(prog, locMap),
    gorgonia.BindDualValues(m.learnables()...))
solver :=
gorgonia.NewRMSPropSolver(gorgonia.WithBatchSize(float64(bs)))
    defer vm.Close()
```

It's not strictly necessary to call `gorgonia.Compile(g)`. This was done for pedagogical reasons, to showcase that the mathematical expression can indeed be compiled down into an assembly-like program. In production systems, I often just do something like this: `vm := gorgonia.NewTapeMachine(g, gorgonia.BindDualValues(m.learnables()...))`.

There are two provided `vm` types in Gorgonia, each representing different modes of computation. In this project, we're merely using `NewTapeMachine` to get a `*gorgonia.tapeMachine`. The function to create a `vm` takes many options, and the `BindDualValues` option simply binds the gradients of each of the variables in the models to the variables themselves. This allows for cheaper gradient descent.

Lastly, note that a VM is a resource. You should think of a VM as if it were an external CPU, a computing resource. It is good practice to close any external resources after we use them and, fortunately, Go has a very convenient way of handling cleanups: `defer vm.Close()`.

Before we move on to talk about gradient descent, here's what the compiled program looks like, in pseudo-assembly:

```
Instructions:
0 loadArg 0 (x) to CPU0
1 loadArg 1 (y) to CPU1
2 loadArg 2 (w0) to CPU2
3 loadArg 3 (w1) to CPU3
4 loadArg 4 (w2) to CPU4
5 loadArg 5 (w3) to CPU5
6 loadArg 6 (w4) to CPU6
7 im2col<(3,3), (1, 1), (1,1) (1, 1)> [CPU0] CPU7 false false false
8 Reshape(32, 9) [CPU2] CPU8 false false false
9 Reshape(78400, 9) [CPU7] CPU7 false true false
```

```
10 Alloc Matrix float64(78400, 32) CPU9
11 A × Bᵀ [CPU7 CPU8] CPU9 true false true
12 DoWork
13 Reshape(100, 28, 28, 32) [CPU9] CPU9 false true false
14 Aᵀ{0, 3, 1, 2} [CPU9] CPU9 false true false
15 const 0 [] CPU10 false false false
16 >= true [CPU9 CPU10] CPU11 false false false
17 ⊙ false [CPU9 CPU11] CPU9 false true false
18 MaxPool{100, 32, 28, 28}(kernel: (2, 2), pad: (0, 0), stride: (2,
                        2)) [CPU9] CPU12 false false false
19 0(0, 1) - (100, 32, 14, 14) [] CPU13 false false false
20 const 0.2 [] CPU14 false false false
21 > true [CPU13 CPU14] CPU15 false false false
22 ⊙ false [CPU12 CPU15] CPU12 false true false
23 const 5 [] CPU16 false false false
24 ÷ false [CPU12 CPU16] CPU12 false true false
25 im2col<(3,3), (1, 1), (1,1) (1, 1)> [CPU12] CPU17 false false false
26 Reshape(64, 288) [CPU3] CPU18 false false false
27 Reshape(19600, 288) [CPU17] CPU17 false true false
28 Alloc Matrix float64(19600, 64) CPU19
29 A × Bᵀ [CPU17 CPU18] CPU19 true false true
30 DoWork
31 Reshape(100, 14, 14, 64) [CPU19] CPU19 false true false
32 Aᵀ{0, 3, 1, 2} [CPU19] CPU19 false true false
33 >= true [CPU19 CPU10] CPU20 false false false
34 ⊙ false [CPU19 CPU20] CPU19 false true false
35 MaxPool{100, 64, 14, 14}(kernel: (2, 2), pad: (0, 0), stride: (2,
                        2)) [CPU19] CPU21 false false false
36 0(0, 1) - (100, 64, 7, 7) [] CPU22 false false false
37 > true [CPU22 CPU14] CPU23 false false false
38 ⊙ false [CPU21 CPU23] CPU21 false true false
39 ÷ false [CPU21 CPU16] CPU21 false true false
40 im2col<(3,3), (1, 1), (1,1) (1, 1)> [CPU21] CPU24 false false false
41 Reshape(128, 576) [CPU4] CPU25 false false false
42 Reshape(4900, 576) [CPU24] CPU24 false true false
43 Alloc Matrix float64(4900, 128) CPU26
44 A × Bᵀ [CPU24 CPU25] CPU26 true false true
45 DoWork
46 Reshape(100, 7, 7, 128) [CPU26] CPU26 false true false
47 Aᵀ{0, 3, 1, 2} [CPU26] CPU26 false true false
48 >= true [CPU26 CPU10] CPU27 false false false
49 ⊙ false [CPU26 CPU27] CPU26 false true false
50 MaxPool{100, 128, 7, 7}(kernel: (2, 2), pad: (0, 0), stride: (2,
                        2)) [CPU26] CPU28 false false false
51 Reshape(100, 1152) [CPU28] CPU28 false true false
52 0(0, 1) - (100, 1152) [] CPU29 false false false
53 > true [CPU29 CPU14] CPU30 false false false
54 ⊙ false [CPU28 CPU30] CPU28 false true false
```

```
55 ÷ false [CPU28 CPU16] CPU28 false true false
56 Alloc Matrix float64(100, 625) CPU31
57 A × B [CPU28 CPU5] CPU31 true false true
58 DoWork
59 >= true [CPU31 CPU10] CPU32 false false false
60 ⊙ false [CPU31 CPU32] CPU31 false true false
61 0(0, 1) - (100, 625) [] CPU33 false false false
62 const 0.55 [] CPU34 false false false
63 > true [CPU33 CPU34] CPU35 false false false
64 ⊙ false [CPU31 CPU35] CPU31 false true false
65 const 1.8181818181818181 [] CPU36 false false false
66 ÷ false [CPU31 CPU36] CPU31 false true false
67 Alloc Matrix float64(100, 10) CPU37
68 A × B [CPU31 CPU6] CPU37 true false true
69 DoWork
70 exp [CPU37] CPU37 false true false
71 Σ[1] [CPU37] CPU38 false false false
72 SizeOf=10 [CPU37] CPU39 false false false
73 Repeat[1] [CPU38 CPU39] CPU40 false false false
74 ÷ false [CPU37 CPU40] CPU37 false true false
75 ⊙ false [CPU37 CPU1] CPU37 false true false
76 Σ[0 1] [CPU37] CPU41 false false false
77 SizeOf=100 [CPU37] CPU42 false false false
78 SizeOf=10 [CPU37] CPU43 false false false
79 ⊙ false [CPU42 CPU43] CPU44 false false false
80 ÷ false [CPU41 CPU44] CPU45 false false false
81 neg [CPU45] CPU46 false false false
82 DoWork
83 Read CPU46 into 0xc43ca407d0
84 Free CPU0
Args: 11 | CPU Memories: 47 | GPU Memories: 0
CPU Mem: 133594448 | GPU Mem []
``` ` `
```

Printing the program allows you to actually have a feel for the complexity of the neural network. At 84 instructions, the convnet is among the simpler programs I've seen. However, there are quite a few expensive operations, which would inform us quite a bit about how long each run would take. This output also tells us roughly how many bytes of memory will be used: 133594448 bytes, or 133 megabytes.
```

Now it's time to talk about, gradient descent. Gorgonia comes with a number of gradient descent solvers. For this project, we'll be using the RMSProp algorithm. So, we create a solver by calling `solver :=`
`gorgonia.NewRMSPropSolver(gorgonia.WithBatchSize(float64(bs)))`. Because we are planning to perform our operations in batches, we should correct the solver by providing it the batch size, lest the solver overshoots its target.

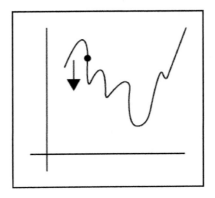

To run the neural network, we simply run it for a number of epochs (which is passed in as an argument to the program):

```
batches := numExamples / bs
log.Printf("Batches %d", batches)
bar := pb.New(batches)
bar.SetRefreshRate(time.Second)
bar.SetMaxWidth(80)

for i := 0; i < *epochs; i++ {
    bar.Prefix(fmt.Sprintf("Epoch %d", i))
    bar.Set(0)
    bar.Start()
    for b := 0; b < batches; b++ {
        start := b * bs
        end := start + bs
        if start >= numExamples {
            break
        }
        if end > numExamples {
            end = numExamples
        }

        var xVal, yVal tensor.Tensor
        if xVal, err = inputs.Slice(sli{start, end}); err != nil {
            log.Fatal("Unable to slice x")
```

```
        }

        if yVal, err = targets.Slice(sli{start, end}); err != nil {
            log.Fatal("Unable to slice y")
        }
        if err = xVal.(*tensor.Dense).Reshape(bs, 1, 28, 28); err !=
nil {
            log.Fatalf("Unable to reshape %v", err)
        }

        gorgonia.Let(x, xVal)
        gorgonia.Let(y, yVal)
        if err = vm.RunAll(); err != nil {
            log.Fatalf("Failed at epoch  %d: %v", i, err)
        }
        solver.Step(gorgonia.NodesToValueGrads(m.learnables()))
        vm.Reset()
        bar.Increment()
    }
    log.Printf("Epoch %d | cost %v", i, costVal)
}
```

Because I was feeling a bit fancy, I decided to add a progress bar to track the progress. To do so, I'm using `cheggaaa/pb.v1` as the library to draw a progress bar. To install it, simply run `go get gopkg.in/cheggaaa/pb.v1` and to use it, simply add `import "gopkg.in/cheggaaa/pb.v1` in the imports.

The rest is fairly straightforward. From the training dataset, we slice out a small portion of it (specifically, we slice out `bs` rows). Because our program takes a rank-4 tensor as an input, the data has to be reshaped to `xVal.(*tensor.Dense).Reshape(bs, 1, 28, 28)`.

Finally, we feed the value into the function by using `gorgonia.Let`. Where `gorgonia.Read` reads a value out from the execution environment, `gorgonia.Let` puts a value into the execution environment. After which, `vm.RunAll()` executes the program, evaluating the mathematical function. As a programmed and intentional side-effect, each call to `vm.RunAll()` will populate the cost value into `costVal`.

Once the equation has been evaluated, this also means that the variables of the equation are now ready to be updated. As such, we use `solver.Step(gorgonia.NodesToValueGrads(m.learnables()))` to perform the actual gradient updates. After this, `vm.Reset()` is called to reset the VM state, ready for its next iteration.

Gorgonia in general, is pretty efficient. In the current version as this book was written, it managed to use all eight cores in my CPU as shown here:

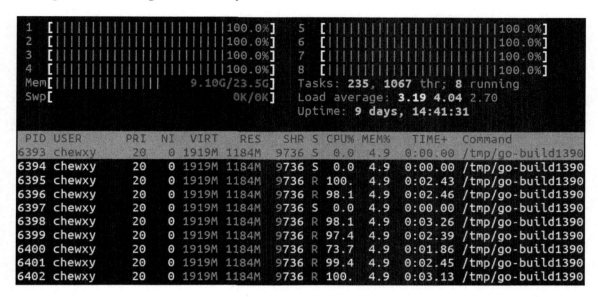

Testing

Of course we'd have to test our neural network.

First we load up the testing data:

```
testImgs, err := readImageFile(os.Open("t10k-images.idx3-ubyte"))
if err != nil {
   log.Fatal(err)
}

testlabels, err := readLabelFile(os.Open("t10k-labels.idx1-ubyte"))
   if err != nil {
      log.Fatal(err)
   }

testData := prepareX(testImgs)
testLbl := prepareY(testlabels)
shape := testData.Shape()
visualize(testData, 10, 10, "testData.png")
```

In the last line, we visualize the test data to ensure that we do indeed have the correct dataset:

Then we have the main testing loop. Do observe that it's extremely similar to the training loop - because it's the same neural network!

```
var correct, total float32
numExamples = shape[0]
batches = numExamples / bs
for b := 0; b < batches; b++ {
    start := b * bs
    end := start + bs
    if start >= numExamples {
        break
    }
    if end > numExamples {
        end = numExamples
    }

var oneimg, onelabel tensor.Tensor
        if oneimg, err = testData.Slice(sli{start, end}); err != nil {
            log.Fatalf("Unable to slice images (%d, %d)", start, end)
        }
        if onelabel, err = testLbl.Slice(sli{start, end}); err != nil {
            log.Fatalf("Unable to slice labels (%d, %d)", start, end)
        }
        if err = oneimg.(*tensor.Dense).Reshape(bs, 1, 28, 28); err != nil
    {
            log.Fatalf("Unable to reshape %v", err)
        }
```

```
gorgonia.Let(x, oneimg)
gorgonia.Let(y, onelabel)
if err = vm.RunAll(); err != nil {
    log.Fatal("Predicting (%d, %d) failed %v", start, end, err)
}
label, _ := onelabel.(*tensor.Dense).Argmax(1)
predicted, _ := m.outVal.(*tensor.Dense).Argmax(1)
lblData := label.Data().([]int)
for i, p := range predicted.Data().([]int) {
    if p == lblData[i] {
        correct++
    }
    total++
}
}

    fmt.Printf("Correct/Totals: %v/%v = %1.3f\n", correct, total,
correct/total)
```

One difference is in the following snippet:

```
label, _ := onelabel.(*tensor.Dense).Argmax(1)
predicted, _ := m.outVal.(*tensor.Dense).Argmax(1)
lblData := label.Data().([]int)
for i, p := range predicted.Data().([]int) {
    if p == lblData[i] {
        correct++
        }
        total++
    }
```

In the previous chapter, we wrote our own argmax function. Gorgonia's tensor package actually does provide a handy method for doing just that. But in order to understand what is going on, we will need to first look at the results.

The shape of m.outVal is (N, 10), where N is the batch size. The same shape also shows for onelabel. (N, 10) means N rows of 10 columns. What can these 10 columns be? Well, of course they're the encoded numbers! So what we want is to find the maximum values amongst the column for each row. And that's the first dimension. Hence when a call to .ArgMax() is made, we specify 1 as the axis.

Therefore the result of the .Argmax() calls will have a shape (N). For each value in that vector, if they are the same for lblData and predicted, then we increment the correct counter. This gives us a way to count accuracy.

Accuracy

We use accuracy because the previous chapter used accuracy. This allows us to have a apples-to-apples comparison. Additionally you may note that there is a lack of cross validation. That will be left as an exercise to the reader.

After training the neural network for two hours on a batch size of 50 and 150 epochs, I'm pleased to say I got a 99.87% accuracy. And this isn't even state of the art!

In the previous chapter, it took just 6.5 minutes to get a 97% accuracy. That additional 2% accuracy required a lot more time. This is a factor in real life. Often business decisions are a big factor in choosing ML algorithm.

Summary

In this chapter, we learned about neural networks and studied about the Gorgonia library in detail. Then we learned how to recognize handwritten digits using a CNN.

In the next chapter, we're going to strengthen our intuition about what can be done with computer vision, by building a multiple facial-detection system in Go.

8
Basic Facial Detection

The previous chapters can best be described as trying to read an image. This is a subfield in machine learning called **computer vision (CV)**. With convolutional neural networks (`Chapter 7`, *Convolutional Neural Networks – MNIST Handwriting Recognition*), we found that the convolutional layers learned how to filter an image.

There is a common misconception that any **machine learning (ML)** worth doing has to come from neural networks and deep learning. This is decidedly not the case. Instead, one should view deep learning as a technique to get to one's goals; deep learning is not the end-all. The purpose of this chapter is to expose readers to some of the insights into making ML algorithms work better in production. The code for this chapter is exceedingly simple. The topic is trivial and widely considered by many to be solved. However, the insights are not trivial. It is my hope that this chapter propels the reader to think more deeply about the problems that they face.

To that end, the algorithms that will be introduced in this chapter began their life in academia. However, the invention of these algorithms was driven by a highly practical requirement, and one can learn quite a lot by analyzing how these algorithms were invented.

In this chapter, we're going to further improve our knowledge about what can be done with computer vision, by building multiple facial detection systems in Go. We will be using `GoCV` and `Pigo`. What we will be building is a program that detects faces from a live webcam. However, this chapter will be different from the previous ones, in that we will be comparing two kinds of algorithms. The purpose is to allow the reader to think more about the actual problems faced, rather than just copy-pasting code.

What is a face?

In order to detect faces, we need to understand what a face is, specifically what a human face is. Think about a typical human face. A typical human face has two eyes, a nose, and a mouth. But having these features isn't enough to define a human face. Dogs also have two eyes, a nose, and a mouth. We are, after all, products of mammalian evolution.

I encourage the reader to think more carefully about what makes a human face. We instinctively know what a face is, but to really quantify exactly what constitutes a face takes work. Often, it may lead to philosophical ruminations about essentialism.

If you watch terrible procedural TV shows, you might see faces being drawn with dots and lines when the detectives on TV are doing facial recognition across a database. These dots and lines are primarily due to the work of Woodrow Bledsoe, Helen Chan, and Charles Bisson in the 1960s. They were among the first people to study automated facial detection. One of the first things noticed is that the standard features of the face—hairline, browlines, gauntness of eyes, height of nose bridge, and so on—are all dynamically definable; that is to say that these features are measured relative to one another. This made automatically detecting features a little bit more challenging than expected.

Their solution was novel: using a device that is an ancestor to today's drawing tablets, annotate the location of eyes, nose, mouth, and other facial features. The distances between these annotations are then used as features for facial recognition. The process today is no different, except a lot more automatic. The works of Bledsoe, Chan, and gang led to an immense effort to quantify how pixels would co-occur to form facial features.

In order to understand the features that make up a face, abstract. What is the minimum possible number of dots and lines required to depict a face? It is instructive to note abstractions in the use of kaomoji. Consider the following kaomoji:

```
(^‿^)
( _ )
( ˘‿˘)
(   )
( ` ´)
```

It's quite easy to see that these depict faces. Contrast them with kaomojis that depict other things (fish, spider, gun, and bomb respectively):

```
<.))))><<
/\/\ ┌( ͡° ͜ʖ ͡°)┐ /\/\
 ⊥╤══─
●~*
```

The process of abstraction—the act of removing details until only the ones that matter remain—allows one to think more clearly about a subject matter. This is true in art, as it is in mathematics. It is equally true of software engineering, though careful implementation of the abstractions needs be made. Going back to the kaomojis, note that, even in their highly abstract form, they are capable of displaying emotions. In order of display, the kaomojis show happiness, indifference, love, dissatisfaction, and anger. These abstract depictions offer us a path to think about the facial features in pictures. To determine whether a face exists, we simply determine if those lines are there. The question now becomes how do we take a photo and draw lines?

Start with the facial structure and assume an evenly-lit room. Barring diseases such as Graves which cause proptosis, eyes are generally sunken. This causes the area of the eyes to be shadowed by the brow ridge of the face, as well as cheekbones. In pictures of an evenly-lit face, eyes would appear in shadow. Noses, on the other hand, would appear more brightly lit, because noses are raised compared with the rest of the face. Likewise, lips have a dark area and a bright area, separated by a dark line. These are all useful features to consider when thinking about detecting faces.

Viola-Jones

Fast forward to the early 2000s. Facial detection methodologies leaped forwards with Viola and Jones introducing a very fast method of detecting objects. The `Viola-Jones` method, while generic enough for the detection of any object, was primarily geared to detecting faces. The key genius to the Viola-Jones method is that it used many small classifiers to classify a region of an image, in a staged fashion. This is called the **cascade classifier**.

 To make the explanation clearer, whenever *classifier* is used in the context of the Viola-Jones method, I mean the small classifiers in the cascade classifier. When referring to the cascade classifier, it will be explicitly mentioned as such.

A cascade classifier is made up of many small classifiers. Each classifier is made up of multiple filters. For a brief introduction to filters, see the previous chapter (How Instagram filters work). To detect faces, first start with a small section (called a **window**) of the image. Run the classifiers one by one. If the sum of the result of applying all the filters in the classifier exceeds a predefined threshold for the classifier, then it's considered to be part of a face. Then, the cascade classifier moves on to the next classifier. This is the *cascading* part of the cascading classifier. Once all the classifiers are done, the window slides to the next pixel, and the process begins anew. Should a classifier in the cascade classifier fail to identify something as part of the face, the entire region is rejected and the sliding window slides on.

The filters work by detecting the aforementioned light and dark areas of the face. Take, for example, the fact that the areas around the eyes are typically sunken and therefore shadowed. If we are to apply a filter to an area, we would highlight only the eyes:

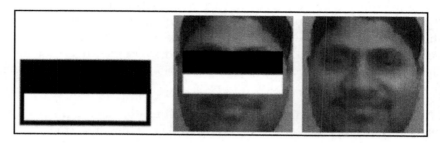

A classifier for eyes would have multiple filters, configured to test against the possible configurations of eyes. A classifier for the nose would have multiple filters specific to the nose. In a cascading classifier, we could arrange the importance; perhaps we define the eyes as the most important part of the face (they are after all windows to the soul). We could arrange it so that the cascade classifier first classifies a region for eyes. If there are eyes, we then look for the nose, then the mouth. Otherwise, the sliding window should slide on:

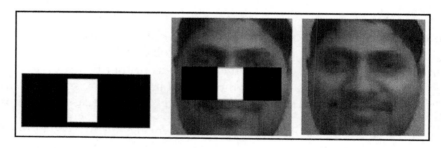

Another point of innovation with Viola-Jones is that the method was designed to work on an image pyramid. What is an image pyramid? Imagine you have yourself a large 1024 x 768 image. This image has two faces of multiple scales. There is one person standing very close to the camera, and one person standing far away. Anyone with any familiarity with the optics of cameras would instantly realize that the person standing close to the camera will have a much larger face in the image compared to the person standing far away from the camera. The question is, how would we be able to detect both faces at different scales?

One possible answer is to design multiple filters, one for each possible scale. But that leaves a lot of room for error. Instead of designing multiple filters, the same filters can be reused, if the image is resized multiple times:

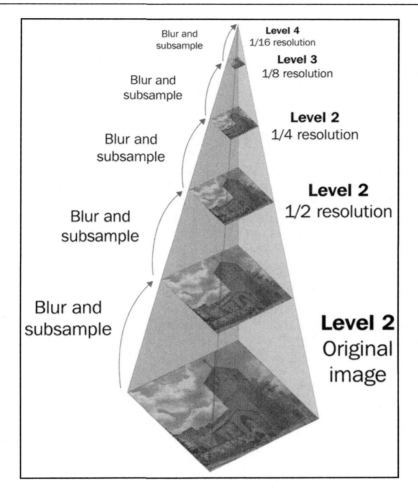

The face that is very close to the camera wouldn't be detected by a filter designed to detect a small face. Instead, in the original resolution, the classifier will detect the smaller face. Then, the image is resized so that the resolution is now smaller, say 640 x 480. The big face is now small, and the small faces are now single dots. The classifier will now be able to detect the large face and not the small faces. But in total, the classifier would have detected all the faces in the image. Because the images are directly resized, coordinates in the smaller image can be easily translated into coordinates in the original image. This allows for detection in the smaller scale to be directly translated into detections in the original scale.

At this point, if you have read the previous chapter, this starts to feel somewhat familiar. **Convolutional Neural Networks (CNNs)** work in a remarkably similar way. In a CNN, multiple filters are applied to a sub-region, producing a filtered image. The filtered image is then passed through a reduction layer (max-pooling, or some other reduction method). The key in CNNs is to learn what the filters would be. In fact, the first layer of each CNN learns filters that are extremely similar to the filters used in the Viola-Jones method.

The primary similarities are that Viola-Jones essentially amounts to having a sliding window and applying filters to the section of the image. This is comparable to convolutions in a CNN. Where CNNs have an advantage is that they are capable of learning those filters, whereas in the Viola-Jones method the filters are manually created. The Viola-Jones method on the other hand has the benefit of cascading: it may terminate searching a section for faces early if one of the classifiers fails. This saves a lot of computation. Indeed, such was the influence of the Viola-Jones method that it inspired the *Joint Face Detection and Alignment Using Multitask Cascaded Convolutional Networks* by Zhang et al. in 2016, which used three neural networks in cascading fashion to recognize faces.

It would be tempting to equate the image pyramid with what the pooling layers do in a CNN. This wouldn't be correct. Multi-scale detection in the Viola-Jones method is a neat trick, while pooling layers in a CNN lead to the learning of higher order features. CNNs learn higher order features such as eyes, noses, and mouths, whereas the Viola Jones method doesn't.

In light of this, one may wonder if CNNs may be better. They do detect faces the way humans do—by identifying eyes, noses, and mouths as features, as opposed to filtering patterns on pixels. There are still reasons to use Viola-Jones today. At this point in time, the Viola-Jones method is well understood and well optimized in libraries. It comes built into GoCV, which is what we'll use. The method is also faster than deep learning-based models, at some expense of flexibility. Most Viola-Jones models only detect faces if those faces are front-facing. Additionally, the Viola-Jones method may not detect rotated faces (terrible if you want to detect the face of a head-turning demon as proof to give an exorcist).

Depending on use cases, one might not need deep learning-based systems to perform facial detection at all!

PICO

Another technique we'll be using is **Pixel Intensity Comparison-based Object detection (PICO)**, originally developed by Markus, Frljak, et al. in 2014. It uses the same broad principles as the Viola-Jones method, in that there is a cascade classifier. It differs in two ways. First, a sliding window is not used. This is due to the latter differences. Second, the classifiers of the cascade classifier are different from that of Viola-Jones. In Viola-Jones, a method of applying filters repeatedly and then summing the result is used as a classifier. By contrast, in PICO, decision trees are used.

A decision tree is a tree where each node is a feature, and the branching of the feature is defined by a threshold. In the case of PICO, the decision tree applies for each pixel in the photo. For each pixel considered, the intensity is compared against the intensity of another pixel at another location. These locations are generated from a uniform distribution, obviating the need for a sliding window.

The PICO method also does away with needing image pyramids and integral images. The classifiers are capable of detecting faces straight away from an image. This makes it very fast.

Nonetheless, the legacy of Viola-Jones is evident. The classifiers are applied in stages. First, the simpler classifiers are used. This would eliminate areas where the probability of faces existing is low. Next, more complex classifiers are used on the reduced search areas. This is repeated until the last stage is reached. The results of each classifier are retained for later use.

The reader might come to realize that areas in a picture that definitely has a face will be searched by more classifiers. It is with this intuition that the authors introduced a final clustering step in the PICO classifier. The rule is simple: if there is an overlap of areas searched by the classifier, and the overlap percentage is greater than 30%, it's considered to be part of the same cluster. Thus, the final result is robust to small changes.

A note on learning

You may have noted that in describing the algorithms previously, I have neglected to mention the training procedures for how these models learn. This omission is rather deliberate. As we will not be training any models, how the Viola-Jones method and the PICO method are trained to produce models will be left as an exercise for the reader.

Instead, in this chapter we wish to use already created models. These models are commonly used in practice. We will then compare and contrast the methods to find out their pros and cons.

GoCV

In this chapter, we will be using GoCV. GoCV is a binding for OpenCV and comes with a suite of features from OpenCV that can be used. One of the features from OpenCV is the Viola-Jones classifier, which we will use to our advantage.

Installing GoCV is a little tricky, however. It requires OpenCV to be installed beforehand. At the time of writing, the version supported by GoCV is OpenCV 3.4.2. Installing OpenCV can be quite a painful experience. Perhaps the best place to find out *how* to install OpenCV is a website called **Learn OpenCV**. They have great guides on installing OpenCV on all platforms:

- Installing OpenCV on Ubuntu: `https://www.learnopencv.com/install-opencv3-on-ubuntu/`
- Installing OpenCV on Windows: `https://www.learnopencv.com/install-opencv3-on-windows/`
- Installing OpenCV on MacOS: `https://www.learnopencv.com/install-opencv3-on-macos/`

After the daunting process of installing OpenCV is done, installing GoCV is a piece of cake. Simply run `go get -u gocv.io.x.gocv`, and Bob's your uncle.

API

The API of GoCV matches the API of OpenCV quite well. A particularly good API to showcase is the display window. With the display window, one is able to display the image the webcam is receiving live. It's also a very useful tool for debugging, in cases where one might want to write a new classifier.

I have developed programs for many years. It's fair to say I've seen many design patterns and packages. Among the prickliest problems to have for almost all programming languages is the foreign function interface, when a program has to call a library written in another language. Not many are well done. Most are shoddily done, as if something is plastered over the underlying **foreign function interface (FFI)**. In Go, FFI is handled by cgo.

Very often, library authors (myself included) get too smart, and attempt to manage resources on behalf of the users. While at first blush this may seem to be good UX, good customer service even, this ultimately leads to much pain. At the time of writing, Gorgonia itself had just undergone a series of refactors to make the resource metaphors more clear, specifically with regards to CUDA usage.

With all this said, GoCV is probably one of the most consistent Go libraries with regards to its cgo usage. The part where GoCV is consistent is in its treatment of foreign objects. Everything is treated as a resource; hence, most types have a `.Close()` method. There are certainly other beauties of GoCV, including the `customenv` build tags, which allow library users to define where OpenCV is installed, but the chief compliment I have for GoCV is in its consistency with regards to treating OpenCV objects as an external resource.

The treatment of objects with the resource metaphor guides us in our use of the GoCV API. All objects must be closed after use, which is a simple rule to abide by.

Pigo

Pigo is a Go library for detecting faces by using the PICO algorithm. Compared to the Viola-Jones method, PICO is fast. Naturally, PIGO is fast too. Add this to the fact that GoCV uses cgo, which adds a penalty for speed, and PIGO may seem to be a better option overall. However, it must be noted that the PICO algorithm is more prone to false positives than the original Viola-Jones method.

Using the PIGO library is simple. The provided documentation is clear. However, PIGO was designed to run within the author's workflow. Differing from that workflow will require some tiny amount of extra work. Specifically, the author draws images using external helpers such as `github.com/fogleman/gg`. We shan't. However, the work isn't much.

To install `pigo`, simply run `go get -u github.com/esimov/pigo/...`.

Face detection program

What we want to do is build a program that reads an image from a webcam, passes the image into a face detector and then draws rectangles in the image. Finally, we want to display the image with the rectangles drawn on.

Grabbing an image from the webcam

First, we'll open a connection to the webcam:

```
func main() {
// open webcam
webcam, err := gocv.VideoCaptureDevice(0)
if err != nil {
log.Fatal(err)
}
defer webcam.Close()
}
```

Here, I used `VideoCaptureDevice(0)` because, on my computer, which runs Ubuntu, the webcam is device 0. Your webcam may differ in device numbering. Also, do note `defer webcam.Close()`. This is the aforementioned resource metaphor that GoCV sticks very strongly to. A webcam (specifically, a `VideoCaptureDevice`) is a resource, much like a file. In fact in Linux, this is true; the webcam on my computer is mounted in the `/dev/video0` directory and I can access raw bytes from it by just using a variant of `cat`. But I digress. The point is that `.Close()` has to be called on resources to free up usage.

 The talk about closing resources to free up usage naturally raises a question, given we program in Go. Is a channel a resource? The answer is no. `close(ch)` of a channel merely informs every sender that this channel is no longer receiving data.

Having access to the webcam is nice and all, but we also want to be able to grab images off it. I had mentioned one can read raw streams off the file of a webcam. We can do the same with GoCV as well:

```
img := gocv.NewMat()
defer img.Close()
width := int(webcam.Get(gocv.VideoCaptureFrameWidth))
height := int(webcam.Get(gocv.VideoCaptureFrameHeight))
fmt.Printf("Webcam resolution: %v, %v", width, height)
if ok := webcam.Read(&amp;img); !ok {
log.Fatal("cannot read device 0")
}
```

First, we create a new matrix, representing an image. Again, the matrix is treated like a resource, because it is owned by the foreign function interface. Thus, `defer img.Close()` is written. Next, we query the webcam for information about the resolution. This is not as important right now, but it will be later. Nonetheless, it's quite nice to know what resolution a webcam runs at. Last, we read the webcam's image into the matrix.

At this point, if you are already familiar with Gorgonia's tensor libraries, this pattern may seem familiar, and yet feels funny. `img := gocv.NewMat()` does not define a size. How does GoCV know how much space to allocate for the matrix? Well, the answer is that the magic happens in `webcam.Read`. The underlying matrix will be resized as necessary by OpenCV. In this way, the Go part of the program does no real memory allocation.

Displaying the image

So, the image has been magically read into the matrix. How do we get anything out of it?

The answer is that we have to copy the data from the data structure controlled by OpenCV into a Go-native data structure. Fortunately, GoCV handles that as well. Here, we write it out to a file:

```
goImg, err := img.ToImage()
if err != nil {
log.Fatal(err)
}
outFile, err := os.OpenFile("first.png",
os.O_WRONLY|os.O_TRUNC|os.O_CREATE, 0644)
if err != nil {
log.Fatal(err)
}
png.Encode(outFile, goImg)
```

First, the matrix has to be converted to `image.Image`. To do that, `img.ToImage()` is called. Then, it is encoded as a PNG by using `png.Encode`.

And you will have a test image. This was mine:

In the picture, I'm holding a box with a photo of Ralph Waldo Emerson, famed American author. Readers who are familiar with writing instruments may note that it's actually a brand of inks I use for my writing.

So, now we have the basic pipeline of getting an image from the webcam and writing out the image to a file. A webcam continuously captures images, but we're only reading a single image to a matrix, and then writing the matrix into a file. If we put this in a loop, we would have the ability to continuously read images from a webcam and write to file.

Analogously to having a file, we could write it to the screen instead. The GoCV integration with OpenCV is so complete that this is trivial. Instead of writing to a file, we can display a window instead.

To do so, we need to first create a window object, with the title `Face Detection Window`:

```
window := gocv.NewWindow("Face Detection Window")
defer window.Close()
```

Then, to show the image in the window, simply replace the parts where we write out to a file with this:

```
window.IMShow(img)
```

When the program is run, a window will pop up, showing you the image captured by the webcam.

Doodling on images

At some point, we would also like to draw on an image, preferably before we output it, either to the display or a file. GoCV handles that admirably. For our purposes in this chapter, we'll just be drawing rectangles to denote where a face might be. GoCV interfaces well with the standard library's `Rectangle` type.

To draw a rectangle on an image with GoCV, we first define a rectangle:

```
r := image.Rect(50, 50, 100, 100)
```

Here, I defined a rectangle that starts at location (50, 50) and is 100 pixels wide and 100 pixels tall.

Then, a color needs to be defined. Again, GoCV plays very nicely with image/color, found in the standard library. So, here's the definition of the color `blue`:

```
blue := color.RGBA{0, 0, 255, 0}
```

And now, onward to draw the rectangle on the image!:

```
gocv.Rectangle(&amp;img, r, blue, 3)
```

This draws a blue rectangle with the top left of the rectangle at (50, 50) in the image.

At this point, we have the components necessary to build two different pipelines. One writes an image to a file. One creates a window to display the image. There are two ways the input from the webcam may be processed: one-off or continuously. And, we are also able to modify the image matrix before outputting. This gives us a lot of flexibility as scaffolding in the process of building the program.

Face detection 1

The first face detection algorithm we want to use is the Viola-Jones method. It comes built into GoCV, so we can just use that. The consistency of GoCV gives us a hint as to what to do next. We need a classifier object (and remember to close it!)

This is how to create a classifier object:

```
classifier := gocv.NewCascadeClassifier()
if !classifier.Load(haarCascadeFile) {
log.Fatalf("Error reading cascade file: %v\n", haarCascadeFile)
}
defer classifier.Close()
```

Note that at this point, it is not enough to just create a classifier. We need to load it with the model to use. The model used is very well established. It was first created by Rainer Lienhart in the early 2000s. Like most products of the 2000s, the model is serialized as an XML file.

The file can be downloaded from the GoCV GitHub repository: https://github.com/ hybridgroup/gocv/blob/master/data/haarcascade_frontalface_default.xml

In the preceding code, haarCascadeFile is a string denoting the path to the file. GoCV handles the rest.

To detect faces, it is a simple one-liner:

```
rects := classifier.DetectMultiScale(img)
```

In this single line of code, we are telling OpenCV to use Viola-Jones' multiscale detection to detect faces. Internally, OpenCV builds an image pyramid of integral images, and runs the classifiers on the image pyramids. At each stage, rectangles representing where the algorithm thinks the faces are, produced. These rectangles are what is returned. They can then be drawn on the image before being output to a file or window.

Here's what a full windowed pipeline looks like:

```
var haarCascadeFile = "Path/To/CascadeFile.xml"
var blue = color.RGBA{0, 0, 255, 0}
func main() {
// open webcam
webcam, err := gocv.VideoCaptureDevice(0)
if err != nil {
log.Fatal(err)
}
defer webcam.Close()
var err error
// open display window
```

```go
 window := gocv.NewWindow("Face Detect")
 defer window.Close()
// prepare image matrix
 img := gocv.NewMat()
 defer img.Close()
// color for the rect when faces detected
// load classifier to recognize faces
 classifier := gocv.NewCascadeClassifier()
 if !classifier.Load(haarCascadeFile) {
 log.Fatalf("Error reading cascade file: %v\n", haarCascadeFile)
 }
 defer classifier.Close()
for {
 if ok := webcam.Read(&img); !ok {
 fmt.Printf("cannot read device %d\n", deviceID)
 return
 }
 if img.Empty() {
 continue
 }
 rects := classifier.DetectMultiScale(img)
for _, r := range rects {
 gocv.Rectangle(&img, r, blue, 3)
 }
window.IMShow(img)
 if window.WaitKey(1) >= 0 {
 break
 }
 }
 }

` ` `
```

The program is now able to get an image from the webcam, detect faces, draw rectangles around the faces, and then display the image. You may note that it is quite quick at doing that.

Face detection 2

In one fell swoop, GoCV has provided us with everything necessary to do real-time face detection. But is it easy to use with other face detection algorithms? The answer is yes, but some work is required.

The algorithm we want to use is the PICO algorithm. Recall that images in GoCV are in the `gocv.Mat` type. In order for PIGO to use that, we would need to convert that into a format readable by PICO. Incidentally, such a shared format is the `image.Image` of the standard library.

Recall once again that the `gocv.Mat` type has a method `.ToImage()`, which returns an `image.Image`. That's our bridge!

Before crossing it, let's look at how to create a PIGO classifier. Here's a function to do so:

```
func pigoSetup(width, height int) (*image.NRGBA, []uint8, *pigo.Pigo,
                    pigo.CascadeParams, pigo.ImageParams) {
  goImg := image.NewNRGBA(image.Rect(0, 0, width, height))
  grayGoImg := make([]uint8, width*height)
  cParams := pigo.CascadeParams{
                         MinSize: 20,
                         MaxSize: 1000,
                         ShiftFactor: 0.1,
                         ScaleFactor: 1.1,
  }
  imgParams := pigo.ImageParams{
                         Pixels: grayGoImg,
                         Rows: height,
                         Cols: width,
                         Dim: width,
  }
  classifier := pigo.NewPigo()

  var err error
  if classifier, err = classifier.Unpack(pigoCascadeFile); err != nil {
                  log.Fatalf("Error reading the cascade file: %s", err)
  }
  return goImg, grayGoImg, classifier, cParams, imgParams
}
```

This function is quite dense. Let's unpack it. We'll do it in a logical fashion as opposed to in a top-down linear fashion.

First, a `pigo.Pigo` is created with `classifier := pigo.NewPigo()`. This creates a new classifier. Like the Viola-Jones method, a model is required to be supplied.

Unlike in GoCV, the model is in a binary format which needs to be unpacked. Additionally, `classifier.Unpack` takes a `[]byte`, instead of a string denoting the path to the file. The provided model can be acquired on GitHub:
`https://github.com/esimov/pigo/blob/master/data/facefinder`.

Once the file has been acquired, it needs to be read as `[]byte`, as shown in the snippet below (which is wrapped in an `init` function):

```
pigoCascadeFile, err = ioutil.ReadFile("path/to/facefinder")
if err != nil {
  log.Fatalf("Error reading the cascade file: %v", err)
}
```

Once the `pigoCascadeFile` is available, we can now unpack it into the classifier by using `classifier.Unpack(pigoCascadeFile)`. Usual error handling applies.

But what of the earlier parts of the section? Why is this necessary?

To understand this, let's look at how PIGO does its classification. It looks roughly like this:

```
dets := pigoClass.RunCascade(imgParams, cParams)
dets = pigoClass.ClusterDetections(dets, 0.3)
```

When PIGO runs the classifier, it takes two parameters which determine its behavior: the `ImageParam` and the `CascadeParams`. In particular, the details `ImageParam` is illuminating our process. It's defined thus:

```
// ImageParams is a struct for image related settings.
// Pixels: contains the grayscale converted image pixel data.
// Rows: the number of image rows.
// Cols: the number of image columns.
// Dim: the image dimension.
type ImageParams struct {
  Pixels []uint8
  Rows int
  Cols int
  Dim int
}
```

It is with this in mind that the `pigoSetup` function has the extra functionalities. The `goImg` is not strictly required, but it's useful when considering our bridge between GoCV and PIGO.

PIGO requires images to be in `[]uint8`, representing a grayscale image. GoCV reads a webcam image into a `gocv.Mat`, which has a `.ToImage()` method. The method returns a `image.Image`. Most webcams capture color images. These are the steps required in order to make GoCV and PIGO play nicely together:

1. Capture an image from the webcam.
2. Convert the image into an `image.Image`.
3. Convert that image into a gray scale image.
4. Extract the `[]uint8` from the gray scale image.
5. Perform face detection on the `[]uint8`.

For our preceding pipeline, the image parameters and the cascade parameters are more or less static. Processing of the image is done in a linear fashion. A frame from the webcam doesn't get captured until the face detection is done, and the rectangles drawn, and the final image displayed in the window.

Hence, it would be perfectly all right to allocate an image once, and then overwrite the image in each loop. The `.ToImage()` method allocates a new image every time it's called. Rather, we can have a naughty version, where an already-allocated image is reused.

Here's how to do it:

```go
func naughtyToImage(m *gocv.Mat, imge image.Image) error {
            typ := m.Type()
    if typ != gocv.MatTypeCV8UC1 &amp;&amp; typ != gocv.MatTypeCV8UC3 &amp;&amp; typ !=
            gocv.MatTypeCV8UC4 {
        return errors.New("ToImage supports only MatType CV8UC1, CV8UC3 and
                CV8UC4")
    }

    width := m.Cols()
    height := m.Rows()
    step := m.Step()
    data := m.ToBytes()
    channels := m.Channels()

    switch img := imge.(type) {
    case *image.NRGBA:
      c := color.NRGBA{
        R: uint8(0),
        G: uint8(0),
        B: uint8(0),
        A: uint8(255),
      }
```

```
    for y := 0; y < height; y++ {
      for x := 0; x < step; x = x + channels {
        c.B = uint8(data[y*step+x])
        c.G = uint8(data[y*step+x+1])
        c.R = uint8(data[y*step+x+2])
        if channels == 4 {
          c.A = uint8(data[y*step+x+3])
        }
        img.SetNRGBA(int(x/channels), y, c)
      }
    }

  case *image.Gray:
    c := color.Gray{Y: uint8(0)}
    for y := 0; y < height; y++ {
      for x := 0; x < width; x++ {
        c.Y = uint8(data[y*step+x])
        img.SetGray(x, y, c)
      }
    }
  }
  return nil
}
```

This function allows one to reuse an existing image. We simply loop through the bytes of the `gocv.Mat` and overwrite the underlying bytes of the image.

With the same logic, we can also create a naughty version of a function that converts the image into gray scale:

```
func naughtyGrayscale(dst []uint8, src *image.NRGBA) []uint8 {
  rows, cols := src.Bounds().Dx(), src.Bounds().Dy()
  if dst == nil || len(dst) != rows*cols {
    dst = make([]uint8, rows*cols)
  }
  for r := 0; r < rows; r++ {
    for c := 0; c < cols; c++ {
      dst[r*cols+c] = uint8(
        0.299*float64(src.Pix[r*4*cols+4*c+0]) +
          0.587*float64(src.Pix[r*4*cols+4*c+1]) +
          0.114*float64(src.Pix[r*4*cols+4*c+2]),
      )
    }
  }
  return dst
}
```

The differences in function signature are stylistic. The latter signature is better—it's better to return the type. This allows for error correction as follows:

```
if dst == nil || len(dst) != rows*cols {
    dst = make([]uint8, rows*cols)
  }
```

And so our pipeline looks like this:

```
var haarCascadeFile = "Path/To/CascadeFile.xml"
var blue = color.RGBA{0, 0, 255, 0}
var green = color.RGBA{0, 255, 0, 0}
func main() {
var err error
  // open webcam
  if webcam, err = gocv.VideoCaptureDevice(0); err != nil {
    log.Fatal(err)
  }
  defer webcam.Close()
  width := int(webcam.Get(gocv.VideoCaptureFrameWidth))
  height := int(webcam.Get(gocv.VideoCaptureFrameHeight))

  // open display window
  window := gocv.NewWindow("Face Detect")
  defer window.Close()

  // prepare image matrix
  img := gocv.NewMat()
  defer img.Close()

  // set up pigo
  goImg, grayGoImg, pigoClass, cParams, imgParams := pigoSetup(width,
                                                               height)
  for {
    if ok := webcam.Read(&amp;img); !ok {
      fmt.Printf("cannot read device %d\n", deviceID)
      return
    }
    if img.Empty() {
      continue
    }
    if err = naughtyToImage(&amp;img, goImg); err != nil {
      log.Fatal(err)
    }
    grayGoImg = naughtyGrayscale(grayGoImg, goImg)
    imgParams.Pixels = grayGoImg
    dets := pigoClass.RunCascade(imgParams, cParams)
    dets = pigoClass.ClusterDetections(dets, 0.3)
```

```
    for _, det := range dets {
      if det.Q < 5 {
        continue
      }
      x := det.Col - det.Scale/2
      y := det.Row - det.Scale/2
      r := image.Rect(x, y, x+det.Scale, y+det.Scale)
      gocv.Rectangle(&img, r, green, 3)
    }

    window.IMShow(img)
    if window.WaitKey(1) >= 0 {
      break
    }
  }
}
```

There are some things to note here. If you follow the logic, you will note that the only things that really changed are the data in `imgParams.Pixels`. The rest of the things didn't really change as much.

Recall from the earlier explanation of the PICO algorithm—that there may be overlaps in detection's. A final clustering step is required for final detections. This explains the following two lines:

```
dets := pigoClass.RunCascade(imgParams, cParams)
dets = pigoClass.ClusterDetections(dets, 0.3)
```

The `0.3` value is chosen based on the original paper. In the documentation of PIGO, the value `0.2` is recommended.

Another thing that is different is that PIGO does not return rectangles as detections. Instead, it returns its own `pigo.Detection` type. To translate from these to standard `image.Rectangle` is simply done with these lines:

```
x := det.Col - det.Scale/2
y := det.Row - det.Scale/2
r := image.Rect(x, y, x+det.Scale, y+det.Scale)
```

Running the program yields a window showing the webcam image, with green rectangles around faces.

Putting it all together

Now we have two different uses of two different algorithms to detect faces.

Here are some observations:

- The images using PIGO are smoother—there are fewer jumps and lags.
- The PIGO algorithm jitters a little more than the standard Viola-Jones method.
- The PIGO algorithm is more robust to rotations—I could tilt my head more and still have my face detected compared to the standard Viola-Jones method.

We can of course put both of them together:

```go
var haarCascadeFile = "Path/To/CascadeFile.xml"
var blue = color.RGBA{0, 0, 255, 0}
var green = color.RGBA{0, 255, 0, 0}
func main() {
var err error
  // open webcam
  if webcam, err = gocv.VideoCaptureDevice(0); err != nil {
    log.Fatal(err)
  }
  defer webcam.Close()
  width := int(webcam.Get(gocv.VideoCaptureFrameWidth))
  height := int(webcam.Get(gocv.VideoCaptureFrameHeight))

  // open display window
  window := gocv.NewWindow("Face Detect")
  defer window.Close()

  // prepare image matrix
  img := gocv.NewMat()
  defer img.Close()

  // set up pigo
  goImg, grayGoImg, pigoClass, cParams, imgParams := pigoSetup(width,
                                                height)

  // create classifier and load model
  classifier := gocv.NewCascadeClassifier()
  if !classifier.Load(haarCascadeFile) {
    log.Fatalf("Error reading cascade file: %v\n", haarCascadeFile)
  }
  defer classifier.Close()
  for {
    if ok := webcam.Read(&img); !ok {
      fmt.Printf("cannot read device %d\n", deviceID)
```

```
      return
  }
  if img.Empty() {
    continue
  }
  // use PIGO
  if err = naughtyToImage(&img, goImg); err != nil {
    log.Fatal(err)
  }

  grayGoImg = naughtyGrayscale(grayGoImg, goImg)
  imgParams.Pixels = grayGoImg
  dets := pigoClass.RunCascade(imgParams, cParams)
  dets = pigoClass.ClusterDetections(dets, 0.3)


  for _, det := range dets {
    if det.Q < 5 {
      continue
    }
    x := det.Col - det.Scale/2
    y := det.Row - det.Scale/2
    r := image.Rect(x, y, x+det.Scale, y+det.Scale)
    gocv.Rectangle(&img, r, green, 3)
  }

  // use GoCV
  rects := classifier.DetectMultiScale(img)
  for _, r := range rects {
    gocv.Rectangle(&img, r, blue, 3)
  }

  window.IMShow(img)
  if window.WaitKey(1) >= 0 {
    break
  }
 }
}
```

Here we see PIGO and GoCV both managed to detect them rather accurately, and that they agree with each other quite a lot.

Additionally we can see that there is now a fairly noticeable lag between actions and when the actions are displayed on screen. This is because there is more work to be done.

Evaluating algorithms

There are many dimensions upon which we can evaluate the algorithms. This section explores how to evaluate algorithms.

Assuming we want to have fast face detection—which algorithm would be better?

The only way to understand the performance of an algorithm is to measure it. Thankfully Go comes with benchmarking built in. That is what we are about to do.

To build benchmarks we must be very careful about what we're benchmarking. In this case, we want to benchmark the performance of the detection algorithm. This means comparing `classifier.DetectMultiScale` versus, `pigoClass.RunCascade` and `pigoClass.ClusterDetections`.

Also, we have to compare apples to apples—it would be unfair if we compare one algorithm with a 3840 x 2160 image and the other algorithm with a 640 x 480 image. There are simply more pixels in the former compared to the latter:

```go
func BenchmarkGoCV(b *testing.B) {
  img := gocv.IMRead("test.png", gocv.IMReadUnchanged)
  if img.Cols() == 0 || img.Rows() == 0 {
    b.Fatalf("Unable to read image into file")
  }

  classifier := gocv.NewCascadeClassifier()
  if !classifier.Load(haarCascadeFile) {
    b.Fatalf("Error reading cascade file: %v\n", haarCascadeFile)
  }

  var rects []image.Rectangle
  b.ResetTimer()

  for i := 0; i < b.N; i++ {
    rects = classifier.DetectMultiScale(img)
  }
  _ = rects
}
```

There are a few things to note—the set up is made early on in the function. Then `b.ResetTimer()` is called. This resets the timer so that setups are not counted towards the benchmark. The second thing to note is that the classifier is set to detect faces on the same image over and over again. This is so that we can get an accurate idea of how well the algorithm performs. The last thing to note is the rather weird `_ = rects` line at the end. This is done to prevent Go from optimizing away the calls. Technically, it is not needed, as I am quite certain that the `DetectMultiScale` function is complicated enough as to never have been optimized away, but that line is just there for insurance.

A similar set up can be done for PIGO:

```
func BenchmarkPIGO(b *testing.B) {
  img := gocv.IMRead("test.png", gocv.IMReadUnchanged)
  if img.Cols() == 0 || img.Rows() == 0 {
    b.Fatalf("Unable to read image into file")
  }
  width := img.Cols()
  height := img.Rows()
  goImg, grayGoImg, pigoClass, cParams, imgParams := pigoSetup(width,
                                                        height)

  var dets []pigo.Detection
  b.ResetTimer()

  for i := 0; i &lt; b.N; i++ {
    grayGoImg = naughtyGrayscale(grayGoImg, goImg)
    imgParams.Pixels = grayGoImg
    dets = pigoClass.RunCascade(imgParams, cParams)
    dets = pigoClass.ClusterDetections(dets, 0.3)
  }
  _ = dets
}
```

This time the set up is more involved than the GoCV benchmark. It may seem that these two functions are benchmarking different things—the GoCV benchmark takes a `gocv.Mat` while the PIGO benchmark takes a `[]uint8`. But remember that we're interested in the performance of the algorithms on an image.

The main reason why the gray scaling is also added into the benchmark is because, although GoCV takes a color image, the actual Viola-Jones method uses a gray scale image. Internally, OpenCV converts the image into a gray scale before detection. Because we're unable to separate the detection part by itself, the only alternative is to consider conversion to gray scale as part of the detection process.

To run the benchmark, both functions are added into `algorithms_test.go`. Then `go test -run=^$ -bench=. -benchmem` is run. The result is as follows:

```
goos: darwin
goarch: amd64
pkg: chapter9
BenchmarkGoCV-4 20 66794328 ns/op 32 B/op 1 allocs/op
BenchmarkPIGO-4 30 47739076 ns/op 0 B/op 0 allocs/op
PASS
ok chapter9 3.093s
```

Here we can see that GoCV is about 1/3 slower than PIGO. A key reason for this is due to the cgo calls made in order to interface with OpenCV. However, it should also be noted that the PICO algorithm is faster than the original Viola-Jones algorithm. That PIGO can exceed the performance of a highly tuned and optimized Viola-Jones algorithm found in OpenCV, is rather impressive.

However, speed is not the only thing that matters. There are other dimensions that matter. The following are things that matter when considering face detection algorithms. Tests for them are suggested but left as an exercise for the reader:

```
| Consideration | Test |
|:---:          |:---:|
| Performance in detecting many faces | Benchmark with image of crowd |
| Correctness in detecting many faces | Test with image of crowd, with
                                        known numbers |
| No racial discrimination | Test with images of multi-ethnic peoples
                             with different facial features |
```

The last one is of particular interest. For many years, ML algorithms have not served people of color well. I myself had some issues when using a Viola-Jones model (a different model from the one in the repository) to detect eyes. In a facial feature detection project I did about five years ago, I was trying to detect eyes on a face.

The so-called **Asian** eyes are composed of two major features—an upward slant away from the nose to the outside of the face; and eyes that have epicanthic folds, giving the illusion of a *single* eyelid—that is, an eyelid without crease. The model I was working on couldn't detect where my eyes were on occasion because the filter looked for the crease of the eyelid, and the creases on my eyelids are not that obvious.

On that front, some algorithms and models may appear accidentally exclusionary. To be clear, I am NOT saying that the creators of such algorithms and models are racist. However there are some assumptions that were made in the design of the algorithms that did not include considerations of all the possible cases—nor could they ever. For example, any contrast-based detection of facial landmarks will fare poorly with people who have darker skin tones. On the flipside, contrast-based detection systems are usually very fast, because there is a minimal amount of calculation required. Here, there is a tradeoff to be made—do you need to detect everyone, or do you need to be fast?

This chapter aims to encourage readers to think more about use cases of machine learning algorithms and the tradeoffs required in using the algorithms. This book has mostly been about thinking about the tradeoffs. I highly encourage the reader to think deeply about the use cases of the machine learning algorithms. Understand all the tradeoffs required. Once the appropriate tradeoffs are understood, implementation is usually a piece of cake.

Summary

In this chapter, we learned about using GoCV and PIGO, and built a program that detects faces from a live webcam. At the end of the chapter, we implemented a usable facial recognition system, got familiar with notions of hashing of facial features, and saw how to make fast inferences using the Gorgonia suite of libraries as well as GoCV, which is a binding for OpenCV.

In saying that, in the next chapter, we'll look at some of the implications of not having built your algorithm by yourself.

Hot Dog or Not Hot Dog - Using External Services

9

In the previous chapters, I stressed the importance of understanding the mathematics behind algorithms. Here's a recap. We started with linear regression, followed by a Naïve Bayes classifier. Then, the topics dovetailed into one of the more complex topics in data science: time series. We then detoured and discussed clustering by means of K-means. This was followed by two chapters on neural networks. In all these chapters, I explained the mathematics behind these algorithms, and showed that, with much surprise, the programs yielded are short and simple.

The purpose of this book is to walk a delicate line between the math and the implementations. I hope I have provided enough information so that you have an understanding of the mathematics and how they may be useful. The projects are real projects, but often they are in various forms, simplified and rather academic. And so, it may be a bit of a surprise that this chapter will not contain many mathematical explanations. Instead, this chapter is aimed at guiding readers through more real-world scenarios.

In the previous chapter, we discussed facial detection. Given an image, we want to find the faces. But who are they? In order to know who the faces belong to, we'd need to perform facial recognition.

MachineBox

As mentioned, we will not focus on the math going on behind the scenes of face detection. Instead, we will use an external service to perform the recognition for us. The external service is MachineBox. What it does is quite clever. Instead of having to write your own deep learning algorithms, MachineBox packages up the commonly-used deep learning functionalities into containers, and you simply just use them straight out of the box. What do I mean by commonly-used deep learning functionalities? Nowadays people are relying more and more on deep learning for tasks such as facial recognition.

Just like Viola-Jones in the early 2000s, there are only a few commonly used models—we used the Haar-like cascades generated by Rainer Lienhart in 2002. The same is becoming true of deep learning models, and I shall talk more about the implications of that in the next chapter. By models, I mean the actual weights of the deep learning networks (for a more in-depth coverage, see `Chapter 7`, *Convolutional Neural Networks – MNIST Handwriting Recognition*, on deep neural networks). These commonly-used models are packaged up by MachineBox and you're able to just use it out of the box.

One thing that must be kept in mind is that MachineBox is a paid service. They do offer a free tier, which is sufficient for the needs of this chapter. I am in no way affiliated with MachineBox. I just think they're a cool company and deserve some recognition for the work they do. Plus, they do not do sketchy things such as secretly charging your credit card, so that's a plus from me.

What is MachineBox?

MachineBox is a service, first and foremost. The machine learning algorithms are packaged nicely as a cloud service. Further, because MachineBox cares about the developer experience, they have provided SDKs and local instances for you to develop against. This comes in the form of containers. Set up Docker, run the commands found on the MachineBox website, and you're done!

In this project, we wish to use a facial-recognition system to recognize faces. MachineBox provides such a service, called facebox.

Signing in and up

First, we need to sign into MachineBox. Go to `https://machinebox.io` and click on **Sign Up**. Conveniently, the sign in page is the same. MachineBox will then email you a link. Clicking the link should send you to this page:

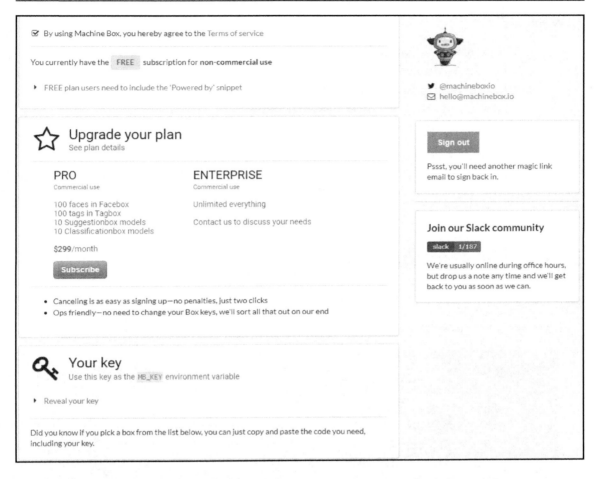

Click on **Reveal your key**. Copy the key. If you're using a UNIX-based operating system, such as Linux or MacOS, in your terminal, run the following:

```
export MB_KEY="YOUR KEY HERE"
```

Alternatively, if you want to persist this environment variable, simply edit your terminal configuration file (I use bash on Linux and MacOS, so the file I'd edit is .bash_profile or .bashrc depending on which OS I'm on).

In Windows:

1. Go to **System** | **Control Panel**
2. Click on **Advanced System Settings**
3. Click on **Environment Variables**
4. In the section **System Variables**, click **New**
5. Add MB_KEY as the key and the variable is the key.

MachineBox relies on another piece of technology built on Go: Docker. Most modern software developers already have Docker installed on their machines. If you haven't already done so, you can install Docker by going to `https://docs.docker.com/install/` and install the Community Edition of Docker.

Docker installation and setting up

Once that's all done, we're ready to get our MachineBox running with the following command:

```
docker run -p 8080:8080 -e "MB_KEY=$MB_KEY" machinebox/facebox
```

```
File  Edit  View  Search  Terminal  Help
$ docker run -p 8080:8080 -e "MB_KEY=$MB_KEY" machinebox/facebox
2018/11/29 08:54:37 Number of MB_WORKERS is set to 4
[INFO]     starting...

          Welcome to Facebox by Machine Box
          (facebox 7f66aba)

          Visit the console to see what this box can do:
          http://localhost:8080

          If you have any questions or feedback, get in touch:
          https://machinebox.io/contact

          Please consider buying a subscription:
          https://machinebox.io/#pricing

          Report bugs and issues:
          https://github.com/machinebox/issues

          Tell us what you build on Twitter @machineboxio

[INFO]     box ready
```

Using MachineBox in Go

To interact with MachineBox, simply go `http://localhost:8080`. There, you'll see an array of options on the box. But we want to interact with the service programmatically. To do so, MachineBox has provided an SDK. To install it, run `go get github.com/machinebox/sdk-go/facebox`. This installs the SDK for us to interact with facebox.

The project

This is the last project of this book. So, for a bit of fun, let's build on the previous chapter's project, but give it a twist. There's an Asian rapper called **MC Hot Dog**. So let's build a face-recognition system to determine whether a face is HotDog or Not HotDog.

What we want to do is to read an image off a webcam, and use MachineBox to determine whether MC Hot Dog is in the picture. We'll once again be using GoCV to read images off the webcam, but, this time, the image will be sent to MachineBox for classification.

Training

MachineBox is a machine learning system as a service. It has, presumably, in some backend somewhere, a general model—say, a convolutional neural network that has been trained with many faces, such that it knows what a face is. It does not provide the specific model that you may require for the task at hand. So instead, we would need to fine-tune the model provided by MachineBox by giving it training data. Per MachineBox's terminology, this is called **teaching**. As part of a curiosity collection, I have collected a small but usable number of images of MC Hot Dog's face that are suitable for the task of teaching the MachineBox what MC Hot Dog looks like.

For this project, the images are in the `hotdog.zip` file. Unzip the file into a folder called `HotDog`. This folder should be at the same level as `main.go` for this project.

Training the MachineBox model is simple with the SDK provided. The following code illustrates the program:

```
import "github.com/machinebox/sdk-go/facebox"

func train(box *facebox.Client) error {
    files, err := filepath.Glob("HotDog/*")
    if err != nil {
```

```
            return err
    }
    for _, filename := range files {
        f , err := os.Open(filename)
        if err != nil {
            return err
        }

        if err := box.Teach(f, filename, "HotDog"); err != nil {
            return err
        }
        if err := f.Close(); err != nil {
            return err
        }
    }
    return nil
}

func main(){
    box := facebox.New("http://localhost:8080")
    if err := train(box); err !=nil {
        log.Fatal(err)
    }
}
```

And there you have it—a complete tutorial on how to teach MachineBox how to recognize MC Hot Dog. MachineBox makes it easy—so easy that you don't need to know the mathematics behind the deep learning systems.

Reading from the Webcam

By this point, I hope you have already read the previous chapter and have GoCV installed. If you haven't, then read the *GoCV* section in the previous chapter to get started.

To read from the webcam, we simply add the following lines to the main file. You may recognize them as snippets from the previous chapter:

```
// open webcam
webcam, err := gocv.VideoCaptureDevice(0)
if err != nil {
    log.Fatal(err)
}
defer webcam.Close()

// prepare image matrix
img := gocv.NewMat()
```

```
defer img.Close()

if ok := webcam.Read(&img); !ok {
    log.Fatal("Failed to read image")
}
```

The confusing bit of course, is how to pass `img`, which is of the `gocv.Mat` type, to MachineBox. There exists a `Check` method on the MachineBox client that takes `io.Reader`. `img` has a method, `ToBytes`, that returns a slice of bytes; coupled with `bytes.NewReader`, one should be able to easily pass `io.Reader` into `Check`.

But if you try that, it won't work.

Here's why: MachineBox expects an input that is *formatted* as a JPEG or PNG. If it is not, you will get a **400 Bad Request** error. Poorly-formatted images would also cause these sorts of problems, which is why the error returned by `box.Teach()` is purposefully unhandled in the preceding line. In real-life settings, one might want to actually check whether it's a **400 Bad Request** error that was returned.

The raw bytes of an image in `img` are not encoded as a known image format. Instead, we have to encode the image in `img` as a JPEG or a PNG and then pass it into MachineBox, as follows:

```
var buf bytes.Buffer
prop, _ := img.ToImage()
if err = jpeg.Encode(&buf, prop, nil); err != nil {
    log.Fatal("Failed to encode image as JPG %v", err)
}

faces, err := box.Check(&buf)
fmt.Printf("Error: %v\n", err)
fmt.Printf("%#v", faces)
```

Here, we make use of the fact that `*bytes.Buffer` acts as both `io.Reader` and `io.Writer`. This way, we don't have to write directly to the file—rather, everything stays in memory.

Prettifying the results

The program prints the results. It looks something as follows:

```
Error: <nil>
[]facebox.Face{facebox.Face{Rect:facebox.Rect{Top:221, Left:303, Width:75,
Height:75}, ID:"", Name:"", Matched:false, Confidence:0, Faceprint:""}}
```

This is a rather boring result to be printed on the terminal output. We live in the age of GUIs now! So let's draw our results.

As a result, we want the window to show whatever the webcam is showing. Then, when a key is pressed, the image is captured, and processed by MachineBox. If a face is found, a rectangle should be drawn around it. If the face is recognized as MC Hot Dog, then label the box HotDog, followed by the confidence. Otherwise, the box should be labelled Not HotDog. The code for this looks a bit convoluted:

```
// open webcam
webcam, err := gocv.VideoCaptureDevice(0)
if err != nil {
    log.Fatal(err)
}
defer webcam.Close()

// prepare image matrix
img := gocv.NewMat()
defer img.Close()

// open display window
window := gocv.NewWindow("Face Recognition")
defer window.Close()

var recognized bool
for {
    if !recognized {
        if ok := webcam.Read(&img); !ok {
            log.Fatal("Failed to read image")
        }
    }

    window.IMShow(img)
    if window.WaitKey(1) >= 0 {
        if !recognized {
            recognize(&img, box)
            recognized = true
            continue
        } else {
            break
        }
    }
}
```

But if we break it down, we can see that the code in the main function can be split into two parts. The first part deals with opening a webcam and creating a window to display the image. A more complete account of this is covered in the previous chapter.

In particular, let's turn our focus to the infinite loop:

```
for {
    if !recognized {
        if ok := webcam.Read(&img); !ok {
            log.Fatal("Failed to read image")
        }
    }

    window.IMShow(img)
    if window.WaitKey(1) >= 0 {
        if !recognized {
            recognize(&img, box)
            recognized = true
        } else {
            break
        }
    }
}
```

What this says is simply this: first check whether the recognition process has been done. If it hasn't, grab an image from the webcam, and then show the image using `window.IMShow(img)`. This constitutes the main loop—the webcam will continuously capture an image and then immediately display it in the window.

But what happens when a key is pressed? The block of code that follows says to wait for a keyboard event for 1 millisecond. If there is an event, any event at all, we check whether the image had previously been recognized. If not, call `recognize`, passing in the captured image from the matrix, and the MachineBox client. Then we set the `recognized` flag as true. Thus, upon the next key press, we exit the program.

`recognize` is where the meat of the drawing is done. If you have gone through the previous chapter, this should be quite familiar to you already. Otherwise, here's how `recognize` looks:

```
var blue = color.RGBA{0, 0, 255, 0}

func recognize(img *gocv.Mat, box *facebox.Client) (err error) {
    var buf bytes.Buffer
    prop, _ := img.ToImage()
    if err = jpeg.Encode(&buf, prop, nil); err != nil {
        log.Fatal("Failed to encode image as JPG %v", err)
    }

    // rd := bytes.NewReader(prop.(*image.RGBA).Pix)
```

```
        faces, err := box.Check(&buf)
        // fmt.Println(err)
        // fmt.Printf("%#v\n", faces)

        for _, face := range faces {
            // draw a rectangle
            r := rect2rect(face.Rect)
            gocv.Rectangle(img, r, blue, 3)

            lbl := "Not HotDog"
            if face.Matched {
                lbl = fmt.Sprintf("%v %1.2f%%", face.Name,
face.Confidence*100)
            }
            size := gocv.GetTextSize(lbl, gocv.FontHersheyPlain, 1.2, 2)
            pt := image.Pt(r.Min.X+(r.Min.X/2)-(size.X/2), r.Min.Y-2)
            gocv.PutText(img, lbl, pt, gocv.FontHersheyPlain, 1.2, blue, 2)
        }
        return nil
    }
```

Here, we see the familiar code used to first encode the image as a JPEG, and then send it to the MachineBox client for classification. Then, for each face found, we draw a blue rectangle around it. `facebox.Face` is defined as follows:

```
type Face struct {
    Rect       Rect
    ID         string
    Name       string
    Matched    bool
    Confidence float64
    Faceprint  string
}
```

`facebox.Face` allows us to identify the faces, if they are matched, and the confidence level. So if there is a `face` found, these fields would be accessible to the programmer.

But first, we must solve the issue of rectangles. MachineBox does not use the same definition of rectangles as `image.Rectangle`, which is found in the standard library.

Thus, a helper function to convert `facebox.Rect` into `image.Rectangle` is required:

```
func rect2rect(a facebox.Rect) image.Rectangle {
    return image.Rect(a.Left, a.Top, a.Left+a.Width, a.Top+a.Height)
}
```

There are only a handful of ways to define a rectangle. Conversion among the two different types is trivial.

After the rectangle has been drawn, a label is written. If the face is recognized as MC Hot Dog, we'll label it as `HotDog`. MachineBox also provides a confidence score, which is a number between 0 and 1 on whether a face is `HotDog` or `Not HotDog`. So we'll draw that into the label as well.

The results

You're probably curious about the results. Here are some of them: my face is classified as HotDog with 57% confidence. In fact, using my phone and an image of several other people, I have found that some people are more HotDog-like than others as shown in the following images:

What does this all mean?

Does this mean that MachineBox's algorithm is not good? The short answer is no: we cannot say that the MachineBox algorithm is not good. The longer answer requires a more nuanced understanding that combines engineering understanding and an understanding of machine learning. As far as the algorithm of facebox goes, there are no exact details about what facebox is composed of. But we can deduce what goes on.

First, note that the images with matches are all over 50% in their confidence. We can then assume that facebox considers a match being found only if the confidence level greater than 50%. I verified this by running the recognizer on a directory of over 1,000 images of faces. Only those that are matched have a greater-than 50% confidence. The program is as follows:

```go
func testFacebox() error {
    files, err := filepath.Glob("OtherFaces/*")
    if err != nil {
        return err
    }
    var count, lt50 int
    for _, filename := range files {
        f , err := os.Open(filename)
        if err != nil {
            return err
        }
        faces, err := box.Check(f)
        if err != nill {
            return err
        }
        for _, face := range faces {
            if face.Matched && face.Confidence < 0.5 {
                lt50++
            }
        }
        if err := f.Close(); err != nil {
            return err
        }
        count++
    }
    fmt.Printf("%d/%d has Matched HotDog but Confidence < 0.5\n", lt50, count)
    return nil
}
```

With this in mind, it also means that we cannot directly use facebox's .Matched field as the truth value, except for very rudimentary use cases. Instead, we'd have to consider the confidence of the results returned.

We could, for example, set a higher threshold for a match to be considered HotDog. Setting it to 0.8 shows that only images of MC Hot Dog are recognized as HotDog.

The lesson learned here is that APIs created by other people require some understanding. The code provided in this chapter is remarkably short. This is a testament to MachineBox's developer friendliness. But that does not absolve the developer from having at least the most basic of understanding of things.

Why MachineBox?

I personally prefer to develop my own machine learning solutions. One may, of course, chalk this up to ego. However, in the first chapter, I introduced the notion that there are different types of problems. Some of these problems may be solved by machine learning algorithms. Some problems may only require general machine learning algorithms, while some require specialized algorithms derived from the general algorithms. In the majority of this book, I've shown the general algorithms, and readers are free to adapt these to their own specific problems.

I, too, recognize the value of having general machine learning algorithms as being part of the solution. Imagine that you are developing a program to reorganize your personal photos on your computer. There is no need to spend a protracted amount of time getting a convolutional neural network trained upon a corpus of faces. The main task is to organize the photos, not facial recognition! Instead, one may just use a model that is already trained. These sorts of ready-made solutions are suitable for problems in which the ready-made solution is a small part. Increasingly, there is a demand for such solutions.

As such, many machine learning algorithms are provided now as a service. Amazon Web Services has its own offering, as do Google Cloud and Microsoft Azure. Why did I not choose to introduce those in this chapter? Here's another thing you should know about me: I like to work offline. I find being connected to the internet while working only serves as a distraction—Slack messages, emails, and various other sites compete for my scarce attention. No, I prefer to work and think while offline.

The cloud companies do offer machine learning as a service, and they all require internet access. MachineBox, to its credit, provides a Docker image. A Docker pull is all that is required. A once-off internet connection is required to download the files. But once that's done, the entire workflow may be developed offline—or as is the case for all the code in this chapter, on a plane.

This is MachineBox's main benefit: you are not beholden to a corporate entity that requires an always-on connection to their cloud services. But of course, that's not all. MachineBox is famous for its developer friendliness. That I am able to write the majority of this chapter's code in-flight is testament to their developer friendliness. To be fair, even as a seasoned machine learning library author, facial recognition is still pretty awesome.

Summary

In closing, it's only fair to mention that MachineBox does have some limitations for its free tiers; but for personal projects, in my experience, you won't run into them. Despite my personal reservations on the various machine learning-as-a-service systems out there, I do think they provide value. I have used them from time to time, but I generally do not need them. Nevertheless, I highly recommend that the reader check them out.

This chapter, in combination with the previous chapter, has shown the breadth of machine learning in the industry. Not all machine learning algorithms have to be handwritten from scratch if your main problem does not call for it. I am lucky enough to have a career in doing what I love: building customized machine learning algorithms. This may have tainted my views on this issue. You may be an engineer on a deadline who has to solve some bigger business problems. For that, these two chapters are for you.

The next chapter will list further avenues for ML in Go.

10 What's Next?

The projects covered in this book can be considered bite-sized projects. They can be completed within a day or two. A real project will often take months. They require a combination of machine learning expertise, engineering expertise, and DevOps expertise. It would not quite be feasible to write about such projects without spanning multiple chapters while keeping the same level of detail. In fact, as can be witnessed by the progression of this book, as projects get more complex, the level of detail drops. In fact, the last two chapters are pretty thin.

All said and done, we've achieved quite a bit in this book. However, there is quite a bit we have not covered. This is owing to my own personal lack of expertise in some other fields in machine learning. In the introductory chapter, I noted that there are multiple classification schemes for machine learning systems and that we'd be choosing the common view that there are only unsupervised and supervised types of learning. Clearly, there are other classification schemes. Allow me to share another, one that has five classifications of machine learning systems:

- Connectionist
- Evolutionary
- Bayesian
- Analogizer
- Symbolist

Here, I use the term machine learning. Others may use the term artificial intelligence to classify these systems. The difference is subtle. These five classes are technically schools of thought within artificial intelligence. And this sets a much larger stage for the topics at hand.

Except for two, we have, in this book, explored the different schools of thought in artificial intelligence. In the Connectionist school, we started with linear regression in Chapter 2, *Linear Regression – House Price Prediction*, and the various neural networks from Chapters 8, *Basic Facial Detection*, and Chapter 10, *What's Next?*. In the Bayesian school, we have Naive Bayes from Chapter 3, *Classification – Spam Email Detection*, as well as the DMMClust algorithm in Chapter 6, *Neural Networks – MNIST Handwriting Recognition*; we also have the various distance and clustering algorithms, which somewhat fall into the analogizer school of thought.

The two schools of thought on artificial intelligence that are not covered are the Evolutionary school and the Symbolist school. The former I only have theoretical experiences of. My understanding of the Evolutionary school of artificial intelligence is not great. I have much to learn from the likes of Martin Nowak. The latter, I am familiar with—I have been told that my introduction to Go betrays a lot of my experience with the Symbolist school of thought.

The main reason why I didn't write anything about the Symbolist school of thought is that as a subject matter it is too dense, and I am not a good enough writer to actually tackle the subject. It opens up hairy philosophical implications more immediately than the Connectionist school does. These implications are something I am not yet ready to deal with, though the reader might be.

Having said that, one of the most exhilarating times in my life was building DeepMind's AlphaGo algorithm in Go. You can find the code here: https://github.com/gorgonia/agogo. It's a behemoth of a project, and successfully pulled off by a small team of four. It was an immensely rewarding experience. The AlphaGo algorithm merges Connectionist deep neural networks with Symbolist tree search. Despite pulling off such a feat, I still do not think I am ready to write about the symbolic approach to artificial intelligence.

All of this brings up the question: what's next?

What should the reader focus on?

This question has been asked of me every time I give a class on machine learning and artificial intelligence. I mentioned in the introductory chapter that one may want to be a machine learning practitioner or a machine learning researcher. My professional role straddles both. This allows me some experience to provide a bit of advice for readers interested in either field.

The practitioner

To the practitioner, the most important skill is not in machine learning. The most important skill is in understanding the problem. Implicit in this statement is that the practitioner should also at least understand which machine learning algorithms would be suitable for the problem at hand. Obviously this entails understanding how the machine learning algorithm works.

New people in the field often ask me whether deep learning will solve all their problems. The answer is emphatically no. The solution must be tailored to the problem. Indeed, often, non-deep-learning solutions outperform deep learning solutions in terms of speed and accuracy. These are typically simple problems, so that's a good rule of thumb there: if the problem is non-compositional, you most likely do not need to use deep learning.

What do I mean by non-compositional? Recall from `Chapter 1`, *How to Solve All Machine Learning Problems*, when I introduced the types of problems, and how problems may be broken down into subproblems. If the subproblems are themselves composed of further subproblems, well, that means the problem is *composed* of subproblems. Problems that aren't compositional do not need deep learning.

Granted, this is a very gross overview of the issue. A finer understanding of the problem is always required.

The researcher

To the researcher, the most important skill is understanding how a machine learning algorithm works at a high level. Following this, understanding data structures is the most important. From there, an actual algorithm may be written.

Of note would be the difference between data representation and data structure. Perhaps some day in the future—hopefully not too far from now—we will have programming languages where data representation does not matter. But now, data representation still matters. A good representation will yield an efficient algorithm. A poor representation yields poor algorithm performance.

For the most part, my advice is to start simple, by making things as understandable as possible as first. Then start subtracting the parts that are not necessary. A good example is shown in `Chapter 3`, *Classification – Spam Email Detection*, in Naive Bayes. A direct representation of the Bayesian function would be quite clunky. But in understanding the moving parts of the algorithm, we are able to make it efficient and small.

Sometimes, some complexity is unavoidable. Some complexities are unavoidable because the algorithm is fundamentally complex. Some complexities are tradeoffs that are required. An example of this is the use of Gorgonia. Deep learning is at its heart, just writing a long mathematical expression. To update the weights, backpropagation is used. Backpropagation is simply differentiation. But nobody wants to manually calculate the differentiation! We want to mechanically evaluate our calculus! Therefore some complexity is unavoidable.

Wisdom lies in knowing when these complexities are unavoidable. Wisdom comes from experience, so to the researcher, my advice is to do as much as possible. Doing things at different scales also brings out different experiences. For example, performing K-means at scale across multiple machines is a very different code from the one presented in the previous chapters.

The researcher, the practitioner, and their stakeholder

A word on scale—there is a tendency to reach out to packages or external programs, such as Spark, to solve the problem. Often they do solve the problem. But it's been my experience that ultimately, when doing things at scale, there is no one-size-fits-all solution. Therefore, it's good to learn the basics, so that when necessary, you may refer to the basics and extrapolate them to your situation.

Again on the topic of scale—both researchers and practitioners would do well to learn to plan projects. This is one thing that I am exceedingly bad at. Even with the help of multiple project managers, machine learning projects have a tendency to spiral out of control. It does take quite a bit of discipline to manage these. This is both on the implementor's part and on the stakeholder's part.

Last, learn to manage the expectations of stakeholders. Many of my projects fail. That I can say the projects fail is itself a qualifying statement. For most projects I enter into, I have defined success and failure criteria. If it's a more traditional statistics-based project, then these are your simple null hypotheses. Failing to reject the null hypothesis would then be a failure. Likewise, more complicated projects would have multiple hypotheses—these come in form of F-scores and the like. Learn these tools well, and communicate them to your stakeholders. You must be aware that a large majority of machine learning projects fail on their first few attempts.

What did this book not cover?

There are a number of things that we can explore in Go. Here's a non-exhaustive list of some things you may want to explore:

- Random trees and random forests
- Support vector machines
- Gradient-boosting methods
- Maximum-entropy methods
- Graphical methods
- Local outlier factors

Perhaps if there is a second edition to this book, I will cover them. If you are familiar with machine learning methods, you may note that these, especially the first three, are perhaps some of the highest-performing machine learning methods, when compared with the things written in this book. You might wonder why they were not included. The schools of thought that these methods belong to might supply a clue.

For example, random trees and random forests can be considered pseudo-Symbolist—they're a distant cousin of the Symbolist school of thought, originating from decision trees. Support vector machines are analogizers. Maximum entropy and graphical methods are of the Bayesian school of thought.

This book is biased toward the Connectionist school of thought for a good reason: deep learning is popular right now. If the winds of favor had been different, this book would have been markedly different. There is also the issue of explainability. I can explain support vector machines quite well, but it would consist of pages and pages of mathematical analogy. Opting not to explain how SVMs work, on the other hand, would lead to a very thin chapter—the standard implementation of SVMs is to use libsvm or svmlight. Simply call the functions provided by the library and the job's done! So an explanation of SVMs is warranted.

Where can I learn more?

I strongly believe machine learning methods should not be tied to programming languages. If tomorrow a new language comes out that offers better performance than Go, while keeping the developer friendliness of Go, I'd move to that language in a heartbeat. I wouldn't have to be worried about having to relearn new machine learning methods. I already know them. I can simply rewrite them in that new language. As such, my recommendations would be language-agnostic.

If you want to learn more about machine learning algorithms, I recommend Christopher Bishop's, *Pattern Recognition and Machine Learning*. It's a slightly older book, but you'll be surprised at how many new developments in machine learning have their roots in that tome.

If you want to learn more about deep learning, I recommend Ian Goodfellow and Yoshua Bengio's, *Deep Learning*. It's a new book—it's extremely theoretical, with no code, but the insights gained will be priceless.

If you want to learn more about deep learning using Go and Gorgonia, there is an upcoming book by Darrell Chua and Gareth Seneque, published by Packt. It covers a wide range of deep-learning-related topics.

If you want to learn more about data science and machine learning in Go, I also recommend Daniel Whitenack's, *Machine Learning with Go*. It's one of the first books on machine learning in Go, and to this day, it still stands as an excellent resource.

If you want to learn more about Go, I highly recommend *The Go Programming Language*, by Alan Donovan and Brian Kernighan. **Kernighan** is the **K** in the famous **K&R** book on C. Here, he performs a similar feat.

Thank you

Thank you for reading this book; I hope it has been useful to you.

Other Books You May Enjoy

If you enjoyed this book, you may be interested in these other books by Packt:

Machine Learning With Go
Daniel Whitenack

ISBN: 978-1-78588-210-4

- Learn about data gathering, organization, parsing, and cleaning
- Explore matrices, linear algebra, statistics, and probability
- See how to evaluate and validate models
- Look at regression, classification, clustering
- Learn about neural networks and deep learning
- Utilize times series models and anomaly detection
- Optimize machine learning workflow techniques

Hands-On Go Programming
Tarik Guney

ISBN: 978-1-78953-175-6

- Manipulate string values and escape special characters
- Work with dates, times, maps, and arrays
- Handle errors and perform logging
- Explore files and directories
- Handle HTTP requests and responses
- Perform CRUD operations on a relational database

Leave a review - let other readers know what you think

Please share your thoughts on this book with others by leaving a review on the site that you bought it from. If you purchased the book from Amazon, please leave us an honest review on this book's Amazon page. This is vital so that other potential readers can see and use your unbiased opinion to make purchasing decisions, we can understand what our customers think about our products, and our authors can see your feedback on the title that they have worked with Packt to create. It will only take a few minutes of your time, but is valuable to other potential customers, our authors, and Packt. Thank you!

Index

Printed in Great Britain
by Amazon